East Is West and West Is East

In the series ASIAN AMERICAN HISTORY AND CULTURE
edited by Sucheng Chan, David Palumbo-Liu, Michael Omi, K. Scott Wong, and Linda Trinh Võ

Lan P. Duong, *Treacherous Subjects: Gender, Culture, and Trans-Vietnamese Feminism*

Kristi Brian, *Reframing Transracial Adoption: Adopted Koreans, White Parents, and the Politics of Kinship*

Belinda Kong, *Tiananmen Fictions Outside the Square: The Chinese Literary Diaspora and the Politics of Global Culture*

Bindi V. Shah, *Laotian Daughters: Working toward Community, Belonging, and Environmental Justice*

Cherstin M. Lyon, *Prisons and Patriots: Japanese American Wartime Citizenship, Civil Disobedience, and Historical Memory*

Shelley Sang-Hee Lee, *Claiming the Oriental Gateway: Prewar Seattle and Japanese America*

Isabelle Thuy Pelaud, *This Is All I Choose to Tell: History and Hybridity in Vietnamese American Literature*

Christian Collet and Pei-te Lien, eds., *The Transnational Politics of Asian Americans*

Min Zhou, *Contemporary Chinese America: Immigration, Ethnicity, and Community Transformation*

Kathleen S. Yep, *Outside the Paint: When Basketball Ruled at the Chinese Playground*

Benito M. Vergara, Jr., *Pinoy Capital: The Filipino Nation in Daly City*

Jonathan Y. Okamura, *Ethnicity and Inequality in Hawai'i*

Sucheng Chan and Madeline Y. Hsu, eds., *Chinese Americans and the Politics of Race and Culture*

K. Scott Wong, *Americans First: Chinese Americans and the Second World War*

Lisa Yun, *The Coolie Speaks: Chinese Indentured Laborers and African Slaves in Cuba*

Estella Habal, *San Francisco's International Hotel: Mobilizing the Filipino American Community in the Anti-Eviction Movement*

(Additional titles in this series can be found at the back of this book.)

East Is West and West Is East

Gender, Culture, and Interwar Encounters between Asia and America

KAREN KUO

Temple University Press
PHILADELPHIA

Temple University Press
Philadelphia, Pennsylvania 19122
www.temple.edu/tempress

Published 2013

LIBRARY OF CONGRESS CATALOGING-IN-PUBLICATION DATA

Kuo, Karen J.
East is West and West is East : gender, culture, and interwar encounters between Asia and America / Karen Kuo.
p. cm. — (Asian American history and culture)
Includes bibliographical references and index.
ISBN 978-1-4399-0586-9 (cloth : alk. paper)
ISBN 978-1-4399-0587-6 (pbk. : alk. paper)
ISBN 978-1-4399-0588-3 (e-book)
1. United States—Relations—Asia. 2. Asia—Relations—United States. 3. Gender identity—Cross cultural studies. 4. Sex—Cross cultural studies. I. Title.
E183.8.A78K86 2012
327.7305—dc23

2012017783

♾ The paper used in this publication meets the requirements of the American National Standard for Information Sciences—Permanence of Paper for Printed Library Materials, ANSI Z39.48-1992

Printed in the United States of America

2 4 6 8 9 7 5 3 1

THE AMERICAN LITERATURES INITIATIVE

A book in the American Literatures Initiative (ALI), a collaborative publishing project of NYU Press, Fordham University Press, Rutgers University Press, Temple University Press, and the University of Virginia Press. The Initiative is supported by The Andrew W. Mellon Foundation. For more information, please visit www.americanliteratures.org.

Contents

Acknowledgments

This book was written with the support and help of many people. Its glimmerings began as a PhD dissertation under the guidance of Priscilla Wald, Caroline Chung Simpson, Shawn Wong, and Susan Jeffords at the University of Washington. Over the years, I have benefited from the comments of Judy Tzun-Chun Wu, Andy Chih-ming Wang, Victoria A. Davis, Traise Yamamoto, Claudia Sadowski-Smith Chong-suk Han, Mary Ting Yi Lui, Gordon Chang, Vincente L. Rafael, Camilla Fojas, Kandice Chuh, and Karen Shimakawa. Celine Parreñas-Shimizu's reading of the manuscript encouraged me in the final stages of revision.

At Arizona State University, friends and colleagues contributed to my growth as a scholar: Aaron Baker, Lisa Aubrey, Lisa Anderson, Eric Margolis, and Sherril Tomita; Montye Fuse, Michelle Chin, Sudarat Musikawong, and Hyaeweol Choi. Some of these friends and colleagues also remind me that work and pleasure are not necessarily incompatible. During my first few years as a tenure-track faculty member, my writing group, which included Seline Szkupinski-Quiroga, Marivel Danielson, and Alesha Durfee, was a pleasure to be a part of every time we met. The Institute for Humanities Research's Jenny Norton Grant in Feminist Epistemologies provided food for thought these past couple of years. I want to thank Sally Kitch, director of the Institute for Humanities and Reverend Jenny Norton for providing the space and funding for the intellectual musings with graduate students and colleagues. Myla Vicenti Carpio and Carol Takao always manage to draw me out for Thai food, video games, and laughs. I am enormously blessed to have wonderful colleagues in the Asian Pacific American Studies program, some still at APAS and others who have moved on or will be moving on: Melinda de Jesús, Rudy Guevarra, Brandon Yoo, Wei Li, and Wendy Cheng prove that you can have a department with brilliant colleagues who are also fun to hang out with.

Old friends and new friends have contributed to the book in significant ways. Karen Felts had faith in this project and in me since our graduate school years. Steve Tanaka reminds me that I need to put on my queer thinking cap when things get rough. Daniel Bernardi has always been there to lend a helping hand. Rachel Duclos's enduring friendship has been a comfort to me in hard times. Tina Kotecha's inside jokes remind me of my roots. Lisa Schamus gave good company over food, movies, and playing/watching hockey.

I want to thank my chair Kathy Nakagawa for providing much-needed time to write the book, and Mary Margaret Fonow for providing other forms of institutional support as the director of the School of Social Transformation. Mary Romero, who was my chair for one year, continues to be a model scholar, mentor, and dear friend. A consistent and persistent presence in Asian Pacific American Studies, Roisan Rubio has given me his time, a sympathetic ear, his own brand of constructive criticism on everything (but the book), tea, and snacks, all of which I will always be grateful for.

And of course, this book could not have been written without these individuals. Karen Leong read multiple drafts even when she did not have the time. Her historian's keen eye and her reminders that sentences should not be five lines long have taught me a lot about being honest and clear in one's work. My copyeditor, Ann Gelder, my writer's therapist, went beyond the call of duty. Janet Francendese at Temple University Press stuck with this project and with me. Her thoroughness, patience, and kindness are remarkable. I have the deepest gratitude and respect for David Palumbo-Liu, the series editor of Temple, for not only having faith in this project but for also showing me what it means to really write your first book and how transformative and fulfilling that process can be.

The individuals closest to my heart have also sustained and nourished me. My brother, Kevin, who became the little brother turned friend. Joe has always provided a home from which to write no matter where we lived: Los Angeles, Seattle, or Phoenix. For Massimo and Luc, my two sons, who have lived with this project their entire lives, I can finally tell them that this book is done. They make me marvel at life and inspire me to be a better person every day. This book is dedicated to my parents, Han Fu and Jolene Kuo. They are, quite simply, courageous, fabulous, and inspiring. Much of the book would not have been written without their support and love.

East Is West and West Is East

Introduction

BILLY: Oh, it's a long story. I'll tell you all about it later. But look at her. Isn't she sweet?

MRS. BENSON: She certainly is. But what are we going to do with her?

BILLY: She can live here in the house with us?

MING TOY: I stay here in this house?

EAST IS WEST

In the 1930 film *East Is West*, international businessman Billy Benson brings a Chinese sing-song girl, Ming Toy, into his parental home. While abroad in China, Benson had urged his Chinese American friend Lo Sang Kee to buy Ming Toy from a notorious Chinese American gangster in order to protect her. Kee originally agrees to keep Ming Toy at his house in San Francisco's Chinatown. However, she starts to become a problem—the Chinatown missionaries believe that she is a prostitute because of the way she behaves. Ming Toy unabashedly flirts with men on the street as she sits on Kee's balcony. The film's crisis begins with the question of Ming Toy's presence in the Benson home and spirals downward from there. Will Ming Toy's living in the Benson home compromise the racial and moral integrity of the white American family? Most troubling is Billy Benson's budding romance with Ming Toy, which raises the question of whether white racial purity can be preserved: will the American family of the future be interracial? Having stirred up all these fears, the film seems to put them to rest at the end. In the bizarre final plot twist of *East Is West*, Ming Toy is not Chinese after all but white. It turns out that she was adopted as a young child by a Chinese family after her missionary parents died in China.

While through this plot device the film seems to eradicate fears of miscegenation, its unique racial drama actually presents a subversive commentary on white women's sexuality, particularly their autonomy. This suggestion of the sexual autonomy of the white female, of her capacity to indulge in "wild" sexual behavior typically associated only with the exotic Oriental female, was an equally, if not more, anxiety-provoking idea than that of a Chinese prostitute in the white American home. The film implies that since a white woman can so convincingly appear "Asian," then perhaps the gulf that seemingly separates them is not so great after all. The female behavior associated with Asian women may actually be shared by all women, regardless of race. *East Is West* reveals how rapidly the distance between East and West may contract to a dangerous proximity in two ways. First, the Asian Other easily passes through the United States' national borders and can threaten to actually change not just the racial composition of the nation but also white gender and sexual norms. She can penetrate the white domestic space and might indeed lure the white American male into a forbidden interracial tryst that would pollute the white race. And second, even after she is revealed to be white herself, "Ming Toy" still is a threatening female in the sense that she has displayed, seemingly effortlessly, the sexual behavior associated with Asian women.

The film, in a strong sense, represents the radical possibilities of East and West merging and in doing so exposes the possibility that the greatest threat to the nation and the home may be not necessarily the foreign Other but something that resides within the nation already as a constituent part of its assumed white racial identity.

Hence the inspiration for the title of my book comes from this 1930 Hollywood film, a film initially barred from commercial release in the United States by the Motion Picture Production Code because of its depiction of Chinese-white miscegenation. Yet, as I argue in a detailed analysis of the film in chapter 1, I believe that a more subtle, unconscious motive for its censorship might have been that it presented white and Chinese female sexual identity as similar in essential ways. This instance of cinematic censorship was only part of a larger system of control and surveillance of not just Asian women but also white women, a mechanism put in place to contain the threat of modern female sexuality. Social and legal surveillance and control over Asian immigrant women and white women between the late nineteenth and early twentieth centuries were primarily rationalized as protecting the white family, either from the sexual and racial infiltration of Chinese prostitutes or from the immorality of sexually promiscuous white women who refused to conform to the standards of respectable white femininity. *East Is West* presents fears not only of Asiatic female sexuality but also of the fragility of white racial and gender norms in the modern world. Together these anxieties represent an overriding ontological fear: that of modernity itself. As I show, in this period in the United States, fears of modernity's profound changes found voice precisely through articulations of mutual encounters, real and imagined, between Asia and America.

In the books and films I examine, "Asia" and "America" both took on an array of imaginative projections that tested the capaciousness of American modernity—white and Asian subjects defined their respective racialized formations of modern identity, femininity, masculinity, and sexuality through and against each other. These attempts by Asians and white Americans at understanding better their new locations in modern history reveal anxiety about the nation's changing domestic makeup and sociocultural life. Books written at the time, such as Lothrop Stoddard's *The Rising Tide of Color* and Madison Grant's *The Passing of the Great Race*, warned of the imminent decline of the US nation and its culture should the United States continue to allow the immigration of nonwhite and non-Anglo-Saxon people from Asia and eastern and southern Europe.[1] Stoddard and Grant and their supporters were especially afraid that these new immigrants would inevitably mix with Anglo-Americans, resulting in the racial mongrelization of America. As a result, notions of white racial purity depended heavily on the maintenance of the cultural, racial, and social norms evinced in the space of the white family and home.

White women usually bore the greatest burden of maintaining the family's racial and sexual purity; the regulatory regimes enacted to control white female sexuality in the early twentieth century resulted directly from fears that white women could not, in fact, discipline themselves. They were deemed constitutionally susceptible to giving in to sexual behaviors that defied social norms and proprieties. But white men also bore some responsibility for upholding racial purity: they were charged with embodying the proper identifications of masculinity, strength, and virility and were to steel themselves against the temptations presented by the Ming Toys of the world. Whiteness thus was defined according to a set of proper and normative gendered and sexual identifications, behaviors, beliefs, and expressions that constantly defended against incursions of otherness, both racial and sexual, and "Asia" seemed to present a particularly alluring and dangerous otherness. Equally important, however, along with my inquiries into how white American men and women imagined their gendered and sexual lives through a comparison with Asians, I also look through the other end of this scope to examine the ways Asians, through their real and imagined relations with white Americans, reconsidered their own racial and cultural identities, particularly in the realms of gender and sexuality. My book thus asks how *both* Asian and white genders, sexualities, and domesticities come together in a deciphering of race, and how these formations continually intersect in ways that are sometimes oppositional and sometimes collaborative and integrative.

Rereading Racial, Gendered, and Sexual Formations through Asian Exclusion

The racial exclusion of Asians should be seen as a symptom of the crisis in America's management of race, gender, and sexuality that was unfolding within the nation itself in the early twentieth century. In this crisis, the sexual, gendered, and reproductive regulation of Asian men and women as offsetting "Others" helped construct and normalize white sexuality and domesticities. In fact, the American notions of Asians as sexually deviant (usually the extremes of asexual or hypersexual) that still exist today came out of the historical conditions of Asian immigration and settlement in the United States during the early twentieth century.

More recent historical works about the exclusion period reveal the heterogeneity and unevenness in the sexualization of Asians, particularly as it serves to repress white narratives of anxiety over sex, gender, and race. The sexualities of both Asian women and Asian men were often represented as either completely innocuous or extremely threatening, rarely as anything in between. Representations of Asian women in the late nineteenth through the early twentieth centuries introduced the figure of the submissive and docile Japanese geisha, in Madame Chrysanthemum and Madame Butterfly. Euro-Americans latched onto these exotic Asian female stereotypes, seeing them as indications of Oriental feminine beauty and docility.[2] Since these figures, for the most part, existed "out there" in Asia, and not in the United States, they did not threaten to compete or mix with Americans in the United States. Asian immigrant women, however, were typically viewed in a different light from this nonthreatening Oriental femininity.[3] For example, Chinese immigrant women were routinely seen as prostitutes and as disease carriers who infected respectable white families through liaisons with white men, and this view affected Americans' perceptions not only of Asian immigrant women but also of white men and their families, who were seen as vulnerable to this particular Asiatic "invasion."[4]

Exclusion laws essentially codified what constituted sexually normative behavior, presumably exhibited by whites but not by Asian men or women.[5] These gendered and sexual regulations of difference between Asians and whites were therefore based on ideas of what constituted heteronormative and middle-class sexualities and gendered identities, as well as based on race. And containing sexual behavior had its racial implications. Exclusion also shaped antimiscegenation laws that barred Asians and whites from marrying and procreating. Hence the intimate connection can be seen between the regulation and disciplining of sexual behavior and racial consequence. In this scenario, racial identity signaled sexuality. Yet just as racial identities were multivalent, so were the sexual characteristics associated with them. For instance, exclusionary and restrictive laws depended on the social construction of Asian men as sexually deviant and, in particular, a danger to white women and the reproduction of white families.[6] Filipino male immigrants in the early twentieth century were seen as hypersexual menaces. Moreover, Chinese immigrant men living in "bachelor societies" in the United States had long been seen as particularly suspicious because of the men's cohabitation with other men and the seeming absence of women and children in their midst.[7] Ignorant of how these Asian immigrant male communities were the products of exclusion and antimiscegenation laws, most white Americans viewed Asian males as sexually abnormal, emasculated, and even feminized. In short, Asian men were characterized as either wildly predatory or questionably asexual, both threatening and nonthreatening, respectively.[8]

My readings of Asian and American texts of the early twentieth century complicate homogeneous representations of Asian men and women during this period to argue that other, more significant and complex characterizations and articulations of Asian sexuality and gender existed. I reinterpret this period's exclusion of Asians as a point of departure from which to read the internal weaknesses of white racial and gendered identities and how those weaknesses shaped, and were shaped by, new formations of gender, sex, and race that came about as Asians in America were starting to become what we now call Asian Americans.

During these years, white women of different classes were defined by their sexual and gendered differences from Asian women or, in other cases, actively defined their sexual and gendered identities through strategic differences from and similarities to Asian women. The early twentieth century's "girl problem" identified young unmarried white women and their sexual independence as a threat to the erosion of white domesticity. For example, my reading of the film *East Is West* reveals how the representation of deviant Asiatic (Chinese) female sexuality gives voice to the "girl problem" that was actually at the center of debates about white women and sexuality in the early twentieth century. The popularity of the New Woman and the early feminist and reproductive-rights movements sustained the notion that women, regardless of class, were becoming a problem in the maintenance of normative white domesticity.[9] In the 1920s and into the 1930s, white middle-class women's marriage and reproduction rates were dropping, lending support to the fears of race suicide promulgated by Madison Grant and Lothrop Stoddard.[10] I read *East Is West* as taking part in this debate over white female sexuality, not as simply a set orientalist piece of lurid exotica.

Similarly, white and Asian men tested out their sexual, gendered, and racial identities through each other, constructing specific national identities that overlapped with the new global definitions of manhood. Studies on American masculinity during the early twentieth century reveal representations of middle-class white men that were very similar, in their contradictions, to those of Asian men. The representations of white and Asian men within American national culture describe various cultural instances of emasculation, through either racism or changes related to gender and sexuality in the nation and often the compensatory need to reestablish and redefine a hegemonic masculinity defined as white, American, and middle class.[11] In the case of white men, the sense of emasculation resulted from a number of factors: women's growing power in the public sphere, immigration, and the rise of the working-class man. All these factors compelled a renewed claim to a virile masculinity reaffirming the power and privilege that middle-class men had enjoyed in the United States throughout the nineteenth century.[12]

In the texts I examine the constantly shifting images and representations of Asian and white genders and sexualities reveal the ultimate instability of gender and sexuality as concepts during this period. In these texts, both Asian and white subjects seize this instability as an invitation and a means to construct new and more nuanced gendered and sexual identities for themselves—that is, modern identities. Within this comparative racial and cultural frame, the texts I examine depict how the intermingling and interpenetration of Asian and white identities in America, within and against the constraints of the exclusion period, continue to point to the instability of race, gender, and sexuality and, at the same time, our efforts to disentangle the making of modern white and Asian identities as they began to emerge during the early twentieth century.

Encountering Modernity through the Other

In departing from scholarly works in Asian American cultural studies that predominately examine either white US subjects' representations of Asia and the East or Asian American representations of the United States and the West, my aim in this book is to show how both Asians *and* white Americans made sense of racial, gendered, and sexual identities, nationally and internationally, through their encounters with each other.[13] On the one hand, the US films I examine, *East Is West* (1930) and Frank Capra's *Lost Horizon* (1937), present white American subjects' interpretations of Asia and Asians. While both films illustrate the projection of the West's desire for exotica and difference onto Asia, I argue that on closer examination, these films also used Asia to reconsider white gendered and sexual identities. On the other hand, in examining two literary pieces, an early Korean American novel by Younghill Kang, *East Goes West: The Making of an Oriental Yankee* (1937), and a Japanese feminist autobiography, Baroness Shidzué Ishimoto's *Facing Two Ways: The Story of My Life* (1935), I show how Asian authors understand the changes (economic, political, social, cultural) brought on by modernity and the effects of these changes on gender, sex, and race through the authors' interactions, assimilation, and relationships, both real and imagined, with Americans.[14] My interdisciplinary analysis of literature and film uses a multidirectional focus to demonstrate how both white American and Asian subjects came to define racialized gender formations and even sexual identities for each other during the early twentieth century, when these categories were being challenged in unprecendented ways due in particular to the United States' territorial expansion overseas and the concomitant immigration of large numbers of Asians to the United States. Next I connect the ways Asians and white Americans, through what I call a "mutual gaze," tested out different notions of gender and sexuality to the ways they used their imaginings of each other's national and cultural identities to test out how both Asia and America fit into the modern world.

The Asian authors in my study express the desire to see the United States as an exemplary modern nation-state and culture. Adopting this view of America was a way of exploring the range of modernity's possibilities. In fact, these authors soon discovered how America illustrates the limitations of modernity, as racial and gender biases were inscribed into the very laws of the land. For example, in my discussion of Younghill Kang's *East Goes West*, the protagonist, Chungpa Han, a Korean exile and new migrant, seeks rebirth in the United States as he leaves behind an untenable situation in Korea under Japanese colonization. Kang's novel couples the narrative of exile with that of the immigrant dream, one that promises the "Village spirit," "the artist's and rebel's life," and "free love" supported by the American mythos of individualism and enterprise.[15] Similarly, Japanese feminist Baroness Shidzué Ishimoto, like many other Japanese women of her time, admired American women not only for their supposed disregard of gendered and domestic conventions but also for their being on the vanguard of feminism. Nevertheless, both authors come to see how visions of US modernity as democratic and liberated are ultimately challenged by the realities of racism, exclusion, and imperialist domination. Both Kang and Ishimoto keenly felt the contradiction between their idealistic view and their pragmatic understanding of the growing US hegemony in the political and cultural relations between the United States and East Asia in the 1930s. For these Asian authors, then, the United States ultimately represented both an enlightened modern nation and the failings of modernity, and their narratives must be understood as exploring both of these facets as a way to reflect back on the ability of Western liberal ideals to serve the demands of a new modern world that now contained Asia in a powerful and increasingly present manner.

As David Palumbo-Liu argues, in the aftermath of World War I the United States was internationally seen as an example of a modern nation-state, that is, as a pluralistic and democratic society. Yet this projection of the United States as the embodiment of modernity was peculiarly coexistent with the United States' racist policies of immigration exclusion (of Asians in particular but also other ethnic groups, such as Jews and southern and eastern Europeans) and even segregation:

> One of the most interesting aspects of early twentieth-century redefinitions of the American state was the particular blend of exclusionist practices coupled with liberal ideology, the latter used to distinguish the United States as the modern nation above all. Specifically, after the Treaty of Versailles, America held itself up as the nation that would lead in the reformation of the modern world, and such reformation had a particular connection to the modern state's ability to assimilate migrant populations. America was to be "a living exemplar of pluralistic assimilation."[16]

For this reason in particular, Kang and Ishimoto were highly skeptical of any idealistic view of American modernity. Kang's novel expresses shock at the continual racism faced by his Korean narrator, who, like Kang himself, was a migrant and exile from Korea living in the United States. Ishimoto's relationships with US feminists Margaret Sanger and Mary Beard gave her a taste of not only a promising, liberatory view of the "Modern Woman" but also the Eurocentrism of that image. At times Ishimoto felt misunderstood and undervalued as a Japanese woman by her American friends; she also describes how American women framed her as "exotic" and sometimes dismissed her as not a "real" feminist.

Both Kang and Ishimoto also saw—as did many of their contemporaries in Japan, Korea, and the United States—that the United States as a growing world power was a dangerous by-product of the nation's progress in technology and industry in this period. As Ishimoto points out, Japan's military rise at the beginning of the twentieth century, while enabling it to become an imperialist power that challenged European and US global hegemony, was viewed ambivalently by many Japanese intellectuals, artists, and activists: the adoption of Western capitalism and the rapid industrialization of the nation not only resulted in a restructuring and severing of Japanese culture and traditions in emulation of Western models of consumption and individualism but also created uneven relations of power between workers and industrialists and between the nation's government and its people.[17] Ishimoto cannot help but view her country's capitalist exploitation of women and children and its imperialist exploitation of the Koreans and Chinese as originating in Japan's fixation on competing with Western/US modernity in those terms. And from the position of the subject of Japanese colonization, Kang describes how his protagonist's forced exit from Korea, now a "dying" country, propels him into a differently colonized subject position in the United States. While not as explicit as Ishimoto's critique of Japan's US-style imperialism, Kang's novel draws parallels between the United States' internal colonization of its nonwhite subjects and Japan's colonization of Koreans, confronting the reader with a subtle yet powerful question: how is the United States' treatment of its nonwhite subjects any different from Japan's subjugation of Koreans? Just as Asians projected their visions and understandings of modernity through the West and American Other, white America's fantastic orientalist imaginings of Asia and Asians reflected their own fears and desires about modernity.

American orientalist perceptions and representations of Asia and Asians imagined them as immutable racial Others, on a polarity of degeneracy, or exemplary Other. Through an orientalist lens, white Americans paradoxically viewed Asia as an imaginary and exotic place, as a menacing yellow peril, and, at still other times, as a hypercivilized nation, representing the pinnacle of modernity's ambitions. On the one hand, yellow peril representations of Asians demonstrate a Manichean logic of good versus evil: if Asians are diabolical, uncivilized, and irrational, then white Americans are virtuous, civilized, and rational. This dualism is seen most ostensibly in the film *East Is West* where the Chinese prostitute becomes a sign of Chinese racial and cultural degeneracy. The Chinese practice of selling Chinese women into prostitution is barbaric and immoral, but the Chinese prostitute is also morally in question. On the other hand, another orientalist perception of Asia and Asians is as the exemplary Other: Asia represents an enlightened and highly advanced civilization in *Lost Horizon*'s representation of Shangri-La, a utopia that can exist only in Tibet and China, not the West. Locating the exact nature of America's orientalisms requires that one understand the historical reasons why Asia as the ultimate Other figured so prominently and complexly into America's interpretation of modernity during the early twentieth century.

At the same time that the United States was expanding its territory overseas through acquisition and commerce, it was contracting its own national borders through laws excluding Asian immigrants. These twin phenomena influenced the ways white Americans saw Asia and Asians as simultaneously signifying the ills and possibilities of modernity, illustrating Palumbo-Liu's point that "the formation of 'modern America' in the early twentieth century is so deeply and particularly attached to the Pacific region" that "managing the modern was inseparable from managing Asian America."[18] From the mid-nineteenth to the early twentieth century, the United States' economic and territorial expansion into Asia and the Pacific put the United States on a trajectory of economic global success and domination.[19] However, territorial expansion and overseas commerce started to dissolve economic borders between nations, also potentially fracturing cultural borders. Amy Kaplan has shown that at the center of debates over US domestic policies were questions about geographical and ideological borders, as the United States engaged in an accelerated imperialism through the conquest, invasion, and territorialization of noncontiguous lands and countries such as the Philippines, Puerto Rico, Cuba, Hawaii, and Alaska.[20] The United States suddenly required a new rationale and justification for the maintenance of its national boundaries vis-à-vis these newly territorialized and/or incorporated countries.[21] The inclusion of nonwhite countries and nonwhite populations challenged the notion of an American nation whose citizens were predominantly white, because the ramifications of the United States' desire for territory and commerce in the Asia Pacific could not be contained "out there"; rather, these desires inevitably affected the US nation by entailing the importation of labor.

Industrialization and economic development within the United States demanded and depended on cheap labor, and the inclusion of Asian immigrants in the US population for these purposes seriously threatened white America's need to maintain its racial identity. Fears over the implications of Asian immigration set in motion a series of legal, social, and cultural actions to forestall it, and these immigration exclusion acts ended up being instrumental in defining the stark racial otherness of Asians. The 1875 Page Law, which prevented the immigration of Chinese prostitutes, along with the 1882 Chinese Exclusion Act and the 1924 National Origins Act specifically identified Asians as excludable from the United States.[22] Domestic laws that prevented Asians from becoming Americans accompanied these exclusion acts: naturalization laws excluded Asians from US citizenship, while other laws, such as the Cable Act of 1922, penalized American women with the loss of their citizenship if they married an "alien ineligible to become a citizen."[23] These laws maintained a perception of Asians as essentially unassimilable within the American melting pot, contributing to the pervasive image of Asians as an always foreign and menacing yellow peril, and therefore as a racial Other to be expelled.[24] Thus, although by the 1930s, laws excluding and restricting Asians had been in place for many years, the imagined threat posed by Asians had not been erased. In fact, as I have argued, these fears and anxieties were simply displaced, from concerns about labor and economic competition to issues of sexuality, which, while always present, were now brought to the surface in new ways because of American anxieties over changes in traditional gender roles and even definitions of normative (hetero) sexualities. For example, the rise of the notion of the New Woman presented the female as open to new behaviors that seemed to mimic those found in the image of Asian female sexuality. But alongside this powerful revision of female gendered and sexual behavior, both Asian and white, came a revision of masculine behavior, as my study demonstrates.

The phenomenon of expansion and contraction indicates that modernity as a cultural experience and even space was essentially more fluid, less fixed, and destabilizing, not just in revising notions of race, nation, and culture but in challenging both Asian and American normative concepts of race, gender formation, and sexuality. America's historical relationship to Asia and Asians, through expansion and ideological contraction, thus created a continual tension. This tension can be translated into the experiences of modernity's polarities: on the one hand, the fantastic possibilities of East and West merging and coming together, and, on the other, what those fantastic possibilities portend—that mixing and merging challenging the norms of race, gender, and sexuality. This tension at work can be seen in my reading of the films *East Is West* and *Lost Horizon*. Both reveal how censorship and reediting erased or muted the fantastic possibilities of East and West merging, essentially containing the spread of nonnormative gendered and sexual behaviors and identities depicted in the films. Eventually, these fantasies contracted into reestablishing normative racial (white), gender, and sexual beliefs and identities.

In this respect, the forms of American orientalism reflecting this tension between expansion and contraction can take an array of seemingly contradictory and heterogeneous meanings and representations, but importantly, as my book shows, these orientalist forms must be seen specifically and understood within the co-encounter and mutual gazing of Asia and America. Lisa Lowe rightly argues in her consideration of orientalism's multiple forms and trajectories that orientalism is itself "heterogeneous and contradictory," consisting "of an uneven matrix of orientalist situations across different cultural and historical sites." She writes that one can look at representations of race, gender, and sexuality as always unstable and contestable: "I suggest that the elucidation of these heterogeneous sites may prove useful, in terms of both method and political strategy, because they mark the places where orientalism is vulnerable to challenge."[25] My book argues that retaining this usage of "orientalism" remained locked in a nineteenth-century formulation. Lowe's critique opens the way to see better the fissures and weak spots of orientalist discourse thus defined, but it helps less in seeing how "orientalism" in the early twentieth century contained very different kinds of "contradictions," ones that are better understood within the dynamic I have suggested—a mutual gazing across the Pacific by Asians and Americans. For instance, the works of Americans Frank Capra and Margaret Sanger show a strong residue of earlier orientalist tropes and images and beliefs and cannot be taken outside the context in which Capra and Sanger each sought to merge America quite selectively and purposefully with Asia in a new global imaginary, an imaginary that had very new roles for men and women to play. For Capra, it was a modern man who turned away from aggression and nationalism to pacifism and cosmopolitanism. For Sanger, it was a vision of what might be called an incipient transnational feminism, facilitated in part by her contact and work with Baroness Ishimoto. Similarly, in my book the active querying of Western liberalism by Asian authors discloses their own efforts to revise traditional Asian notions of masculinity and femininity within the context of increasing contact with, and residence in, America. As I noted above, these authors tested out the capaciousness of liberal idealism (specifically regarding the modern individual) against not just "orientalism" but also its material manifestations in law and history. How were modern Asians to navigate lives in America that were still circumscribed in this way? How did "assimilation" for the Korean male in exile require a new set of strategies in the face of abiding restriction? How would Japanese women align themselves with their Western "sisters" while sorting through the specifics of both Japanese sexism and Western Eurocentrism?

In chapter 1, I examine how the film *East Is West* discloses the ways US domestic space was troubled by modern urbanization's economic and sexual "intercourses," phenomena that were coterminous with increased immigration from decidedly "Asiatic" spaces. I argue that the depiction of a racially ambiguous Chinese/white woman draws together the histories of the nation's legal and social control over Chinese prostitution and immigration, as well as of white female sexual autonomy. The early twentieth-century fascination with the Oriental woman reveals contradictory constructions of Asiatic femininity in relation to constructions of white female sexual and gendered identities. In fact, the image of the Chinese woman as sexual and social menace to white domesticity, as referenced in *East Is West*, tells us more about the vulnerabilities of white domesticity than it does about the actual dangers of Chinese female sexuality. The sexualized surveillance of white women during the early twentieth century is eerily similar to the ways the US nation racialized Chinese women through the policing of their sexuality in the late nineteenth century. Missionaries and law enforcement policed the boundaries of white respectable society from the racialized society inhabited by the Chinese and Chinese women in the late nineteenth century. Likewise, during the early twentieth century an entourage of social workers, parents, police, and authority figures found it necessary to regulate the social autonomy of young women as a way to control their sexuality. The policing and surveillance of young white women helped create the notion of the "girl problem" and of white women's potentially aberrant sexuality. The depiction of an autonomous female sexuality as embodied in the Chinese prostitute in *East Is West* made it possible to articulate the fears over "woman adrift" in the cities.[26] In both cases, policing Asian/Chinese and white female sexuality was rationalized as a means of protecting white families, yet was rationalized in different ways. Asian and Chinese women's threat was highly racialized and based on the belief that they endangered white families through the possibility that white fathers and sons had sex with Chinese prostitutes. In the case of white women, it was their own sexuality and promiscuity that was in question. They threatened either their own families or those of others. And more disturbing, their potential for cross-racial intimate relations (with nonwhite men) threatened to bring down the entire institution of white femininity and domesticity.

While Asian women are treated in contradictory and paradoxical ways in the film *East Is West*, the Asian man in the novel I discuss, Younghill Kang's *East Goes West*, demonstrates and yet complicates the racializing emasculation that ensues from his contact with America. In my second chapter, through an examination of Kang's novel, I reveal how racial and national exclusion constructed the Asian man simultaneously as a potential American citizen and as an unassimilable subject. Asian American historians have argued that the laws of exclusion, citizenship, and antimiscegenation of the early twentieth century created a "bachelor" society of Asian male immigrants, thus negatively affecting their ability to marry and produce families.[27] In my reading of Kang's novel, I argue that class differences among

Asian men constructed different forms of racialized masculinity and even of sexuality that rereads the historical representation of the Asian "bachelor" as not necessarily emasculated or oppressed. My reading of Kang's novel in terms of its sexual politics and constructions of Korean and white masculinity reconsiders Asian American historical theories about Asian masculinity, especially as they have been typically read along the binary constructions of deviancy versus normalcy, foreign versus domestic, homosexual versus heterosexual, emasculation versus masculinization, and authentic versus inauthentic. While his novel lucidly reflects on how Korean and Asian masculinities were repeatedly defined as sexually and socially unassimilable, Kang also presents the ways legal and cultural prohibitions over miscegenation fostered specific sexual and gendered masculine identities that did not merely challenge white heteronormativity but provided alternative possibilities for imagining Asian masculinity. Thus, in my first two chapters, different narratives of Asian women's and men's integration into the United States reveal how Asia tested the capacity of US modernity and of the United States *as* modernity. To what extent could the United States accommodate Asian women and men as subjects or even citizens, but also how could white American male and female identities accommodate new formations of Asians as (potential) Americans?

The first two chapters also show how the insertion of Asians into the United States—especially into the domestic realm, the locus of constructions of white sexualities and genders—challenged and at the same time normalized white American female and female identities. In contrast, chapters 3 and 4 examine how US white subjects, by traveling to Asia and collaborating with Asians, reformulated racial, gendered, and sexual identities both at "home" and "abroad." "Asia" in these cases was envisioned as a frontier for the construction of new social imaginaries—as a place of freedom rather than constriction. Specifically, white US men and women conceived of Asia as an ideological frontier that could transcend national boundaries, enabling transnational definitions of American masculinity and new transnational forms of feminism: in this way Asia becomes the projection of the United States as the ideal modern nation, which in reality it has failed to become.

In chapter 3, I examine Frank Capra's film *Lost Horizon* to show how the white US male subject, through his integration into Asia, provides a counterpoint to the gendered and sexual constructions of Asian men in *East Goes West*. In the early twentieth century, women's growing power and autonomy as it was represented in the popular sphere whether through the girl problem, the woman adrift, or the New Woman affected not only the ways Americans viewed women but also how they viewed white men. If white patriarchy could not contain women, as more women were considered promiscuous and unmarriageable (or more likely unwilling to marry), then white masculinity was equally in question, because, without women as the angel of the house, men were no longer the image of strength that defined masculinity in earlier ages. Moreover, historical circumstances of the early twentieth century, the shock and devastation of the First World War and then, little more than a decade later, the Great Depression, challenged normative white male roles: as stoic and virile and as the breadwinner and patriarch. These challenges to a hegemonic definition of masculinity thus made it more acceptable to broach the limitations of men as masculine and powerful patriarchs. In *Lost Horizon*, the remaking of a specific masculinity in Asia at the dawn of World War II was a response to the ways the modern condition seemed to have sapped the American man of his strength and virility, leaving him helpless among strong women, growing immigrant settlement, and economic devastation during the Depression era. Capra's 1937 film reveals "Asia" as a catalyst for the imagining of a radically different white male identity that discards a destructive and aggressive Western masculinity for one that is pacifist and rational. In a surprising reversal, Capra's film inverts the US empire's "manifest" masculinity by presenting a white male figure who recoils from the expectations of the West's policy of aggression and territorial acquisition. For a brief moment after the film's first release, this displacement of West onto East allowed audiences to contemplate notions of anti-imperialism, pacifism, alternative masculinities, and indeed an alternative society—a utopia. Unfortunately, *Lost Horizon*'s subsequent reediting by the US government for propaganda purposes during World War II changed its focus and meaning entirely: its utopian and pacifist imaginary became bounded by an antifascist and then a neo-imperialist agenda. Ultimately, the reedited version recuperated an aggressive masculinity and erased the film's original depiction of a pacifist and even emasculated alternative white male identity. In this way, the white masculinity of Capra's original film, resignified within the context of World War II, ultimately gave birth to a white masculinity characterized as benevolent and paternal, fitting the purposes of the US nation-state's desire to softly forward its imperialist aims in a new postwar global era.

Thus the integration of West into East in this period is both a catalyst for presenting provocative and telling possibilities for masculine identity and, in the hands of government editors, a means of limiting those possibilities. As mentioned previously, in both *East Is West* and *Lost Horizon*, the censorship and/or reediting of the films changed the more radical representations of gender and sexuality that resulted from merging East and West, Asia and America. The original depictions, even the intent of the films, presented a kind of raw ambiguity of Asian and white racial, gendered, and sexual identities and identifications, revealing the entanglements of Asia and America in the co-constructions of modern identities. One sees in these films that the contradictions and ambiguities cannot remain.

In chapter 4, I examine how the exchange of feminist knowledge between Japanese and American women affected Japanese and American feminists' definitions of feminism, internationalism, femininity, domesticity, and woman. While in reading *East Is West* in chapter 1 I explore the destabilization of Asian and white female racial and sexual identities within the conditions of immigration and urbanization, in this chapter I examine how those very conditions also informed the imaginings of alternative forms of female agency and gendered identities through the politics of New Women not only in the United States but also in Japan. Like Kang, Ishimoto in her autobiography, *Facing Two Ways: The Story of My Life*, uses US race and gender politics to expand notions of Japanese female and male identities. These encounters were not one-way streets, or mere impositions of the West upon the East. The New Women and American feminists defined their modern gendered identity and sexuality through a play of difference and separation from Asian women, but also through alliances and similarities with those women. In some cases, white feminists' alliances with Asian feminists gave them an international audience that fueled American feminism's global ambitions and shaped a universalizing rhetoric of gender and sexuality. The Japanese feminist Ishimoto, in turn, used her alliances with American feminists to cultivate a unique and even transnational feminist sensibility that served her political and existential purposes, either to develop a Japanese feminism as a critique of existing Japanese feminisms at the time or to chart new ways of being a mother, a wife, and a woman within an imperializing and militarizing Japan.

Ishimoto's autobiography, *Facing Two Ways: The Story of My Life*, is part socialist and feminist manifesto and part life story. She describes how her transformation from an obedient Japanese wife and mother into a birth control activist and feminist made her a New Woman of Japan. I suggest in this chapter that Ishimoto's synthesis of Western and Japanese progressive politics allowed her to theorize a more expansive and transcendent vision of feminism that challenged racial and class boundaries, unlike those espoused by her American feminist friends, who often regressed to American notions of race. Ishimoto had strong ties to the United States because of the publication of her autobiography in English and because of her relationship with notable white American feminists, including birth control activist Margaret Sanger and feminist historian Mary

Beard. Her version of feminism questions the racial, national, and cultural boundaries that prevented nations and individuals from eradicating the social hierarchies that oppressed not only women but other classes of people as well. Through such critical reconsiderations she hoped to construct a new female identity that was not merely Japanese or Asian but international and even transnational, formed in dialogue between Asia and the West, especially the United States. In Ishimoto's view, Japanese and American women shared alliances as subjects under patriarchy. However, her autobiography shows that, in practice, such alliances were severed under the United States' cultural, national, and racial hegemony and, at times, US feminists' own global ambitions. In comparison to Ishimoto's vision of a transnational feminism, for example, Sanger saw Asia primarily as an intellectual and ideological frontier for the expansion of her birth control movement. Sanger's efforts could have opened the opportunity for Asian and American feminists to forge stronger ties across and outside of nation and cultures; however, her entrenched orientalist notions about Asia and Asian women made them not collaborators but objects that fueled her ambitions.

In each of these chapters, contact between East and West, Asia and America, forces a reassessment of the normative boundaries of race, sex, gender, class, home, and nation. This contact permits us a closer look at American modernity as it was envisioned in the interwar period, and the texts I examine allow us to look at modernity from the perspectives of both Asians and whites and to see what happens when they direct their gazes toward each other. These texts suggest the transcendent possibilities that can emerge from intercultural and interracial contact, even as I show how Asian and white subjects struggle against constant efforts at recontainment due to persistent fears over racial, sexual, and cultural mixing that endure even today.

1 / How Yellow and White Women Are Sold: Controlling Chinese and White Female Sexuality and the Making of US Domesticity in *East Is West*

In the infinite, Ming Toy, whence all things come, there is no East, there is no West. West is East, and East is West.

LO SANG KEE IN *EAST IS WEST*

BILLY: *A Love Boat? What do you mean?*

LO: *Just as I would sell rugs in my store in San Francisco, so they sell women here upon the river.*

BILLY: *Oh woman market, huh? I should think that would be illegal.*

LO: *So is boot-legging in our beloved United States.*

EAST IS WEST SCRIPT

The beginning of the 1930 film *East Is West* unabashedly introduces us to a Chinese "woman market," where Lo Sang Kee (E. Alyn Warren), a Chinese American businessman, brings his good friend Billy Benson (Lew Ayres), an international man of trade and son of the US ambassador to China, to browse the nubile female goods that are bought and sold every day in the Chinese sex slave market. One Chinese "sing-song girl," Ming Toy (Lupe Vélez), stands out as distinctively different from the other Chinese girls on the auction block: she is vocal and rebellious.[1] While the other Chinese girls acquiesce to their sale, Ming Toy argues with her father (who is selling her) and physically assaults one of the auctioneers, biting him when he goes to inspect her teeth. Benson is immediately drawn to her, though he has shown very little interest in the other Chinese girls and is even seemingly untouched by their misery at being sold.[2] Just as Ming Toy is about to be sold to a Chinese man, Benson's Chinese American friend, Lo Sang Kee, intercedes and secretly purchases Ming Toy, whom he brings with him to San Francisco's Chinatown. Eventually, Benson and Ming Toy fall in love, and all seems well, except for one problem—she is Chinese and he is white. In the end, Ming Toy's Chinese father, Hop Toy (Tetsu Komai), discloses to Benson that Ming Toy is not his true daughter but a white girl adopted from missionaries. The taboo against interracial intimacy is lifted upon this discovery, and therefore the film can end happily . . . or so it seems.

The Hays Commission prevented *East Is West* from ever being distributed.[3] Its domestic division disapproved of the film's depiction of miscegenation and prostitution, but especially of the fact that the film implied that white women could be sold into sexual slavery as *Chinese* women. In 1935, after five years of attempting to obtain approval from the Hays Commission, Universal Pictures finally shelved *East Is West* in its archives as an "unreleased film."[4]

In some respects, the Hays Commission's decision reflected the persistence of earlier fears of white female victimization during the white slavery scare of 1910–15, as well as fear in the late nineteenth century of an epidemic of Chinese prostitution. The concern that Chinese prostitution and white slavery were rampant phenomena was contrary to the historical case: there is no evidence that either existed in high numbers. Moreover, the Chinese prostitution trade had been virtually eliminated in the United States since the passage of the 1875 Page Law, which prohibited the importation of Chinese prostitutes.[5] Thus it is the nature and the abiding power of these fears, contrary to actual evidence, that draws our attention. Censors remained concerned not only by the danger of suggesting miscegenation between Chinese and whites but also, and perhaps more important, by the danger of presenting an equivalency between Chinese and white women, in which both were seen as sexually deviant and threatening to white middle-class families.

While the idea of interracial sexual desire was abhorrent to Americans during the height of anti-immigrant and antimiscegenation sentiments in the early twentieth century, it was still fairly commonly found in mass pulp fiction, soft-porn literature, and serials depicting sexual relations between Asians and whites.[6] However, splashed across the cinematic screen, such vivid and realistic images of interracial intimacies were feared to be more stimulating and alluring to the collective psyche. Cinema cast forth moving and graphic images in a way that enhanced their verisimilitude and presented the public with a far more alarming depiction of the possibility that the East and the West could breach their boundaries in a graphically sexual exchange for money. Yet as I show, what made this film especially problematic for censors is not simply the possibility of miscegenation between the white man and the "Chinese" woman but also the depiction that (racialized) female sexuality is dubiously contained.

My reading suggests that the film was troubling to censors because of its narrative focus on visuality and female sexuality and particularly the ways racial difference disappears within these frames. The film's narrative of racial passing and racial misrecognition, in which the Chinese prostitute comes to discover that she is actually pure white, draws on the riddle of the film's title: unbeknownst to viewers, the heroine is really white, but her behavior reveals that such racial differentiation is shaky to begin with. The Chinese Ming Toy's outrageous behavior can at first be attributed to her racial identity. Nevertheless, that this dangerous figure turns out to be white, although she may have her wild "Chinese" side, is recontained when she moves into Benson's home. Taking Ming Toy out of Chinatown and into Benson's white home seems to quiet her more sexually provocative (though generally innocent) behavior. Still, that Asian sexuality has been found in a white woman means that female sexuality in general can transcend racial specificity. And in fact, it is the film's portrayal of the heroine's sexual breach that makes her undecipherable as a white woman. Here, when East "is" West, the film reveals the possibilities of imagining cross-racial equivalences between Chinese and white women and unveils the anxieties that such an equation implies. Even while the film's resolution tries to divest the film of its visual potency in depicting the alarming contradictions of female sexuality, which can be racially other and sexually deviant, the harsh censorship it drew suggests that what cannot be seen can still be imagined. In this chapter, I consider how this blending of East and West gives imaginative expression to the dangers that Asian and white female sexuality poses to the white family and home. In particular, I show how the film draws on the ways visuality, exercised outside of cinema, was integral in the construction of Chinese women as sexually deviant.

It is important to note that one of the key ways Chinese immigrant women became codified by the state as prostitutes was through the use of surveillance and visual inspection. Immigration officials and police often watched how Chinese and Asian women behaved, how they dressed, and whether their faces and facial expressions bore traces of lasciviousness. The visual scrutiny of Chinese and Asian immigrant women during exclusion attempted to distinguish the women who were respectable wives and mothers from those who were prostitutes, in order to prevent the latter from entering the United States. As a result, the audaciousness of *East Is West* was precisely its representation of the failure of the visual to discern not just race but, more important, sexual deviancies as they defined the racial difference of Chinese and white women.

I argue that, as viewers of the film, our supposed inability to determine Ming Toy's real racial identity only intensifies in the end anxieties over race and sexuality. There seems to be no way to ascertain the behavioral differences between Asian and white women. And the film tantalizes us with the possibility that there is no difference, that East is West—a prospect that is just too frightening. What happens when "they" (the Chinese) actually appear to be just like "us" (whites)? Thus the film's racial displacement never fully contains the fears over white female sexuality and contradictorily reveals that neither Chinese nor white female sexuality can adequately be controlled. Even though the heroine is revealed as white at the end, the riddle of the title, *East Is West*, haunts the film. Is the Chinese woman's deviant behavior erased when she is discovered to be white? Does this then mean, now she is white, that white women are also deviant? The film's racial reversals, the misrecognition, and the passing reveal just how dangerous white women are when they behave like Chinese women. The racial passing alludes to the anxiety over the inability to differentiate these two women because, being one and the same, they exhibit the same sexually deviant and potentially morally corrupt behavior. The ambiguity surrounding Ming Toy's racial and sexual persona thus indexes the latent anxieties over the continued purity of white domesticity and thereby our nation's racial purity—if white women can be mistaken for Chinese women, and if women in general are understood as inclined to sexual promiscuity, then there is a real crisis in maintaining the racial and sexual purity of the white family, given that white women are no longer the angels of the home but questionable sexual figures.

In other words, when East *is* West, such a merging offers a way to signify and express the deep anxieties over white female sexuality and the threats it poses to the white family. As white women moved away from traditional family and domestic values, the threat became not merely external, in the form of the racial and sexualized Other (the racialized rapist or the Chinese prostitute), but internal, residing within the white home and the family—in white women themselves.

East Is West discloses the ways the white family was troubled by modern urbanism's economic and sexual "intercourses," phenomena that were coterminous not only with increased immigration from decidedly "Asiatic" spaces but also with the effects of migration in general, which were particularly visible in the urban industrial centers: as immigrants from Asia and Europe mingled with white Americans, Mexicans, and African Americans in the cities and in the workplace, there was an increased chance for racial mixing. I explained in the introduction how migration from the East resulted in both the real and perceived shifting of domestic space, economics, and demography in the West, causing gender, race, class, sexuality, and national identity to be dynamically redefined and understood throughout the early twentieth century in the United States. Thus female sexuality became an indissociable part of the discussion over immigration. Some groups, such as the Progressives, argued that the rise of crime and especially prostitution left young unmarried white women particularly vulnerable to unscrupulous men, who lured them into lives of prostitution, in which, as purchasable white women, they were open to cross-racial intercourse.[7] Immigrant men (and black men) were particular targets for the anti-white-slavery movements. Pressure to pass laws to protect white women resulted in the Mann Act, otherwise known as the White-Slave Traffic Act (1910). While the specter of white female victimization loomed large, however, what was most troubling was the idea of white female sexual autonomy.[8] If white women were indeed their own agents, not victims, then the sanctity and purity of white domesticity as the bedrock of the US nation would begin to crumble. Such fears of white female promiscuity and sexual autonomy also reflected the social and cultural climate of the times, notably the increasing number of women living and working in cities, the liberalizing of notions of gender and sex, and the rise of the women's movement and the New Woman. White women were seen as becoming more sexually promiscuous and less inclined toward marriage and family.

In this chapter, I begin by describing the different historical dangers that Chinese and white female sexuality in particular posed to the sanctity of the white home and family. While the Chinese prostitute threatened to infect white families through sexually transmitted diseases, white women's sexual autonomy (read as promiscuity) endangered the integrity of the white family: how would the white family be maintained when white women no longer represented home and hearth? I then examine the ways the film *East Is West* draws on these fears of racialized female sexuality and re-presents them in a way that further troubles the distinctions between Chinese and white female sexuality and thus race. And even more troubling are the ways the film implicates white men in the exchange of women, equating them with Chinese men. To untangle this crossing of racial identities on the basis of sexuality, it is important first to trace the historical context of the laws that sought to prevent Asian/American crossings.

The Chinese Prostitute Invades the White Family

The late nineteenth-century panic over the Chinese prostitute's infiltration of the white home and family was linked to the fear of the Chinese prostitution slave trade invading the United States. Yellow slavery stories customarily represented a "Mongol invasion" that included Asian women who were bought and sold by lecherous Chinese men right in the middle of Chinatown, USA. These yellow peril tales augured what the film's title announces: that the East is not only coming to the West, but the East is (already in) the West. Although such prostitution was hardly pervasive, it seemed so to the American public. By the time the Page Law was passed in 1875, anti-Chinese sentiments had helped fuel the perception of an epidemic. Horace F. Page, the congressman who underwrote the bill, made a claim based on a few missionary sources that 90 percent of Chinese women in the United States were prostitutes.[9]

The actual number of Chinese prostitutes was much lower and constituted a very small percentage of prostitution overall, even at the height of the Chinese prostitution trade (1860–75).[10] According to Lucie Cheng, the number of Chinese prostitutes in San Francisco during the late nineteenth century was nominal, but anti-Chinese activists and legislators often gave contradictory accounts of how many Chinese prostitutes lived in the city: "These estimates contradicted one another and revealed the witnesses' political biases and self-interests. Because of those contrasting interests, the estimates of Chinese prostitutes in San

Francisco differed widely, ranging from 200 to 2,700. In neither hearing [on Chinese immigration, conducted by the California State Senate and by the US Congress, in 1876] did witnesses or legislators cite the census figures."[11] Ronald Takaki explains that in 1862, of the 63,199 Chinese in the United States, 4,566 were Chinese women. Further, in the heyday of Chinese prostitution, 1870 census figures indicated that 61 percent of the 3,536 Chinese women living in San Francisco were listed as prostitutes.[12] Clearly, the number of Chinese women in the United States was highly disproportionate to the number of Chinese men. Yet these statistics did not quell the anti-Chinese sentiment directed at Chinese women. More likely the figure of the Chinese prostitute was a convenient scapegoat and rationale for rising anti-Chinese sentiments over immigration resulting from foreign trade with China.[13] Chinese prostitution was singled out as an epidemic because Chinese women were construed as dangerous by-products of industrialization, which allowed unchecked immigration of people from China and Asia. Moreover, the racial difference of Chinese women connected them to the dreaded Chinese coolies who were believed to be taking jobs away from white workers. Both workers and prostitutes threatened to infect the United States in different ways, but more dangerous was the Chinese prostitute, who was seen as silently infiltrating white families and thereby corrupting white, middle-class domesticity.

What made the Chinese prostitute especially "dangerous" was the surreptitious and invisible way she could permeate the white family through passing on sexually transmitted diseases to white men.[14] Nayan Shah argues that Chinese women in particular were viewed as potential carriers of syphilis.[15] Because the Chinese prostitute did not cater exclusively to Chinese men but also performed services for white men, the rise of venereal disease in white men was pinned on the Chinese prostitute. Such illicit sexual racial crossings were thus of urgent moral and public health concern. Social reformers argued that Chinese prostitutes could infect white men with venereal diseases and their families would not find out until it was too late. In San Francisco's Chinatown, social workers and hygiene officials told sordid stories about the "crib girl," the lowest common denominator of prostitute, who was exclusively Chinese. She was displayed in a small "crib," in a narrow alley between buildings in Chinatown, with a tiny barred window from which she peered out, beckoning prospective clients.[16] The commonly held belief that Chinese prostitutes were cheaper and more available than white prostitutes constructed the former as irresistible sexual commodities that simply could not be passed up: they were available and affordable to working-class white men and even boys. As Shah explains: "The most famous testimony came from Dr. Hugh Huger Toland, a member of the San Francisco Board of Health and founder of Toland Medical College (which subsequently became the University of California Medical School). Dr. Toland reported that he had examined white 'boys eight and ten years old' with venereal diseases contracted at 'Chinese houses of prostitution.'" More shocking were the statistics given about the pervasiveness of venereal diseases contracted by these boys: "Toland estimated that 'nine-tenths' of all syphilis cases in white boys and young men were attributable to Chinese prostitutes." As Dr. Toland explained of the Chinese prostitutes, "The women do not care how old the boys are, whether five years old or more, as long as they have money."[17] The peril of infection threatening both adult and adolescent males and the fear that they would bring that disease home seemed to necessitate expedient action to curb the importation of Chinese prostitutes. Thus the Page Law developed methods of exclusion that precisely attempted to make visible and therefore containable the Chinese prostitute's sexual deviancy.

Visuality, Detection, Failure

The process of excluding Chinese prostitutes after the passage of the Page Law relied on methods of scrutiny in the detection of deviancy or normativity that sought to render visible what authorities were unable to see: the sexual transmission of disease through Chinese women. Chinese women were the first immigrants to be scrutinized through photographs as indicators of moral character and potential hidden deviancy. Photography was believed at the time to be a new scientific method of ascertaining the inner character of persons on the basis of their bodily attributes. For example, methods of identifying whether Chinese women were legitimate or "immoral" included physical markers whose photographic interpretation would reveal whether they were destined for prostitution. As Eithne Luibhéid explains: "Photographs provided one of the earliest methods of officially recording the body's distinctiveness and using the record to control an individual's mobility. This system was used on Chinese women before any other group of immigrants, because of the 'threat' of their sexuality to the United States."[18] Because there was a growing belief in the power of the visual, particularly the ways photographs gave people the ability to decipher the inner character of the photographed person, US immigration officials found that in addition to collecting biographical information from Chinese and Asian immigrant women, photographs, usually of their faces, helped provide indisputable evidence of their moral character.[19]

Public health officials in the city and immigration officers at the border believed that signs of sexual and moral deviancy could be seen on the bodies and in the behaviors of Chinese and Asian women who did not appear to "look" like respectable white middle-class women, the domestic ideal of femininity. Indeed, racial difference was one implicit criterion of assumed deviancy in Chinese and Asian women, but there were also more nuanced criteria based on markers of class difference. Sometimes, immorality was ascertained by how the women were dressed. Were they wearing sexually provocative clothing or simply clothing that indicated they were of a working or lower class? At other times, immigration officials argued that they could simply see, on the faces of these women, the signs of immorality.[20] Chinese and Asian women's faces and clothing simply did not exhibit the virtue, chastity, and moral conduct that proper white middle-class women presumably possessed.

Such "insight" into Chinese and Asian female immorality and sexual disease through visual examination of their appearance was underscored by scrutiny of their behavior, a scrutiny that also helped define what would be construed as normative, white female domesticity. The signs of aberrant social behavior among Chinese women became signs of sexual deviancy, which then became interpreted as proof of Chinese women's *foreignness* and intractable racial otherness. Shah explains that, besides the police raids in Chinatowns during the mid- to late nineteenth century, local authorities maintained surveillance of Chinese women entering and leaving their homes. Such surveillance addressed a spectrum of behaviors in an attempt to determine whether or not these women were in fact prostitutes. While a Chinese woman sitting in a crib was undeniably evidence that she was a "Chinese prostitute," by contrast, reports of the surveillance of Chinese women's homes—whether they lingered too long at the window or were seen being visited by too many men—were more open to interpretation.[21] Such occurrences and visitations were often reread as signs that these women were actual or potential prostitutes. Implicitly, police and public officials believed that, contrary to the behavior of Chinese prostitutes, proper women did not loiter at doorways or beckon men from their windows.

The issue of moral deviance was closely linked to a physical contamination that could, it was thought, be rendered visible and thus readable by referencing signifiers of white, middle-class domestic roles and characteristics that supposedly preexisted within the United States' borders.[22] Nevertheless, in spite of the pervasive use of visual technology, surveillance gave unreliable evidence. Sucheng Chan explains that immigration officials often were beset with contradictory and conflicting opinions about whether entering Chinese women, on the basis of their appearance, were destined for a life of immorality.[23] Because of the failure of the visual to provide unequivocal evidence of morality or the lack thereof in Chinese and Asian immigrant women, immigration officials had to engage in repeated scrutiny and visual deciphering.[24]

After the passing of the Page Law, Chinese prostitution became less visible in the United States, and the focus shifted to saving white women from slave traders, as evidenced by the Mann Act, or the White-Slave Traffic Act, of 1910. Although the law was passed to "protect" white women from men, I show that what was most troubling in constructing white women as victims was that oftentimes they were not victims at all. The Mann Act not only sought to prevent the abduction and enslavement of white women but was implicitly aimed to control the sexual agency and autonomy of these women by casting them as victims. Although the most visible race in *East Is West* is the exotic Oriental, my argument is that white and yellow are inextricably linked to a critique of female sexual agency.

White Women: Victims or Agents? White Slavery and the Saving of White Women

Even though the Chinese prostitution epidemic was mostly fictional, sensational stories about yellow slavery reappeared decades later in pulp fiction tales of the early twentieth century, along with the white slavery narrative. By this time, however, what the public was most concerned with was the victimization of white women. Thus yellow slavery stories often overlapped with narratives of white slavery in which Chinese men enslaved white women. Yellow slavery and the yellow peril that Chinese men represented became another way to define, at this historical juncture, the fears over white female sexuality and the perceived decline of white patriarchy and domesticity.

Yellow peril literature and films of the early twentieth century depicted how women, Chinese and white alike, were sexually unpredictable, at once victims and agents. One of the most popular authors of yellow peril literature was Sax Rohmer, whose "Fu Manchu" stories contained accounts of the "Mongol" or "yellow" invasion that took place not in China or Asia but in Britain or US Chinatowns. In these stories, Chinese and white women could be lured into Chinatown's opium dens where Chinese men awaited to trade in their bodies.[25] Critically, these narratives posit the interchangeability of yellow and white prostitutes insofar as white and Chinese men could buy both. In some cases, Chinese women were sold to both Chinese and white men, and in other cases, the white prostitute was *enslaved* by Chinese men in the dungeons of Chinatown's opium lairs. The possession of white women by Chinese men, however, was a breach of racial/sexual boundaries. Here one sees the particular value a white female body held in these yellow peril narratives. These Chinatown stories called upon fears of white slavery, a narrative that constructed white women as victims of Chinese male predators. Yet in other ways, these stories depicted what the public truly feared at the time—white women's sexual deviancy. One of the more famous scenes from an early silent film, *Broken Blossoms*, directed by D. W. Griffith in 1919, reveals in its opening shots a claustrophobic view of an underground Chinatown opium den in London where Chinese men smoke opium side by side with white women.[26] Their eyes glazed over by the opium, these women look longingly toward the camera, their gazes showing desire rather than fear. One understands that they were hardly coerced, but rather were willing participants.

The paradoxical representations of white women as both victims and agents reflect the public's fears over the uncertainty of white women's sexuality, underscoring the discrepancy between appearances and beliefs, on the one hand, and the likely underlying presence of female sexual desire, on the other. The narrative of victimhood constructs Chinese men as perpetrators and white women as sexually innocent, unaware of what Chinese men may want from them. These paradoxical representations also came up in real-life cases of relationships between white women and Chinese men. Mary Ting Yi Lui's examination of a high-profile murder case in turn-of-the-century New York's Chinatown involving a young white woman whose dead body was found in a luggage trunk describes how outraged whites believed that she was killed by licentious and devious Chinese men, inevitably drawing from the stereotype of Chinese men as sexual deviants and savage predators of white women. Yet what emerges from this and other sensational tales of white female victimhood and Chinese aggression is that these women willingly cohabited with Chinese men and quite often approached them. As Lui explains, "What was perhaps most troubling to police and the public at large about this and other similar cases was that these teenage girls and young women had entered the premises of their own free will."[27] What these women should appear to be, passive and innocent, is really, underneath, to the contrary or much more complicated. Similar to the ways Chinese women needed to be policed and kept under surveillance, female sexual desires in general needed to be monitored.

In some cases, the border between white women and adolescent girls was also being increasingly challenged by these interracial liaisons. Victor Jew describes a similar Chinese lynch mob scenario in Milwaukee, where Chinese laundrymen were accused of raping adolescent white girls. In both the New York and Milwaukee cases, the white women (and girls) were the ones who accosted the Chinese men, a fact that overturns the perception that young women and girls were both unaware of sexuality and passive recipients of sexual advances.[28] Reaction to these cases was thus not confined to white society's disapproval of interracial relationships, although those relationships were horrifying in themselves; the response also indicated a larger problem about women and girls. Progressive reformers understood that both adolescent white girls and young white women were not models of Victorian purity and chastity but possessed sexual desire, and rather than persist in the belief in chaste white girlhood and womanhood, they would urge the nation to institute reforms to protect and control these girls and women. What was considered the "girl problem" in the early twentieth-century United States gave rise to reformatories to reeducate "delinquent" teenage girls. At the same time, white working-class girls and women were increasingly the subjects of police surveillance and social worker interventions.[29] Concerns over white women and Chinese men were in fact indicative of larger phenomena aimed at controlling white female sexuality during a time when white women's social and cultural roles were changing.

The larger problems concerning white female sexuality were linked to the problems that modern urbanization generated: flows of migrants from the non-West, along with the irregular internal movements and migrations of populations at the height of America's industrialization. The influx of immigrants from Europe and Asia into US cities, where they were needed as laborers in various growing industries, created a space in which people from different racial and cultural backgrounds could come in contact, making it possible for white women to sexually cross racial boundaries. Industrialization also changed women's work and thus women's roles in both the domestic and public spheres. In particular, an increasing number of female laborers, many of them young, immigrant, and working class, were employed in urban factories. The description of them as "women adrift" refers to their being unanchored to the family and traditional female gender roles: young and unmarried, they lived alone in the city or with other girls and without their families.[30] The convergence of the phenomena of migration, greater contact with diverse people, and an unprecedented number of young women working and living alone contributed to the sense of a lack of control within urban spaces. Middle-class social reformers during the Progressive Era believed that this combination of factors made young white women vulnerable to prostitution and victimization.[31] According to Ruth Rosen:

> Reformers discussed prostitution in terms that reflected their acute anxieties about other unresolved ills and problems of the day: the unrestricted immigration, the rate of venereal disease, the anonymity of the city, the evils of liquor, the growth of a working-class urban culture, and, most important of all, the changing role of women in society. As women from all classes increasingly entered the public arena, either through their participation in the labor force or through their involvement in middle-class

> social reform movements, they implicitly challenged the nineteenth-century doctrine of separate male and female spheres. Moreover, their entry into public life blurred the tidy distinctions between "public" women and respectable wives and mothers. In so doing, these women symbolically threatened the traditional patriarchal values of the dominant group of reformers.[32]

No longer was the nation simply policing the border that divided the foreign from home and the nation, as it had with Chinese women earlier. White female sexuality was now equally in question. More unsettling was the possibility that white women had the ability to navigate the nation's heterogeneous urban terrain by selling themselves, a situation in which their agency in choosing prostitution complicated the narrative of white female victimization.[33] Compared to the threat that the Chinese prostitute posed to the white family, the white prostitute was more insidious because she threatened the very center of the white home. This contamination was all the more deadly because the white prostitute could transmit disease between the races.

Fears about white female sexuality were in fact central to the white slavery narratives. While many of the stories depicted white women as victims, there was always a reminder that many of these women readily chose the profession; in this context, some of these stories equated the lure of sexuality with the lure of commercial profit. Margit Stange argues that in many of the white slavery stories of the turn of the century, the economic bottom line was the most dangerous aspect of white slavery. While young white women were initially lured into prostitution against their will, they often stayed in the profession because of the consumer goods and finery it allowed them to purchase.[34] But these "goods" had a racialized dimension to them in some stories, since the white slave trader in the yellow peril tales was typically the Asian immigrant male Other. While the Page Law's exclusion of Chinese women had disingenuously assumed that sexual deviancy and illicit profiteering were restricted to

Chinese women and men, the white slavery narrative blurred this racial barrier and depicted white women as similarly vulnerable and even liable to sexual deviancy. This blurring of racial distinctions shows up in the film *East Is West* as one of the more ungovernable aspects of modernity.

Therefore, as the Page Law attempted to prohibit Chinese women's racial and sexual transgressions, white women's cross-racial liaisons became a particular concern for lawmakers as well. The fears over cross-racial intimacies between white women and nonwhite men were associated more generally with the commodification of white women and of sex itself. During the height of the white slavery panic, Congress passed several acts to deter prostitution and presumably "protect" women, the most notorious of which was the aforementioned Mann Act (or White-Slave Traffic Act) of 1910, prohibiting the transport of white women across state borders for purposes of prostitution.[35] In 1904 the United States signed the International Agreement for the Suppression of the White Slave Traffic and in 1917 passed the Immigration Act, also known as the Asiatic Barred Zone Act, aimed to redraw geographic boundaries of east and west to prevent immigrants from South Asia, Southeast Asia, and some regions of the Pacific from entering the United States. Among its provisions was a ban on bringing women and girls into the country for prostitution.[36] In many respects, these acts placed more scrutiny on white women, either as victims (of white slave traders) or as agents (prostitutes and sexually promiscuous women), than on Asian women. The concern over white slavery and the passing of these various laws points to the United States' need to protect its domestic borders against foreign elements and also to the urgency of controlling white women's behaviors and actions inside those borders. The perceived epidemic commodification of white women, who could be bought and sold like Chinese women, thus pointed to the very fragility of the boundary between East and West and thereby the vulnerability of the white home and family to Asiatic foreign elements. While Chinese prostitutes and their sexual relations with white men threatened the family and home, their existence did not call into question white female chastity or purity: Chinese women were represented as a disease and pollutant that could be expelled from the family and the nation through immigration exclusion. However, white women threatened the internal structure of the white family and reproduction: these women's sexual autonomy did not guarantee that they would uphold white racial purity. The potential racial crossings by white women point to the erosion of their role in the family and thus to the possible disappearance altogether of the white family. The image of the young white woman as chaste, pure, passive, and naive becomes a cultural belief and desire to see women as such, but underneath, and what we don't see, may be more complicated. The national concern over the internal, interstate flows of commodified female bodies—bodies both sexualized and racialized through this traffic—explains the furor over the film *East Is West*, which becomes a story about the nation and the West disappearing and becoming the East.

Passing, Visuality, and Racial Discovery in *East Is West*

East Is West opens with the depiction of a Chinese woman market, where the practice of selling women into slavery and prostitution articulates and problematizes the idea that what divides East from West is precisely the differences in racialized masculinity. The East reveals its disregard of human life, particularly Chinese women, selling humans as they would livestock; the West, in comparison, reveals its civilizing influence and its humanity by the purchase of the Chinese prostitute. When the film first opens, we see several scenarios of Chinese girls, who will all soon be sold to the Love Boat. In one of these scenes a girl and her mother quietly hold each other, while the mother appears to be reassuring the girl that she will be all right. This scene underscores the depravity of Chinese men, both the fathers who sell their daughters and, later, the men who buy these women. In the last of these scenarios we are introduced to

Ming Toy, who in carrying a litter of piglets is engaged in carefree play, until she is beckoned solemnly by her mother to come into the house. Inside is her father, Hop Toy, and a missionary. Ming Toy's father gruffly tells her that she is going to the Love Boat; she resists, cries not to be taken there, and tells the missionary of her father's intentions. It is the white missionary who, to no avail, tries to convince her father that his plan is wrong. Hop Toy replies angrily, "Ming Toy, my daughter [. . .] I do what I want with Ming Toy."

The presence of the missionary represents a common stereotype of the white Western man's necessary and civilizing mission in the Orient, an enterprise that ultimately is ineffective: another indication of the Orient's failure to modernize. From here the film then cuts to Billy Benson and Lo Sang Kee in the Chinese market, where Kee will introduce Benson to the trade in Chinese women. The foreignness of such a practice, coupled with its exotica, puzzles Benson. When he finally meets Ming Toy on the auction block, he asks her how her father could bear to sell her. As Ming Toy explains to Benson after the auction, her father sold her to the infamous Love Boat in order to acquire a pig:

> MING TOY: My father have sixteen daughters, fourteen pigs. He has too much daughters, not enough pigs. He sell one daughter, buy one pig. Then he have fifteen daughter, fifteen pig. My mother have four quartette, four times.[37]

If Chinese fathers can sell their daughters for pigs, then what will the Chinese man who buys Ming Toy do with her? The film thus underscores that even in this modern age, a Chinese woman's life is less valuable than livestock. Indeed, the film establishes China's historical stasis: "Sometimes even today, it is said—unwanted girls were often placed on the auction block and knocked down to the highest bidder."[38] The continued practice of selling women becomes an obvious indication of China's inability to embrace modernity, and for that reason, it is suggested, China will always lag behind Western countries.[39] In contrast,

Benson's impulse is to buy Ming Toy and bring her to the United States, revealing both his white Western male capacity for compassion and his growing romantic interest in Ming Toy. The film shows that white men are fundamentally different from Chinese men: even as Benson has compassion for Ming Toy, he refuses to purchase her simply because he is an "American":

MING TOY: Billy Benson. That's a sweet name. You buy me Billy Benson. I be nice. If that ugly old man buy me, I be devil.
BILLY: Oh, it's not that. Americans just don't buy women, that's all.
MING TOY: Too bad you Americans not civilized like Chinese.[40]

For Benson, his explanation is enough. Being an American man means that he will not treat women as if they are objects for purchase. Ming Toy's response comically highlights this lack of explanation, reversing what is obvious: that it is indeed Americans and thus white men who are the civilized ones. Benson turns to Lo Sang Kee, inaudibly whispering to him as if imploring. In the 1924 play, Billy asks Lo if he would purchase Ming Toy for him and bring her back to live in Chinatown with Lo. We do not hear this discussion in the film, but one assumes that Billy is asking Lo if other arrangements can be made to save Ming Toy. As Billy walks away, Lo approaches Ming Toy and says to her, "I come to tell you that everything is settled my child." He adds, "Little Jade Lady, this unworthy one has the honor to have purchased you."[41] Even though Lo is the one who actually saves Ming Toy by purchasing her, he does so at Billy's request, as one surmises from the quiet exchange between the two men. However, Billy's refusal to purchase Ming Toy because he is an "American" shows American principle and integrity and also compassion. Thus Benson still represents the white male rescuer and Ming Toy the victim of an archaic and depraved Chinese patriarchy that has persisted into modernity. In this respect, it is both the benevolence and civilized humanity of the white American man and his integrity that reassure American viewers of the differences between East and West, China and the

FIGURE 1.1. Still from *East Is West*. © 1930 Universal Pictures. (Courtesy of Universal Studios Licensing LLC.)

United States. Yet this reassurance will slowly be eroded. Even though the yellow slave trade in China suggests that East and West will remain in wholly different civilizational spheres, this divide between East and West will seem to dissolve with Ming Toy's migration to the United States. Ming Toy's transfer signals the possibilities of trade across civilizational boundaries in a heavily gendered and sexualized manner. "East" may *be* "West" in this transaction across the Chinese woman's body—a body that, this film suggests, overlaps ambiguously with whiteness.

Benson's desire for the Chinese prostitute is a seductive and titillating narrative element, but it also questions what it means to assimilate the feminized racial Other even if, as it turns out, she is white. The story of this budding East/West romance is not an uncommon one during the early twentieth century. Yet one difference is that, unlike the exotic tale of *Madame Butterfly*, this romance takes place in the United States, shrinking the distance between the Orient and the Occident, Chinese and whites. What makes the film uniquely provocative is that Ming Toy, bought as a prostitute by Lo Sang Kee, comes to the United States and eventually becomes situated in the Benson home and family. Even though actual miscegenation is erased when Ming Toy is discovered to be white, the film still leaves open the question of the exchangeability of white and Chinese women. In this respect, the title *East Is West* implicitly asks the viewer to ponder the ambiguity of its significance—does it imply that Ming Toy as the East "is" simply *coming* to the West or that the East *is already* the West in some essential fashion? While the Chinese woman/prostitute's entrance into the United States shows that she can cross national and racial boundaries and even enter the white family, the film's title goes one better—its present-tense verb suggests that East and West are one and the same, and therefore any attempt to regulate their mutual flow is unlikely to succeed. Thus the seduction of the narrative is attributable precisely to the extension of the riddle to the very end. And this seduction has everything to do with the fear of racial and sexual confusion between Chinese and white women, and more likely this fear is also the question of whether the nation, as it has been supported by the white home and family, continues to exist as a Western white nation.

Unlike both the yellow peril and white slavery stories, *East Is West* demonstrated the potential to envision an overlap between yellow and white slavery, such that the distinctions between these narratives of dangerously epidemic female sexual deviance became blurred and historically conflated. While the visual identification of aberrant behavior in Chinese (or white) prostitutes could of course be conveyed through literary description, cinema could display those behaviors as visible truths. Ironically, it is the medium of film that reveals the inability of the visual to absolutely ascertain deviancy from normativity and even white from Chinese. In this respect, the film re-presents the historical problem of visuality and the ways that the visual can be inaccurate and unreliable in its discrimination of moral from immoral, good from bad, wife from prostitute. As I explained above, on the one hand, the ineffective practice of visual scrutiny of Chinese and Asian immigrant women purported to discover those destined to be prostitutes and served to keep most of these women (even legitimate immigrants) out of the United States. On the other hand, the fact that young white women were not always innocent and passive victims pointed to an unseen (and deliberately hidden) truth that demanded an entourage of public officials and social workers to police women's sexuality. The film underscores the inability of visuality to demarcate Ming Toy's racial identity, that is, to "see" racial difference. Yet it also provides us with a wealth of information about Ming Toy's sexuality, at once innocent and provocative, naive yet titillating. This is shown in the ways the film depicts Ming Toy: she insists that she is innocent (passive and a victim of Chinese patriarchy), and this assertion is for the most part believed by the other characters (mostly by those sympathetic to her). At the same time, she appears sexually knowing, mostly to missionaries, who see her as a prostitute, and to Charlie Yong, "the Chop Suey King" of Chinatown and a generally unsavory Chinese character who desires Ming Toy. Thus her racial identity must be read through her performance of a combination of both sexual knowing and passivity. This representation of Ming Toy as sexually provocative, a familiar stereotype of Chinese women at this time, is, however, given more erotic value when she is associated with whiteness and, later, white female sexuality.

Ming Toy is filmed in ways that highlight her literal whiteness to signal the film's ending, in which she not only appears physically white but really is racially white. With the exception of some well-known Asian American actors at the time, such as Anna May Wong, the classic Hollywood film for the most part did not use real Asians to play Asians but instead used whites in yellow face. For example, Madame Butterfly and other leading "Asian" women's parts were all played by white actresses.[42] But in the case of *East Is West*, it was not a white actress but a

Mexican American actress, Lupe Vélez, who played Ming Toy, thus emphasizing the character's racial ambiguity. In the play and original script synopsis, Ming Toy is described as a Chinese girl who, visibly, looks white. The script synopsis's explanation that Ming Toy is a Chinese girl who possesses "features of a pronounced European cast" modifies the play's more explicit description of Ming Toy's whiteness—dialogue that is dropped in the film's adaptation.[43] Instead, the film version uses other methods to subtly accentuate her whiteness, without giving away her true racial identity. Legally, Mexicans were considered white and so were often not subject to antimiscegenation laws; yet they were not considered white culturally. For these reasons, having a fair-skinned Mexican American play a Chinese woman gave the effect the studios wanted: a racial ambiguity that still conformed to the censorship codes, which forbade the portrayal of miscegenation between whites and Asians.[44] Unlike many of the white actresses in yellow face, Vélez does not have any tape on her eyes to mimic the lack of epicanthic folds, which was the typical yellow-face "look" in Hollywood. In addition, the lighting of Ming Toy, especially of her face, is consistently lighter and brighter than that of the other Chinese characters (and sometimes even the white characters). Although it was customary to backlight the main actresses in Hollywood films, lending an ethereal and angelic quality to them, in this case there is a lack of soft focus on Ming Toy; instead, her face exudes a brightness. In this way the film attempts to visually accentuate Ming Toy's racial ambiguity and her whiteness through lighting and not through dialogue (which may have been necessary in the play because of the theatrical audience's inability to see actors close up). Casting Vélez accentuates whiteness in yet another way. Ming Toy, as I explained, is depicted as less passive than the other Chinese girls. As I show below, she is, especially in her sexuality, actually quite assertive, outspoken, and feisty. Vélez herself was often marketed as "the Mexican Spitfire," drawing on the stereotype of Latinas as hot tempered and even sexually aggressive. This image of course represents Latina sexuality as deviant in comparison to representations of white female sexuality, which is chaste and demure. This cross-racial casting, the minimal yellow-face makeup, and the lighting of Vélez in the film thus all contribute to an ambiguous and yet more enticing female sexuality. Yet the film then complicates Ming Toy's sexuality still further. Even while portraying Ming Toy as innately sexually provocative, the film also reveals that she has learned to be that way, not from other Chinese women, but from white women.

The film brings Ming Toy's racial identity into sharp focus by showing how her behavior gives away her real racial identity. As I described at the beginning, during the Love Boat auction, Ming Toy reveals a rebellious streak that makes her unlike the other Chinese sing-song girls, who passively accept their sale. In general, Ming Toy has an exuberance and assertiveness that is absent in the other Chinese girls in the film, including those in the Love Boat auction and the cookie-cutter sing-song girls owned by Charlie Yong. Instead of being quiet, Ming Toy asserts her will: she defines her father, Hop Toy, as a "bad devil," and, importantly, she speaks English.[45] Interestingly, it is Ming Toy's racial ambiguity and disobedience that make her alluring, for they empower the viewer to note how her rebelliousness has "sexual" value as it corresponds to a specific racial identity—that of an Asiatic.

The film presents Ming Toy as a tantalizing mixture of resistance and innocence, on the one hand, and sexual provocativeness, on the other. Interestingly, her removal from China and migration to America does not change her. While staying with Lo Sang Kee, Ming Toy often sits on the balcony on the second story. One day, she sees in the balcony across from hers a white woman pulling gum out of her mouth and chewing it provocatively. The woman then languidly looks down at the people in the street and beckons some men with a "yoo-hoo!"; she takes a flower from her hair and drops it to one of the men below. In imitation of this woman, Ming Toy begins to pull her gum out and tries to chew it seductively. She then starts hailing the men below in the same way and takes the flower from her hair and tries to drop it to one of them. He responds, “Not today, baby!” Ming Toy is portrayed as innocent about what she is doing, seeing her actions mostly as an amusement and not considering what she is inviting. However, her antics on the balcony attract Charlie Yong, whose establishment just happens to be across the street; it is his balcony from which the white woman was beckoning men the day before. The next time Ming Toy goes out to the balcony, instead of seeing the white woman, she sees people dancing. She comes out to her balcony and starts dancing. Her behavior entices Charlie Yong to come over and try to claim her. Eventually, Ming Toy creates such havoc that the Chinatown missionaries are scandalized. Even Lo Sang Kee is surprised when Dr. Fredericks, a missionary in Chinatown, warns him that if Ming Toy’s behavior is not controlled, he will have her deported. Yet even when Lo questions Ming Toy, she appears both unaware of and uncaring about what her actions might mean to men:

LO: Ming Toy, I must ask you to keep away from the balcony.

MING TOY: Honorable sir, I only go on balcony because air tasted sweeter.

LO: I fear you have been making disgraceful contortions like women across the street.

MING TOY: Only jazz-dance. You dance Lo Sang Kee?

LO: I do not. Ming Toy, you have been speaking to men on the street.

MING TOY: Only yesterday. When beautiful man pass window and say hello hotsy-totsy.

LO: You are pleased to be called that? Hotsy-totsy?

MING TOY: I don’t know. It sounds cute.[46]

Ming Toy proceeds to reassure Lo that she is innocent. She puts her arms around Lo and gives him a kiss. In this scene, Ming Toy seems both innocent of the gravity of being called “hotsy-totsy” and dismissive of Lo’s warnings. At the same time, we also sense that she has her own desires when she explains to Lo that she likes being called "hotsy-totsy" by a "beautiful man." Her response suggests that she herself can be the looker even if she is also being "looked" at by a man. Lo concludes that, indeed, Ming Toy has become "just the same like American vamp."[47] For their part, the missionaries already believe that Ming Toy is a prostitute. To them, sitting on a balcony in the middle of the city and winking at men, especially ones entering a cabaret, signals something other than innocent friendliness. Though she may be innocently trying to "please" these men, she reveals an inherent sexual precocity, a predilection toward sexual deviancy that the missionaries construe as seduction and promiscuity. Fearing that the missionaries, who control all of Chinatown, will ban his businesses, Lo Sang Kee eventually decides reluctantly to sell Ming Toy to Charlie Yong. Even though Lo is nearly convinced of Ming Toy's innocence, he also seems resigned that he simply cannot control her even by reasoning with her. Ming Toy's inherent sexual precocity makes it seem fitting, in retrospect, that she was sold to the Love Boat.

The film, while playing to the stereotype of the sexually provocative and deviant Chinese female, also underscores white women's sexual deviancies and suggests that such behavior might very well be white rather than Chinese. Viewers are positioned to watch Ming Toy's dubious behavior and wonder whether her Chinese racial identity will confirm what they suspected all along: the Chinese woman's inherent predisposition toward sexual depravity. Yet the scene in which Ming Toy imitates the white prostitute on the balcony implies that rather being inherently sexually deviant, Ming Toy learns to be immoral and deviant by observing a white American woman in Chinatown, one who happens to be employed by Charlie Yong. The appearance of a white prostitute in Chinatown fulfills white fears that white women are being taken as slaves by Chinese men. Yet the depiction of this white woman is not of victimhood or of passivity. Instead, she looks experienced, downtrodden, and less vibrant than the youthful and bright Ming Toy, with her slick, shiny black hair coiled into two neat buns on either side of her head and her straight-across bangs. The film thus reverses the stereotype of the innocent white female victim sold into white slavery and the immoral Chinese prostitute. And in this way, the film references what at that time was perhaps more disturbing, the sexual autonomy of white women: they can both exercise their sexuality outside the white home and cross racial boundaries, as depicted in the appearance of the white prostitute employed by Charlie Yong. The film suggests through Lo Sang Kee's observation that Ming Toy's imitation of the white prostitute points to an American female trait rather than to a Chinese one, when he says Ming Toy is "just the same like American vamp." In the play version, there is no white prostitute that Ming Toy imitates. Thus the film places more emphasis on white female sexual deviancy than on the sexual deviancy inherent in the Chinese female.

The film attempts to further complicate Chinese/white female crossings, as we see that Ming Toy can behave as a proper white woman while still exhibiting that sexual provocativeness. Later in the film, Lo Sang Kee reluctantly gives Ming Toy to Charlie Yong, in hopes that he will truly take care of her, Benson returns from China and arrives at Kee's place. He smuggles Ming Toy out of Chinatown and from Charlie Yong's possession and places her in his own home. The elderly Mr. and Mrs. Benson take to Ming Toy, seeing her as a charming and exotic plaything. Yet here Ming Toy appears to display some rather white middle-class female behavior and feels more at home at the Bensons' house than anywhere else. She directs the Bensons' butler, Thomas, to do things for the Bensons and for her. In one scene, as Billy is leaving the house, Thomas is about to assist him in putting on his coat and hat when Ming Toy rushes down the stairs, takes them from Thomas, and puts them on Billy herself, giving him a kiss good-bye. Ming Toy creates a domestic atmosphere with her attention to Billy and her positioning of herself as the lady of the house. At the same time, she also introduces an illicit sexuality to this white domestic abode. One night Billy brings home a bag of roasted peanuts for Ming Toy as a gift he calls "the great American institution." After showing Ming Toy how to shell and eat a peanut, Billy playfully takes one of the half-opened shells and clips it onto his ear. Ming Toy laughs and claps her hands but then moves over to Billy's ear and takes the peanut in her mouth. This scene is particularly erotically charged, and, as we saw with the balcony scenes, Ming Toy is a kind of sexual instigator of men's passion and desire. As Ming Toy takes the peanut from Billy's ear, we see his smile fade into an expression of shock and yet pleasure; he puts his arms around her, and his grip on her shoulder visibly tightens. Ming Toy, again unaware of the effect she is having, merely pulls away with the peanut shell in her mouth, takes it out, and starts eating the peanut. Benson wraps Ming Toy in his arms again and breathily exclaims to her, "Oh Ming Toy you're a darling," and kisses her.[48] The camera pans down, showing Ming Toy's daintily slippered feet next to Billy's shoes, and the peanut bag drops, scattering the peanuts about. The dropping and scattering of the peanuts is a visual play of their desire, and more likely of Billy's ejaculation, right in the middle of the white home. This scene again puts to question whether Ming Toy indeed learns her provocative behavior from white prostitutes or whether it simply comes from within after all. The resolution of Ming Toy's racial identity uncovers the possibility of multiple racial and sexual transgressions that cast a shadow over her incorporation into Benson's white family and the possibility of her becoming a true white woman and American.

East Is West provides a cultural map for a reading of the stresses and anxieties about racialized sexualities and whether the terms *white* and *Chinese* adequately demarcate racial "difference." The fact of Ming Toy's whiteness opens up other unsettling issues. Even though Ming Toy is really white, has she adequately reformed into a proper white female and domestic subject? Has she completely sloughed off her Chinese upbringing? Moreover, are the traits learned from the white prostitute really inherent, now that we see that Ming Toy is white herself? Thus, along with the racial question, is the question of sexual norms. The film underlines that visual surveillance, discrimination, and interpretation cannot adequately discern true "white"

FIGURE 1.2. Still from *East Is West.* © 1930 Universal Pictures. (Courtesy of Universal Studios Licensing LLC.)

female behavior from "Chinese" female behavior. This failure to adequately separate Chinese from white behavior means that racial difference is an unreliable index.[49] Ming Toy's race becomes almost inconsequential. Finally, it is the question of sexual deviancy of both Chinese and white women that persists in the film and begins to bring to light not just the associations of white and Chinese women but also of white and Chinese men.

The discovery of Ming Toy's "real" white identity, while removing the threat of miscegenation, instead brings up the possibility of sexual equivalencies not only of Chinese and white women but also of Chinese and white men, through the film's overlapping stories of yellow and white slavery. Just as Ming Toy is about to be sold to Charlie Yong (because the Benson family also highly disapproves of Benson's interest in a Chinese woman), Ming Toy's Chinese father, Hop Toy, appears in San Francisco and confesses that he is not her father at all: he took her for himself after she was left orphaned by the death of her real parents, white missionaries in China. The fact that Ming Toy was abducted as a white child turns the narrative from a story about Chinese prostitution, or yellow slavery, into a story about white slavery, in which white women are victimized and sold by Chinese men. Hop Toy plays out the stereotype of the treacherous Chinese man. As he explains to everyone at the end: "Ming Toy father Christian missionary. I steal her when baby."[50] Chinese men are thus the agents of both yellow and white slavery. The film offers the possibility of a series of Chinese-white liaisons: between white men and Chinese women and between Chinese men and white women, all through Ming Toy. Ming Toy's "whiteness" could be bought and symbolically owned by Chinese men, a possibility that underscores the Chinese man's commodification not only of "yellow" women but also of white ones, since Ming Toy was white when Billy Benson possessed her. Thus the collapsing of white and yellow slavery narratives points to the ways Chinese and white masculinity and cross-racial ownership of white and Chinese women bring up a different and yet more disturbing possibility. Along with the unveiling of deep anxieties over cross-racial female sexuality, it is crucial to note the film's critique of masculinity as well. If female bodies can be sold for sex, then one cannot ignore the masculine role in that transaction, as both buyer and seller. In concluding this discussion, I want to look at how the play and the film's adaptation thereof erase the similarity between white and Chinese men, while still leaving intact the question of women's racialized sexualities. In both the play and the film, the subnarrative of yellow and white money recuperates white American masculinity and reemphasizes the civilizational differences between white and Chinese men. While the play effectively launders out yellow money from the ownership of what in the end turns out to be a white woman, the film retains yellow money's ownership of Ming Toy.

The film actually makes some radical changes by the simple omission of Jim Potter, the social worker and Billy's brother-in-law. I argue that the play, written and produced in the early 1920s, was closer historically to the white slavery epidemics and thus had a greater need to disassociate white masculinity with the monetary ownership of white and Chinese women. Hence the play effectively launders out white and yellow money's ownership of white women in a way that the film does not. In the absence of a mediating figure and subnarrative, the film leaves the trace of yellow ownership of a white woman.

Yellow Money, Women's Bodies, and White Patriarchy in a New Era

In the original play, yellow capital retains its taint despite the altruistic efforts of the white men. The sequence in which Lo Sang Kee purchases Ming Toy and brings her back to San Francisco's Chinatown renders Chinese culture not only morally suspect but contaminating as well, for it is Kee who introduces Benson to the brothel, and it is Kee who, in fact, actually brings Ming Toy into the United States. We must remember that it is Benson who tells Ming Toy and Kee that American men simply do not purchase women.[51]

Significantly, the white American males, Billy Benson and Jim Potter, are motivated by virtuous emotions, morality and romantic desire, in opposition to the raw commercial impulses of Chinese and Chinese-American masculinity. In the play Benson explicitly asks Kee to save the Chinese prostitute from a life of sexual slavery. Even while Benson himself will not buy Ming Toy, he convinces Kee that it is "their" duty to save Ming Toy from the evil Chinese man trying to buy her:

BILLY: (*As he hears coins passing on upper deck.*) Wait a minute. (*To L.*) Why don't you buy her?

LO: Me go back San Francisco next week. What I do with her?

BILLY: Take her with you.

LO: Me honorable merchant San Francisco—got no time for women.

BILLY: I know but we can't let her go to this brute. She's such a sweet little thing.[52]

Later, in Chinatown, when Kee throws Ming Toy out of his household because of the complaints from the Chinatown missionaries, it is Potter, a social worker, who takes Ming Toy and situates her within the Benson household as their maid.[53] White masculinity becomes expressed as a marker of Western cultural superiority, as evident in Benson's and Potter's humane treatment of women, compared to women's mistreatment at the hands of Chinese patriarchy. Nevertheless, in spite of Benson's and Potter's roles in representing the American ethos of individual sympathy and altruism, what the play reveals is the contamination of the domestic through its relation to both Chinese femininity and white female sexual deviance. In this respect, Ming Toy's function is an important one, for she symbolically arbitrates between deviant Chinese domesticity and the normative white-American form, such that she becomes a feminized object of monetary exchange and the commodification of traffic in human labor.

But money produced in the East/West transaction inevitably threatens to taint the Benson family with the contamination of the East. If Benson's one valuable "purchase" via Kee is Ming Toy, then this monetary exchange must be transmuted through narrative displacements involving Kee and Charlie Yong in order to rid white money of its associations with the yellow peril. When Ming Toy is first purchased, it is the proxy Kee who buys her on behalf of Benson, the actual purchaser. Before Ming Toy is directly transferred to Benson physically and monetarily, Yong enters the picture again attempting to purchase her. It is Yong who insists to Kee that a monetary exchange must be made to "seal the deal" and to secure Ming Toy.

LO: I no sell no girls. Just be good to Ming Toy. Don't want no money for her.

CHARLIE YONG: No, no; Charlie Yong don't take girls for present. Girl man get for nothing no good. Man like girl better when he pay for her. Now, how much I pay you?

LO: (*Crossing to him.*) Charlie Yong, you not got enough money to buy Ming Toy from me. But if she cost you something make you like her better, you give me what I pay for her on Love-Boat. Only that, not one cent more.

CHARLIE YONG: All right, how much you pay?

LO: Two thousand *tzien*.

CHARLIE YONG: All right. You give me paper written Ming Toy is mine, I give you check.[54]

Yong's insistence on payment mystifies Benson's own incriminating association with yellow money and specifically with his act of having Kee purchase Ming Toy. Before Ming Toy is "sold" to Yong, the narrative enacts a further displacement of Benson's money; his white money now reappears through the agency of Jim Potter, who just happens to be a social worker in San Francisco's Chinatown. Potter brings Ming Toy to the Benson home to be employed as a personal servant. Potter's transfer of Ming Toy from Kee and Yong to the Benson family underlines Benson's actual connection to Ming Toy's monetary sale. Yet by literally taking Ming Toy off the streets and bringing her into gainful and legitimate employment as a domestic worker, Potter, as an agent for both Benson and the state (as a social worker), whitens the tainted money from its yellow origins at the brothel in China. Given that Ming Toy is dubiously Benson's property, his true role displaced only by his procurer, Kee, the question of ownership becomes resignified through her employment within the Benson house, where Ming Toy goes from illegal Chinese prostitute (and even undocumented immigrant) to a legitimate American domestic worker. Thus the stigma of the "Oriental," and even of sexual slavery, is more accurately the stigma of money, both yellow and white; that is, the mixing of yellow and white money comes to represent both racial and sexual contamination, and this never becomes fully resolved in the film, even after Ming Toy's racial transformation.

Although the dreaded connection to yellow money is *bad*, it is even worse to connect Ming Toy to Benson and thus to US money—especially when she turns out to be a white woman. The film's message is that one can sell Chinese women, but one cannot sell white women. The actual "sale" of Ming Toy therefore has to be "laundered" out of existence, and it is her white male benefactor who performs this cleansing by turning her into a domestic worker. The narrative of trade and money thus becomes a way to differentiate types of "raced" women and their relation to sex and money. The story is no longer about the assimilation of Ming Toy, the poor Chinese girl, through the divestment of her economic value; rather, it is, in fact, about the reversal of yellow money's contamination of the white woman. Again, this contamination must be washed clean through the narrative twists of the story. These are for the most part managed by Benson, up to the point when the racial barrier is removed by the discovery of Ming Toy's whiteness. It is then and only then that the two are allowed to be together. This is where the East is decidedly *not* the West—only whiteness can be itself, as the white male hero manages the shifting boundary and parameters of East and West.

In the film, without Potter to launder yellow money out of its ownership of Chinese and white women, that money retains the ownership of Ming Toy, who is actually a white woman at the end. In some respects, cinema's ability to manipulate the visual field, by bringing attention to certain elements through lighting, close/distant focus, and editing, allows it to leave out dialogue and characters that, while necessary in a play to convey meaning, are either unnecessary in film or demand that the film adopt alternative ways to say the same thing; however, in this case, Potter's absence from the film is not compensated by visual manipulation. Hence even as the film portrays white masculinity as unsullied by the monetary exchange of women, white or Chinese, the film leaves intact the ownership of white women by yellow money (and thus yellow men). This lingering effect is only partially compensated by the recuperation of white masculinity through Billy Benson and, in particular, how he comes to represent US masculinity in China and abroad.

Significantly, the film also serves to emphasize the United States' presence in China but resignifies this as cultural and racial superiority through the depiction of white masculine benevolence. As I explained in the introduction, the United States' economic and territorial expansion into Asia also entailed flows of commodities and people into the United States, changing the way the United States envisioned itself as a white nation. One can see in different regulations for Chinese and white women that they represented the perils of US expansion, expansion that took place not only "out there" in Asia but also in the United States through immigration. Essentially, many white and nativist Americans believed that Asian immigration brought into the United States foreign elements that would challenge the need to maintain white racial purity. The immigration of Chinese men and women thereby increased the possibility of racial mixing and would change the racial and cultural makeup of the nation. Hence the control over Chinese and white female sexuality that I discuss here was one way the United States could contain these foreign elements and their influences that were seen as eroding the sanctity and purity of the white home and family.

Benson represents a new era of economic internationalization, of a United States–China commerce that reveals the United States' moral and benevolent side. Not only does Benson refuse to participate in the exchange of women for money, but he is compassionate, choosing to intercede rather than ignore the barbaric practices of the Chinese. Chinese men are presented in contrast to this ideal, especially the Chinese American Charlie Yong, who has been both successful in his Love Boat trade of Chinese women and dishonest in his business practices, making a fortune by selling his inauthentic Chinese food, "chop suey," to Americans. As Lo Sang Kee defines the dish to Ming Toy: "Chop suey is a very depressing and melancholy food which for some unaccountable reason the Americans find highly intriguing. A dish-washer invented it."[55] In contrast, white patriarchy and masculinity, as a symbol of US integrity, shows the nation's ability to resist the potential contaminating effects of the foreign element that inevitably appears through the United States' contact with Asia in economic trade and territorialization.

Benson's saving of Ming Toy also symbolizes a change in US foreign policy signified by its displacement of missionaries. In the film, the missionaries are seen as quite the opposite of benevolent, threatening to have Ming Toy deported because of her questionable behavior. In their place is Billy Benson, the white American man whose international economic ties place him in a position to witness firsthand China's barbarism and lack of regard for human life. Benson, furthermore, represents another side of US foreign policy, specifically, diplomacy.[56] As a representative white American man in China, Benson negotiates to save Ming Toy from the rapacious exploits of lecherous Chinese men such as Charlie Yong. Benson becomes characterized as a figure of American exceptionalism within an unfolding narration of modernity, and the film intimates that this exceptionalism is rooted in Benson's particular position as a paternalistic figure, even while abroad in China.

The film also shows how, in the transformation of the global endeavor into a privatized one, the Chinese woman becomes incorporated into the US nation in specific ways. Ming Toy emerges as a pivotal figure: as both subject and object, her character revises "our" presence abroad and constructs our role as one of American paternalism and altruism represented by Billy Benson, the good-hearted American businessman who brings the poor Chinese girl to America in order to save her. Here, managing the foreign is depicted as an increasingly personal endeavor. As the symbol of this new US era through business and trade, Benson represents a shift in the burden of effecting change, from the state to the individual. Further, his bringing Ming Toy to America suggests not only US benevolence but also a benevolence that fosters the United States' interaction with Asia through trade, immigration, and labor. In bringing Ming Toy home, Benson underscores that how we manage our presence abroad is also a reflection of America at home. Upon the United States' global image projected abroad and specifically in China,

Benson's character thus builds a new form of patriarchy within domesticity. Nevertheless, as "fatherly" as Benson may appear, this East/West liaison is haunted by a sexual desire that must be contained because of the audience's fear of miscegenation.

East Is West tantalizes us with the crossover of female sexuality, Asian and white, and raises the unsettling possibility that white and Asian women might be closer in nature than previously thought. In the film, attempts to recontain these transgressions of sexuality and racial mixing through the surveillance and disciplining of white and yellow women prove unsuccessful. By stretching the boundary of racial identification between white and yellow, America and Asia, the film lures us into contemplating the fears of modern urban life (white slavery, undisciplined women, Chinese prostitution, and immigration) and then attempts to neutralize the racial and sexual ambiguity that it raises. This recontainment becomes necessary when the fantasy of equating East with West is transported in actuality (via the body of the Chinese woman) into the national and domestic (home and family) spaces of the United States. No longer a relatively "safe" (because distant) fantasy, the equation of Asian and American racial and sexual identity captured in the film's title has to be broken back down into its different parts.

Conclusion

East Is West uncovers the intimate connection to and dependence on the constructions of Asian women's sexual deviance as a means to articulate white domesticity. The film signals a critical imagining of the relation between Asian and white women and shows how the integration of Asian women actually reveals the vulnerabilities of American domesticity at this given point in time. In this convoluted narrative, it is precisely the saleability of the Chinese prostitute, within a story of interracial romance, that brings up the discomforting possibility of the sexual deviancy of white women and the frailty of the domestic structures that maintain the racial, classed, and gendered hegemony of the white family. It is this connection among sex, capital, and Asian women that raises the specter of white slavery, which was both an international and domestic fear. In the next chapter, I examine how the integration of Asia through the narrative migration of a Korean man into the United States in Younghill Kang's novel *East Goes West* illustrates a different kind of racial and sexual equivalency between men, white and Korean/Asian. Kang's novel narrativizes how the United States disciplines and contains the aspirations of the Asian American male, rendering him sexually impotent and racially stigmatized despite his cultural class and education. While my discussion of the film *East Is West* provides a more static image of Chinese and white women, as they were cinematically seen through American cultural fears, in the next chapter I examine "America" and "Asia" from the Asian and Asian American perspective, one that provides a more dynamic picture of the ways race, gender, and sexuality can be negotiated by the Asian male migrant/exile, Kang's narrator Chungpa Han. Kang's novel tests the limits of US modernity's capaciousness, and rather than see Korean and Asian men through racial exclusion, it demonstrates that class and sexuality can change and modify the terms of integration even among Korean/Asian men. Kang's novel shows how the privileged and educated Korean/Asian man functions as a screen for the remaking of white masculinities. Yet while in *East Is West*, Asian/Chinese and white women are constructed as threatening and deviant because of their similarity, in the case of the integration of the Asian man in the United States, he is racially, sexually, and culturally domesticated in such a way as to differentiate him from white men.

2 / Masculine Racial Formations in Younghill Kang's *East Goes West: The Making of an Oriental Yankee*

When Younghill Kang published his second novel, *East Goes West: The Making of an Oriental Yankee*, in 1937, literary reviewers equated Kang with his fictional character and narrator, Chungpa Han, seeing both as successfully integrated Asians who became Americans. A *New York Times* reviewer wrote that Kang's story

> attracts and holds the attention as if it were a novel. . . . But of course, *East Goes West* is not a mere novel. It is the candid record of "the making of an Oriental Yankee" as its subtitle states, and its author has been so successfully Americanized as to become Assistant Professor of Comparative Literature in New York University and a member of the Department of Far Eastern Art at the Metropolitan Museum.[1]

Another reviewer expressed a similar sentiment, triumphantly declaring that Kang succeeded by finally obtaining "an American wife and achieving the first rung of an intellectual career."[2] These reviews are fascinating precisely because they portray the Korean man's becoming "American" through both class ascension and the attainment of normative gendered sexual identity, the latter even reliant on an act of Asian-white miscegenation, and because they implicitly suggest that race was not a barrier.[3]

However, Kang's life was not a simple manifestation of the American immigrant dream, as these reviewers believed. Kang's class privilege did not render him immune to immigration exclusion laws or allow him to benefit from the naturalization laws reserved only for whites. Kang was able to enter the United States only because he arrived right before the passage of the 1924 National Origins Act, which essentially cut off Asian immigration; yet even as the first Asian American to receive a Guggenheim Fellowship, Kang was prevented from becoming a citizen.[4] Kang's bill for citizenship in 1937 argued for his exception as an Asian intellectual, but it was never heard in the US House of Representatives (HR 7127), even though Congressman Kent E. Keller argued on Kang's behalf that "[the exclusion law] was [passed] for the purpose of preventing the competition with American labor and not with American scholarship."[5] The campaign also included statements of support from prominent American intellectuals, writers, and politicians such as John Chamberlain, Pearl S. Buck, Lewis Mumford, Malcolm Cowley, and Charles Scribner.[6] None of these appeals worked. Thus, while Kang lived in the United States with his family for the rest of his life, he was never quite at home because of his "alien" status. This contradiction was familiar to many Asians who came to the United States in the early twentieth century.

Nevertheless, Kang's education and his class background present an Asian American experience different from that of the mostly working-class Asian immigrants entering the country at this time. Few could have had a citizenship bill introduced by a US congressman and signed by illustrious American authors. In addition, Kang's marriage to an upper-middle-class white woman, Frances Keely, described as "the pampered daughter of a Virginia industrialist turned professor," was unusual given the social disapproval of Asian-white marriages at this time.[7] These exceptions underwrote the literary critics' belief that Kang had indeed "made it." I have drawn from their reviews to underscore the contradictions between Kang's exceptional status as an Asian American man at this time and the fact that he could not fully take advantage of that status. This contradiction is explored in the novel through various Korean male characters. However, any interpretation of Kang's novel as simply biographical discounts Kang as a serious creative writer and, more important, prevents us from seeing how his imaginative fiction probes the nature and degree of the marginalization of Korean and Asian men at that historical moment, even of highly educated men such as Kang himself. No straightforward autobiography would do what I demonstrate that Kang's novel is able to do.

Most important for this study, Kang's novel illustrates the variegated images of Asian American masculinity at this time, images that did not always fit into the prevailing narrative of the Asian immigrant male laborer. Kang paints a picture of Korean and Asian men who, far from having "made it" in America, continually negotiate their marginalized positions not only through race but also through class and sexuality.[8] The novel also contemplates how, like many Asians in the United States in the 1920s, when anti-Asian sentiments were at their height, Korean men continually experienced the daily disparity of supposedly living in "the greatest democracy in the world" (273) while feeling the sting of racism and exclusion in their public and personal lives. Even the possession of certain forms of cultural capital, money and education, did not assuage the experiences of racism. The narrator of Kang's novel, Chungpa Han, and his Korean compatriots work as busboys, house servants, and laborers, despite their education, and all are thus essentially downwardly mobile in the United States. Kang's novel shows how the legal problems engendered by exclusionary laws and restricted rights to citizenship, when inflected by class differences, add importantly to our understanding of the history of Asian immigrant men during this period. That Kang's novel offers a different glimpse of Asian American men during this time makes it not only an important historical document but an index as well of how class can also change the racial playing field for both Asians and whites. Again, it is precisely in the modalities of his fictional account that we find the blurring and blending of racial and sexual identities, a testing out of the results of the movement of East to West, and the exact problematic of *making* a "Yankee" from the raw material of an "Oriental."

For example, through Kang's seemingly naive protagonist, Han, the novel explores how Korean/Asian and white men define their racial and class identities through each other. Han's education continually places him alternately in the positions of "foreign student" and Asian immigrant laborer. In this and other moments of vacillation between the roles assigned to Asian males, the novel depicts how exploiting such indeterminacy becomes a means of creating mobility across social, sexual, and racial spaces in the United States, even challenging white racial and sexual masculine hegemony. Social disapproval of miscegenation between Asians and whites, the effects of exclusion laws on the presence of Korean/Asian women in the United States, and the absence of Korean/Asian families in the novel all are felt in diverse ways by the various characters. In the course of the novel these male characters negotiate how race and class determine gendered identity, sexual expression and desire, and domestic arrangements. Class and sexuality define different pictures of Korean (and Asian) masculinity especially as these are made legible through the interactions between Korean men.

For example, Kang paints two pictures of Korean men that he initially sets in diametric opposition to each other: George Jum, whom Han calls the working-class "pagan," and his friend Wan To Kim, the "Oriental intellectual." Both men are in love with white women they cannot fully, if at all, possess. George's claimed (hetero) masculine virility works against the ways Asian men are seen at the time as sexually deviant bachelors and, as I show, allows him some marginal integration into the United States. While I reveal the limits and possibilities of George's self-image, his survival and integration must be read alongside the figure of Kim, the elite Korean intellectual who refuses the terms of marginal integration and ends his life miserably. At the novel's end, Kang's protagonist, Han, an intellectual like Kim, contemplates how he can escape Kim's fate. Kang also shows that in spite of George's compromised integration, his marginalization may also be viewed as a critique of the racialized gendered and sexual norms that constrain Korean men in the United States.

I begin my discussion with the Oriental scholar / foreign student, a figure that identifies a crucial form of integration for the educated Korean/Asian man in the United States. As we come to see, not only is this identity projected onto Han, but he finds that it is a necessity for his survival. Importantly, I show how the foreign student in particular functions as a screen for the constructions of both white and Asian masculinity in the novel. The complex and uneven negotiations of race, class, gender, and sexuality, via the foreign scholar figure, illustrate how the making of racialized masculinities depends on the ways that white males locate Asian males in particular racial and cultural frames. Similarly, I examine the relations the novel draws between Korean men and the stereotypes of Asian men in general. My interpretation of the novel's characterization of the Asian bachelor shows how this racial/sexual compromise made by different Korean men deconstructs the class, gender, and sexual dynamics of marginalized integration.

The Oriental Scholar / Foreign Student

Readers are introduced to Kang's protagonist and narrator, Chungpa Han, with his observation about the contradictions of his American life: it is one that persists throughout the novel and is marked by his particular status as a Korean exile. Upon landing in New York, Han declares, "It was always of New York I dreamed" (6), echoing many an immigrant's vision of America. The opening pages suggest optimism—Han describes his arrival in the United States as a rebirth, drawing on a metaphor embedded in the Korean language to describe his travel via steamer from the East to the West: "In Korea *to come out from the boat* is an idiom meaning *to be born*, as the word 'pai' for 'womb' is the same as 'pai' for 'boat'" (5). In this rebirth, Han draws on the idealism of America's promise of individual freedom, especially as it contrasts with Korea, which at this time is being crushed by Japanese colonization. Indeed, Han's desire to be a scholar and poet in Korea has been thwarted by Japanese colonization. In 1910 Japan annexed Korea as a territory as part of its growing imperialist expansion across Asia and the Pacific. As a result of colonization in 1910, Japan cut off all emigration out of Korea. Political exiles who were able to leave during the period of Japanese occupation (1905) and even after annexation constituted one of the strongest nationalist movements in the Korean diaspora; many resided in Manchuria and Russia's far east, with a smaller number in the United States, including political activists Syngman Rhee (who became the first president of South Korea), Park Yong-man, and Ahn Ch'ang-ho.[9] Kang himself took part in Korea's March First movement of 1919, in which more than one million Koreans protested Japanese colonization. Kang was imprisoned and beaten by the police after the protest and subsequently attempted to escape Korea, succeeding finally in 1921 with the aid of missionaries, who smuggled him into the United States.[10] Kang's novel thus depicts a Korean American community that is more exilic than immigrant, the result of Japanese colonization. Even the seven thousand Koreans who emigrated to the United States and Hawaii before 1910 suddenly found themselves with no nation to return to.[11] The position of Kang and his Korean male compatriots as exiles rather than immigrants underscores the in-between and often ambiguous status of Koreans during this time. Despite this situation, Han persists in seeing the United States as a place where he can "seek roots for an exile's soul" (5). If in Korea he exhibits the "futility of the martyr," of "the death-stifled scholar," then in the United States he sees opportunity in the birth of the "individualist," who "demand[s] life and more life, fulfilment, some answer to his thronging questions, some recognition of his death-wasted life, some anchor in thin air to bring him to earth though he seems cut off from the very roots of being" (9).

Yet even at this early stage, Han perceives the thinness of the ideological message of Americanization: “Magic words—opportunity, enterprise, prosperity, success—just business words out of world-wide commerce from a land rich in natural resources” (5). Filled with excitement and enthusiasm, Han is also well aware of his tenuous position in the United States. With little more than four dollars in his pocket, he arrives right before the “the law against Oriental immigration was passed,” a reference to the National Origins Act of 1924, which placed strict quotas on immigration from countries within the Eastern Hemisphere. So with little money and few resources or contacts, Han spends the next few weeks essentially homeless, sleeping on park benches, rubbing shoulders with other homeless men in New York City, and running up a bill in Chinatown restaurants, hoping to make contact with fellow Koreans who can help him find a job and a place to live. As the novel progresses, Han’s journey in the United States will continue to demonstrate the contradictions of his life as a Korean man who comes to America with an education and dream and finds himself limited by American racism. His prerogatives to obtain some advantage because of his class and education are thus doubly negated by Japanese colonialism and US racism.

Han’s attempt to capitalize on his education—to become a man of letters, notably as a scholar of American and British literature—is continually interrupted by his need to earn a wage. He travels up and down the northeastern US coast, as far north as Newfoundland, in search of a university that will accept him as a student and provide funding. But because of anti-Asian legislation and racially discriminatory laws, Han is denied scholarships.

Han eventually discovers that the terms of his integration in the United States depend upon a specific molding of the Korean man as an Oriental scholar or foreign student: these terms include being “taken in” as an Asian ward of white paternalistic benevolence. Near the end of the novel, Han describes this limited and unsatisfying version of the intellectual life he once envisioned: "In a way I might have starved if I had not been a student. It was a kind of racket. Just by being a student, I had got fed, clothed, sheltered, as guest in the house of Western civilization. And I thought to myself cynically, now I understand why there are so many quasi-professional students here from the Orient, like Mr. Ok" (281). Working as a "foreign student," Han is given food and shelter, exempting him from the world of manual labor (to some extent), but only if he agrees to play the good "Oriental child":

> "But professors in Boston have great sympathy for any adopted Oriental child. As long as you are willing to be docile and obedient."
>
> "That's just it!" I agreed indignantly, and Kim smiled. "I hate being nicey-nice." (255)

In this exchange between Han and Wan To Kim, Han expresses his weariness at having to return to yet another professor's home, a necessity if he wants to keep up his education, but, more important, if he wants to eat. The novel therefore demystifies how Han's survival in the United States depends upon his insertion into the particular subject position as Oriental scholar. Clearly, the joke between Han and Kim underlines the knowledge that the Korean/Asian man must play a racial token.

Kang's novel shows how the construction of the foreign student originates in the geopolitical relations between the United States and Asia and how, in that respect, the Oriental student becomes a token beneficiary of that relationship. Han's position derives from the impact that US imperialism in Asia had on US culture. By the early twentieth century, between colonization and US imperialism, "Asia" had a particularly visible material presence in the United States, as its acquisitions included not only Asian lands and goods but also immigrant labor, as well as Asia's cultural productions of art and literature. Han is a beneficiary of these acquisitions, to the extent that they gave rise to liberal intellectuals' scholarly fascination with Asia.[12] Yet this interest in Asia in the early and mid-twentieth century arose at the same time that the United States passed a series of stringent exclusion laws aimed at Asian immigrants and the Asian American population. This contradictory engagement with Asia therefore situates the Asian subject within various competing domestic interpretations. Indeed, these contradictions give Han the opportunity to become a foreign student boarder with educated white families, even to obtain entry to prestigious universities such as Harvard, albeit temporarily. Han's experience of token privilege under white benevolence occurs because the educated Asian subject is categorized as a rare, living cultural artifact of the East, ensconced in the orientalist corner of the West. The educated Korean/Asian man is thus situated within Western and US orientalisms as an object of white Asiaphilia and as a racial token of white benevolence.

Infantilized as a kind of child/pet in the homes of educated white Westerners, Han realizes that no matter how averse he is to this identity, Americans will foist it upon him. The projection of Han and the other Korean men in the novel as "foreign students" is also one reason for Han's fateful meeting with D. J. Lively, the founder and owner of the Universal Education Publishing Company, which issues *Universal Education*, essentially nothing more than a collection of superficial facts, packaged encyclopedia-style in three succinct volumes. Lively recognizes that as an Oriental student/scholar Han himself can be packaged to sell the series. Upon seeing Han, Lively proclaims that he is "a fine clean Christian young Oriental earning his way through college" (134).

At one point, Han even equates his position as an Oriental scholar to that of the missionary subject, whereby the selling of *Universal Education* is uplifted to a kind of spiritual democratic mission. Han is struck by Lively's pitch to acquire him as a future bookseller, listening as Lively extols the spiritual benefits of *Universal Education*:

> "Cultivate your faith in yourself. And in the goods you are selling. Did you ever stop to think what a noble calling for

> any man—that of selling books? selling *Universal Education* to all men?"
>
> "Almost like a missionary," I was thinking. (135)

Lively explains that "faith" in these books is akin to having "faith" in yourself, seeing the commodity as the same as the individual. One could very well substitute "Christianity" for "books" in this instance. Thus the missionary subject of conversion and the Oriental scholar become one and the same, functioning in multiple contexts but essentially doing the same thing, being an object of white Western tutelage, conversion, and labor, all in one. In this episode we see how "American efficiency and American business" (131) result in the degradation of the individual. Han is turned into an orientalized commodity, selling an image of himself to sell the books, products he doesn't even believe in. Here the Oriental scholar holds no deeper meaning: Han is no longer a true scholar; he is merely a cardboard figure emanating an aura of edification to attract prospective buyers.

The Oriental student is a means for Lively to cultivate masculine self-improvement and a revitalized image of white men as pillars of society. Just as each Christian conversion emblematizes the missionary's success, the Oriental scholar is an opportunity for Lively to convert Han into a successful businessman, which he sees as synonymous with being a successful man in all regards. The novel's publication date of 1937 situates it within the Depression era. Accordingly, Lively's entire spiel and philosophy of success is not about selling the product but about the "nobility" of selling yourself and your life through the product. This self is far more valuable and popular when you can cultivate a masculine identity that is likable, trustworthy, empathetic, and genuine, much like the one Dale Carnegie describes in his book *How to Win Friends and Influence People.*

Published in 1936 during the Depression era, Carnegie's book was a list of important attributes each man should cultivate, to make him not only likable and popular but also influential. The book is essentially a sales pitch, not all that different from Lively's. Just a glance at the chapters of Carnegie's book reveals the motivations behind Lively's words: "Fundamental Techniques in Handling People," "Six Ways to Make People Like You," or "How to Win People to Your Way of Thinking." Carnegie's six principles for making people like you are simple psychological tactics to give customers the impression that you care about them and empathize with them and that you are ultimately their friend.

1. Become genuinely interested in other people.
2. Smile.
3. Remember that a person's name is to that person the sweetest and most important sound in any language.
4. Be a good listener. Encourage others to talk about themselves.
5. Talk in terms of the other person's interests.
6. Make the other person feel important—and do it sincerely.[13]

Carnegie's book thus took the burden off the nation's failing economic system and placed it on the individual man, who, if he followed these universal rules of self-improvement, could become just as successful as Carnegie. Carnegie's method of cultivating care and likability in individual men also pointed to the conditions of modern industrialization during the early twentieth century. As Lawrence Levine argues, the conditions of an increasingly "institutionalized, bureaucratized world" demanded new models of success that Carnegie came to represent:

> The latter-day Carnegie's formulas were those of manipulation, of adjustment, of interpersonal relations. They were formulas more appropriate to the rise of the organizational man than to the rise of the traditional rugged individualist. His great success was a testament to the fact that the old success formulas no longer appealed to a population which had finally become conscious of the implications of the institutionalized, bureaucratized world in which it functioned.[14]

In short, Carnegie represents the living proof of his book's tenets. Similarly, Lively presents himself as a living model of emulation for Han, the Oriental boy and scholar. And in this way, Han as the foreign student and Oriental scholar, serves an important purpose for Lively by supporting his vision of an entrepreneurial masculinity, an image of success during a time when joblessness and low wages challenged men's self-image. Kang of course paints a picture of Lively as a veritable scammer. As soon as Han signs up for selling the books, he realizes that he has to pay for the books, so that "in other words, each of Mr. Lively's salesmen automatically became a customer to him before earning any money at all" (136). Suddenly, the picture of successful masculinity becomes an illusion as Han realizes that he is both the object of Lively's masculine self-improvement and the source of his paycheck. However, Lively's self-image depends upon seeing Han as the object of his benevolence and help. And it is crucial to remind ourselves that this benevolence should be read in the context of the United States–Asia relations I outlined at the start of this chapter. We must be aware of the cultural and racial specificities of Lively's relation to Han. This becomes clear in another way—through an episode that foregrounds sexuality and race. Lively's liberal self-image is challenged when Han's friend George shows up with his white girlfriend, June.

The image of interracial intimacies between an Asian man and white woman does not just violate Lively's belief in racial purity: suddenly, the Asian man is no longer just a neutered Oriental pet/scholar for Lively's self-aggrandizements. During the visit to the Livelys' home, George and June are seemingly oblivious to what their hosts may think of them and unabashedly display their affections for each other. After they leave, both Mr. and Mrs. Lively have a "talk" with Han about his friend, "the bad Korean boy" and of the dangers of interracial intimacies.

> "And I can tell you," she burst out again, "it is not wise for an Oriental boy to go round with an American girl. He should marry his own kind, and she should marry hers."

> Elsie [Lively's ten-year-old daughter] had followed us into the library and was listening to all this.
>
> "Oh-h!" she cried, her mouth wide open in surprise. "Mother, if a Chinaman marries an American girl, what kind of baby would they have?" Elsie giggled. "Mother, wouldn't that be funny? I should like to see it." . . .
>
> . . . "My dear boy, see here, I love you just as much as if you were my own boy. But you are getting wrong ideas. I don't want to see you marry an American girl. Neither would I want to see Elsie marrying an Oriental. And all decent people are like that. It is not as the Lord intended."
>
> I was very solemn and silent and unable to open my mouth to say anything. (150)

In the Livelys' view, this display of Asian male sexuality by George taints Han. No longer believing Han to be a "good Christian boy," the Livelys instead continue to chastise him for being ungrateful. Mrs. Lively asks Han, "How is it? Daddy and I have been so wonderful to you, yet you cannot have any gratitude for us. This is very bad taste in you" (149). Clearly, George's open display of desire for a white woman violates the Livelys' sense of right and wrong, or their need to preserve white racial purity.[15] Yet unlike in *East Is West*, where it is the white woman's sexual prerogative that is more threatening, Kang's novel reveals that the Asian man's crossing of racial/sexual boundaries is not just anxiety provoking: George shows that the Asian man is not the passive Oriental student, an empty vessel filled by Lively's sales pitch, and, more important, that he cannot be the screen on which Lively can project his own masculine wish-fulfillments. Thus "neither Mr. Lively nor Mrs. Lively . . . had any use for George" (149).

Masculinity, Sexuality, and the Asian Racial Form

The Oriental scholar / foreign student, who is granted a certain privileged status, is one figure through whom Kang in his novel contemplates how different versions of Korean masculinity can be assimilated, or not, in the United States. To explore this question further, the novel presents two contrasting Korean male figures, George Jum and Wan To Kim. George is a professed nonintellectual and working-class man, who according to Han is the most Americanized Korean man he knows. At the same time, George is also more reflective of Asian Americans of this period, most of them working class and "bachelors." George inhabits the part of the Asian immigrant bachelor and also of an Asian American male sexuality proscribed by racism and immigration exclusion laws. It is a role into which he, for the most part, has been painfully coerced. As a Korean man in America, like other Korean and Asian immigrant men at this time, George resides outside the structures of domestic normativity, and yet, as I argue, he is assimilated into the United States only insofar as he remains the Asian immigrant bachelor. He must pay the price of becoming the Americanized Oriental, and his masculine identity, strongly tied to sex, is intense but strictly limited. By way of contrast, Kang presents the figure of Kim, whose education, money, and Korean aristocratic background would seem to give him the ability to acquire a "white wife" and a university position. US racism ultimately prevents both; Kim's life ends tragically after the loss of his romantic interest, when the woman's parents cannot fathom the idea of an interracial marriage. I argue that through these characters, Kang's novel critically reveals how US integration for the Korean/Asian man is more complicated than racial exclusion. The Korean/male characters' differences of class proscribe their sexual and gendered identifications, which are projected by US culture and its racism and at times adopted by the Korean men themselves. Even while George remains, for the most part, a bachelor and a laborer, he is granted a limited integration on the margins. Kang shows how Kim's access is barred despite his possessing the cultural capital of money and education: a Korean man who appears on the surface to possess the requirements of successful Americanization is shown as an example of the most tragic of circumstances. His fate is not just failed integration but complete disappearance. In this respect, Kang's novel illustrates how class differences between Korean men can also determine access through the adoption, projection, and interpretation of masculinity. George's professed bachelorhood and display of hetero masculinity can be seen as a precursor to this compensatory masculine identity.

Although George came to the United States as a Korean ambassador in Washington, DC, he prefers to work as a cook, as he tells Han: "It's *much* better money than when I was an ambassador for the Korean government in Washington, D.C." (35). George differs from the majority of the Korean men in New York: he does not like to talk about politics, even of Korea's colonial situation, and he has no interest whatsoever in the study of anything but "love." In comparing himself to other more educated Korean men in the community, George tells an audience at the Korean Institute: "I have no degrees from American universities like Reverend Ok. I have no intellect to write that dissertation on American business like Mr. Pang. But love—I study it. Confucius doesn't teach it. Nor does St. Paul. Not all those professors North or South, in literature, commerce, or theology. But in my field I may be said to have the Ph.D." (51). George has chosen to leave the world of politics and a good job in Washington to experience the earthier and lustier side of life in the United States, working as a cook by day, frequenting speakeasies with women by night, and thinking about love. He has entirely given up the cultural capital he had enjoyed, latching onto a more materially remunerative trade. His Asian cultural capital defunct, he cashes in on his sex appeal. In excusing George's overtly amorous displays of love for his white girlfriend, June, Han tells Lively: "George is Americanized. . . . Most Koreans are not like that. My friend has not much education, but he has a good heart" (149).[16] Such a statement sums up George's identity: in Han's eyes, George is perhaps the closest one can get to becoming American.

When Han first meets George, he is an undeniable picture of Asian masculine vigor by virtue of his self-fashioned identity as a womanizer and perennial bachelor. George is one of Han's first friends when he arrives in the United States, and he gives Han numerous tips about how to appear attractive to women. George's sole purpose in life is to seduce women, and he asserts proudly to Han: "I don't believe anybody in New York has gone around with more girls than I have. Still I have more to find out about them. I make a study of them. It's the greatest line of research in the West" (37). George surrounds himself with signifiers of his desire for women, ostentatiously displaying his virile masculinity and also objectifying these women. When Han first arrives at George's apartment, he spies a picture of a woman:

> [George] asked me what I thought of the picture on his dressing table.
>
> "All right. But the girl is very fat."
>
> ..."That picture is the most deceiving thing in the world," he said warmly, taking it up to examine. "She is much much better looking than that. I met her five years ago. In Washington, D.C. . . . If you don't like her, I'll change the picture." And he brought out the photo of a girl in Cossack boots and Russian dancing dress. (37)

George's choice to be with white women rather than Korean women is an attempt also to signify a masculine virility. The novel shows that for George the "inability" to find eligible Korean women is not an obstacle but a choice. When Han asks him about one Korean American woman he seems interested in, George responds that she is "much better by back than by front . . . if all the women in the world could be lined up and covered with a big pillow, all but hands and legs, she'd have a good chance" (50). Soon we find that it is not just Korean women's supposed lack of beauty but also their lack of Americanization that trouble George: "A flirting Korean woman can be the most beautiful in all the world—when she makes up her mind to study American methods outside as well as inside college" (51). George's objection to Korean women and his choice to pursue white women masks the fact that he actually has few options. For the most part, the exclusion of Asian immigrant women from the United States during this period made finding a Korean woman an unviable choice. At the same time, the anti-miscegenation laws in some states and social disapproval made white women a difficult and dangerous choice. Thus George as the Asian bachelor is made by the politics of exclusion to be the unassimilable Asian man. Yet George, despite his on-again, off-again relationship with June, cultivates a masculinity in which he has choice and is able to continually exercise his male heterosexual prerogative. George's projection of heterosexual and masculine potency, more performance and bluster than reality, thus aims to destabilize racial gendered hierarchies and, at the same time, counter the images of Asian men as racially and sexually compromised.

We see in George an aggressive desire both to remake the image of the deviant bachelor and to differentiate himself from the other Korean and Asian men in his community. Scenes at the Korean Cultural Center in the novel portray single Korean men who, in the absence of women, talk incessantly about women, Korean and white, Asian and American, and about marriage and relationships. Despite all the talking and speculating on whether Korean or American women are best, whether American or Asian marriages are better, these scenes present an image not only of despair but also of extinction. As Han's friend Pak finally cries out after all this talking: "Forty-five years old I am. Not yet married. Already I lose at least five children by not marrying. And no children—no more me! This is fault! This is sin! This is crime . . . of the race suicide!" (56) In contrast, George's existence is marginalized, but rather than appear strictly victimized by US racism, he self-fashions a working-class and also masculine bachelor identity: while compromised in his integration, he also illustrates the development of alternative Asian masculinities and domesticities in the face of oppression and exclusion.

George's character questions our impulse to read Asian immigrant men as simply lacking and cast to the margins. Rather than pine for marriage, George sees himself as embodying an alternative lifestyle and, in so doing, exposes the mystique of marriage and monogamy. He poses some astute observations about American marriages even while this institution is essentially denied to him. When Han asks George if he is interested in ever getting married, George responds:

> I am thinking of love, not of marriage. . . . Marriage from love is vinegar from wine, as the poet says. I have done a lot of thinking on this subject. Marriage as an institution here is a failure because it is law-abiding. Anything that law commands in the form of thou shalt not, that thing man wants more. That is the symbol of this Western civilization. Man makes laws. And laws make his wants more complicated. If the law says you should have one wife, then you want more than one. (36)

George tries to explain to Han that laws incite desire rather than extinguish it and therefore also make human desire more problematic. George thus provides a rather modern and at the same time anticapitalist view of marriage and monogamy, seeing them as products that attempt to commodify "love."

Indeed, George's vision of marriage and relationships is so unconventional that it disturbs not only Americans but other Koreans as well. It becomes clear that many of the Korean men disapprove of George's perspective on bachelorhood, marriage, monogamy, and love. George and Chai, a Korean American born and raised in Hawaii and a fellow acquaintance within their circle, show deep antipathy toward each other in their views. Where George is boisterous and gregarious, Chai is reserved and soft-spoken. But Chai is also forthcoming about his viewpoints: "Love is having a wife that is well chosen. All else is fool's play. A wife can make or ruin a man. That is clear" (233). George rejects this view: "Well, love, like poetry or like life, has a thousand definitions. Many are brilliant, suggestive, clever and enlightening. Love, I can't tell you what it is. . . . But just as with life, nobody can define it except by living, so nobody can talk on love except by loving" (233). Chai's more conventional views define love as fixed, possessing definable traits; his pragmatism admonishes George's chosen lifestyle: "Yes, the man who loves many wastes time and energy. . . . Never love wastefully. That is my advice to you" (234). George, in contrast reveals the amorphousness of love and its polydesirous possibilities: "You are all wrong. . . . Love has to be wasteful, or it is no more love" (234). In this way, George provides a definition of love that defies packaging into a product for consumption, and he cautions that modern American marriages have done just that: "Their jobs are like their marriages. In the American civilization, especially in New York civilization, a married woman is no more than a kept woman, and no kept woman could be kept long" (55). Contrary to the perception that the modern American marriage is equal, to many Koreans and Asians in the novel American wives seem to serve no function other than to be bought/married and kept by their husbands. But what is most interesting about George's observations is the equivalency between laborer and wife: both are economically "kept" subjects, intimating a power discrepancy between the keeper/employer/husband and the kept/employee/wife.

George also carves out a space for the possibility of imagining and living, or what Melinda de Jesús calls "polydesirous configurations."[17] In a critique of Asian American studies' assignment of "deviancy" to the Filipino bachelor, de Jesús cautions against a reading of Asian male migrants as living their lives in negative reaction to antimiscegenation and immigrant exclusion laws. Early Asian male migrant experiences "have been given short shrift by literary critics and historians alike because Asian American investment in compulsory heterosexuality has dictated only the recognition of 'deviant heterosexuality' within these texts—and this heterosexist compulsion has played a role in their enduring popularity." Moreover,

> the pervasive and uncritical heterosexism of these readings—what David Eng refers to as "the exclusive regime

> of a compulsive and compulsory heterosexuality"—serves to constrain understandings of Filipino American experience within the narrow confines of heteronormativity. Further, most of these earlier Asian American interpretations assume that there is something gratifying about heteronormativity as if that itself is not deviant and oppressive, a reaction instead to polydesiring configurations of sex and gender, held in check due to the rise of industrialization and capitalism.[18]

According to de Jesús, the measuring of early Asian immigrant males' sexuality against a white and heteronormative standard inevitably paints them as deviant, lacking, and compensating. Although I do not want to discount the effects of racism on Asian American men's sense of sexual and gendered identity, like de Jesús, I too believe that reading George merely as a compromised Asian male figure limits one from seeing the ways Asian immigrant men productively and imaginatively created alternative lives in spite of racism and exclusion.

George's self-fashioned alternative lifestyle illustrates how we can read Korean masculinity beyond the victimhood of the historically consigned (and resigned) deviant bachelor. One has to give George credit for creating sexual and social agency and, more important, for providing some rather astute critiques of marriage and monogamy.

In this way, the repressive apparatuses of racism did not just limit Asian Americans; they could also actually open a space for nonnormative desires and lifestyles. The character of George is a kind of model minority as the "Asian bachelor," who is integrated marginally, but he also is a figure of agency and a critique of the heteronormative. In effect, even Han realizes that unlike the other Korean men, including himself, George "was not a guest in the house. He felt himself quite at home" (282). In the end, however, George surprises everyone, especially Han, by marrying a Korean American woman in Hawaii. Han receives a letter from George in Hawaii in which he rationalizes his choice for marriage: "So here in Hawaii I will spend all my hours in eating, loving and sleeping. Is love the be-all and the end-all, am I still romanticist? I never go back on my words. But what is the difference? Man has to love, and it costs the same amount of energy either way. . . . P.S. For the rest, I have not failed. I have only not succeeded" (367). Even in the end when George decides finally to settle down and shed his bachelor persona, he still leaves room for an alternative imagining of his romantic fate. He may have succeeded in finally becoming married in the traditional sense, but he still holds on to his bachelor bravado.

In contrast to George, Wan To Kim is the veritable cosmopolitan citizen, a modernized Oriental intellectual living uncomfortably in the West. Having lived abroad in Western countries, including sixteen years traveling in Europe during his youth, Kim is one of the few privileged Koreans in the United States who do not need to work; he even anonymously pays for one year of study at Harvard University for Han. Kim is of the worldly and educated Korean elite, an avid collector and scholar of Eastern and Western art, and even quite a sensation within upper-crust New York intellectual circles. But somehow the cultural capital that he possesses—money, education, Korean blue blood—has no currency in the West, and he fails not only to integrate into the United States but even to survive. The novel reveals that there is clearly no place for a cosmopolitan Asian intellectual such as Kim, who can only exist as a "Korean ghost" in America (157). Unlike Han and other Koreans who accept the limited integration available to them as foreign students, Kim remains wholly on the far margins of American culture both because of his subject position as an educated Korean man and by choice.

Kim's lack of integration can be attributed to the differences between his and George's masculine and sexual identities. The equation of Asian American masculinity and sexuality, associated with the sexual prowess that George seemingly possesses, contrasts sharply with Kim's (aristocratic) and romantic impotence. The love of Kim's life, Helen Hancock, a well-bred

Anglo-American, is ultimately unattainable. Her family initially adores Kim, partly because of their interest in Oriental art and culture, but once they find out about the pair's romance, they vehemently disapprove. More important, Kim and Helen's doomed relationship is also the result of Kim's emotional ineptitude. Unlike George, who openly displays his affection for June, even improperly in front of white people, Kim is aloof even to the point of exasperating Han: "I wonder, would [Kim] try to show next that he worshipped not Woman even if he did? Of course he was not one for a genuine Romeo-Julietting, and he had too much pride to be as cheap as George. . . . Yet I wished Kim would not show this pride with Helen. George might get on with better success there, if he had Kim's talents in other directions" (224). What George does possess is his ability to "[make] figurative love" to women, a "talent" that, according to Han, Kim lacks. Indeed, George's and Kim's differences reside not only in lovemaking but also in how lovemaking structures the two men's dissimilarly displayed masculinities. George's masculinity is embodied in the present time and integrated into the United States, contrasting sharply with Kim's, which seems impotent in comparison: "George had all the animalism of the pagan, the lust of the world, the flesh of the twentieth century . . . while Kim's love was the voice of an unseen bird in agony in some mountain solitude, a man of another world, good for nothing in this one" (244). Moreover, the ability to make love to women not only signifies masculine prowess in the novel but also reveals how George's and Kim's class difference enables their integration into the United States.

In this way, Kang reveals how class underpins George's and Kim's sexual and masculine identities. While George, on the one hand, is able to integrate by adopting, hyperbolizing, and remaking the role of the Asian bachelor, Kim, on the other hand, as an educated, worldly, and cosmopolitan Oriental man, is essentially "good for nothing" in this world. Like George, Kim is in love with a white woman; yet George and June's interracial relationship is possible because George does not necessarily expect to marry June and finds marriage distasteful for all the reasons I suggested above. In rejecting marriage, George not only finds a viable option, but, as I argued above, he claims some agency through a resignified bachelorhood, even if it is sometimes more performance than actuality. In addition, George and June accept that their relationship must remain on the margins of US society, mostly within ethnic enclaves. George and June thus allay the prohibitions of interracial intimacy by carving an alternative space out of the prohibitive. However, Kang shows that unlike George, Kim is unable to circumvent the prohibitions of interracial intimacy, not only because of Kim's aristocratic identity but also because of his choice of love object, an educated and upper-class Anglo-American, Helen Hancock, who "came from a conservative background" (244). Kim behaves as a suitor who must court Helen, but Han reveals that such courting is futile: "Her aunt in New York had made a great deal of trouble about Kim, and except the Browns [family friends] everyone in Helen's family was passionately stirred up. This had happened only recently. Now Helen was going home to face the trouble and try to persuade them to have a different attitude toward Kim. Kim had no such illusion" (252). The only time Kim can see Helen is when she is staying with the Browns, who like and approve of Kim as Helen's amour. However, there is still a difference between seeing Kim as an object of orientalized interest and seeing him as a potential husband. Once the Browns realize that the two are becoming more involved, they start to disapprove, and soon Helen can see Kim only in secret. For Kim, the prohibitions against him only "intensified the feeling that he had had all along, that he was an unwanted guest in the house of Western culture" (244). Helen's conservative and Anglo-white background makes it harder for her to break from her family, tethered as she is to their approval. Kim feels utterly helpless and, unlike George, sees no alternative but to "wait until [Helen] made up her mind" (244). Kim passively accepts that he must go through the proper channels to obtain Helen, or at least acquiesce to Helen's desire to do so. Eventually, those proper channels betray Kim. Helen's parents, in order to finally separate her from Kim, ship her off on an around-the-world cruise. As her parents explain in a letter to Kim: "If you love her as we love her . . . the only way you can show it is bravely to keep away. Barriers have been passed that were never meant to be broken" (265). While Kim did not genuinely believe that he would prove an exception to those barriers, the news painfully reminds him that there is "no trespassing" of these racial boundaries (265). Interestingly, Han underscores the class differences between Kim and George and how they structure their approaches to and experiences with love in the United States. In trying to cheer Kim up after he has lost Helen, Han thinks that it is "useless to preach George's doctrine, 'Do not take life too seriously.'" Han realizes that, in response, "Kim would have said, 'What could a fish living way down in a lower well know about the superior regions of air above?'" (244). Han already anticipates that Kim will shrug off this George-esque advice, mostly because Kim views George as beneath him. Han's imaginative response refers to Kim's belief that George "had all the animalism of the pagan, the lust of the world, the flesh of the twentieth century," while Kim resides above him, in the loftier world of love (244).

Kim is also an example of a Korean male subject who refuses to play the role projected onto him. In recognizing the downside to US modernity, he not only refuses participation but criticizes it precisely because of its essential dehumanization of individuals as commodities. Kim echoes Han's own disappointment over Western and US pragmatism and "efficiency." In the United States everything is up for sale and compromised, so that Kim's particular identity in the United States is already lost. In warning Han about his desire to pursue an intellectual life through higher education in the United States, Kim tells him, "You will study a little of everything and not much of anything" (160). Higher education is like D. J. Lively's vision of education—fast, succinct, and portable: "They try to educate too many. You can see the same in the Dearborn assembling plants: It is the business method. It works to turn out Fords . . . but not to turn out scholars" (160). Poetry, art, and knowledge merely "[become] the instinct for self-advertisement" (165). Kim further explains to Helen that not only is money the bottom line in the United States, but for the Korean/Asian man even monetary success does not bring acceptance. "The only goal for a man here is money and power. But money and power in New York are not for men of my race. Even if we succeeded, we would not be admired for that, but only hated and feared" (215). Here Kim describes his particular outlook on modernity. But he is also describing his own situation as an educated and wealthy Asian man. Despite the cultural capital that Kim holds, US racial barriers are uncrossable.

There is both a futility and melancholia in this knowledge, and Kim expresses a nostalgia that typified many Asian intellectuals of his generation. Many Asian writers between the late nineteenth and early twentieth centuries held fond memories of the preindustrial age, which they inevitably equated with pre-Western contact. As I explained earlier, the West is associated with industrialization and modernization, with the United States representing the epitome of the modern. For Kang and other Asian writers during this period, the dystopic side of modernity is a severing of the individual from the organic, of humanity's connection to time, history, and the world. As I show in chapter 4, in an examination of the Japanese feminist Baroness Shidzué Ishimoto, who was a contemporary of Kang, there was a sense that US materialism structured modernity. For Ishimoto this materialism is a sustaining ideology of capitalism, which results in the exploitation of workers and women and the uneven distribution of income. Kang's novel echoes similar themes of disillusionment with US modernity, specifically the ways capitalism (and industrialism) commodifies the Asian man. Han details his own commodification as a foreign student and as Lively's Oriental salesman. Higher education is nothing more than an assembly mill. Nothing in the United States rises above its monetary value, and even the intellect, education, and the human spirit can be quantified. Moreover, US capitalist ideologies change the very pursuit of knowledge. Not only are educational diplomas churned out like cars on an assembly line, but education is essentially severed from the individual and from life, as Kim explains: "But I felt too, about literature . . . here, too, is specialization, of the worst kind. I saw how literature muddles away from life, and without life what is literature? Just as without touching the affairs of human existence, what is education?" (284). In general, Kim has very little faith in the US intellectual tradition and therefore in his place as an intellectual in US society. Those who refuse to be assigned a monetary value and accept the disconnection of the individual from his intellectual pursuits become lost in America. When Han asks Kim, "You have been in the West for sixteen years and you see nothing to it?" Kim responds that there is nothing in the United States to "root man, nothing to anchor him" (165). As he tells Han:

> You and I came to the West to find a new beauty, a new life, a new religion. But is there any? Alas! We have come at the wrong time. It is too late. . . . In former life I was an Eastern poet . . . but tell me, what now is to be our fate? Being unable to go back to that previous existence, being unable to label ourselves in this new world . . . becoming lost within another lost world? (166)

In these words, Kim explains how the West has not effectively integrated the East. Despite the optimism that typified both Kim's and Han's initial entry into the West and the United States, they are disillusioned by its modernity and progress.

In the end, Kim's cultural and social rootlessness in America is compounded by his economic destitution and by his broken heart. After Kim's father died, the family wealth was mismanaged by his half brothers. As Han explains, given the impact of Japanese colonization and how modernity has inevitably changed the traditional structures of Korean society, "the biggest Korean fortune now will often fail, leaving the heirs stranded penniless abroad, on student passports" (355). When Han last sees Kim, he had to sell everything, including his rare Asian books, and was living in a small apartment devoid of furniture on the poorer side of town. Han also finds out that though

Helen had instructed Kim to write her, she never received his letters, as they were most likely intercepted by her family. Kim eventually receives news from the Hancocks' maid that Helen is dead, that "she had died in a rest home outside of Boston" (357)—one surmises from a broken heart and longing for Kim. Soon after Han's visit to Kim, he finds a mysterious obituary in the New York paper that misidentifies Kim as a "friendless 'Japanese' on Bleecker Street" (362). Kim had apparently taken his own life, but no one knows exactly when that happened. His death was reported to the police erroneously as that of a "Japanese" man and he was quickly buried, but Han cannot even find his gravesite. Thus, in the end, even Kim's ethnic and national identity is not his own. Han's observations about Kim as "a man of another world, good for nothing in this one" turn out to have been prophetic (244). In the end, Kim simply ceases to exist.

East Goes West shows how George's and Kim's contrasting class status aligns with their respective and different heterosexual masculine roles and the ways each man's class/sexuality gives unequal access to the nation. The novel's depiction of sexuality and class foregrounds Kim's inability at "lovemaking" as one way to textually play out the negation of whatever Han might have gained because of his class identity. Kim's worldly knowledge, his education, and even his money all fail to provide him with survival skills in the United States. Clearly, there is no place for the cosmopolitan Asian male subject as embodied by Kim. Kim represents the resolution of the contradictions of Han's life in trying to become an Asian/American intellectual.[19] Yet unlike George, Kim, as even he himself observes, "[had] no instinct for self-preservation" (358). Kim lacks the necessary pragmatism and desire not only to lift himself out of poverty but simply to live. Through Kim, Kang expresses the difficult position of the Korean intellectual and writer and his erasure from US life and culture. In contrast, George's survival, as we have seen, is a compromise brought on by racism and exclusionary laws and at the same time a remaking of that compensation by the articulation of nonnormative domesticities and masculinities.

In showing the contrasting integration experiences of Kim and George, the novel remains ambivalent about the paths taken by both men. After his last meeting with Kim, Han becomes frightened by Kim's fate, seeing himself in Kim, and admits, "Almost did I dread the effect of Kim upon myself" (358).

> Yes, I ran from Kim. A silent life, a motionless life, an unpraised life, an unblamed life, and now a wholly undistinguished life at the end—a life that had lived in the ego and in the inner dream, that did not know if it was in inner dream or in outer reality, a life that had never accepted its real worldliness. . . . I ran from Kim . . . (359)

Even while Kim offers a salient critique of modernity's alienation, Han's realization that there is no place in the United States for a Korean man like Kim predicts his own fate.

In the passage above, Han describes Kim as a man who clings to the ideal of modernity that Han described at the beginning of the novel. Although Kim as a Korean man in the United States could not be integrated because of his race, Han also sees that the worldly and cosmopolitan intellectual, who lived in "dreams" and did not accept life's "real worldliness," could not survive. Kim represents a figure caught in the midst of change, "a child of revolution, whose soul passed from one continent to another never to find peace, denying earth as home . . . a strange, gifted creature born with the instinct for noble human things. He was wasted" (363). The ideal of the Western Oriental "sees three different times—not only intellectually but sympathetically" (128). When Han explains that "the Westernized Oriental is a child of the nineteenth century" (128), he means that the Westernized Oriental straddles both place and time. He understands not only the culture of the East but also that of the West because of Western presence and even colonialism in the East during the nineteenth century. The Westernized Oriental thus also exists in the time of pre- and post-Western contact and, in this way, simultaneously sees both the nineteenth century and twentieth-century modernity. Han seems to intimate through Kim's tragic outcome that such an identity is "wasted" in the United States. A creature such as Kim could not finally root himself in the present world, which demands conformity to US hierarchies of race, class, and gender. Although Han feels deeply connected to Kim's visions, he realizes that in the United States, as an Asian man and an exile, one cannot cling to the dead and the impossible. This brings us back to the novel's beginning, to Han's talking about leaving a dying Korea and hoping for rebirth in the United States. Yet as the novel shows, such a rebirth is not without its pains and compromises. The promises of US modernity prove empty, revealing the necessity of adopting racialized roles, participating in a racial and class hierarchy in order to survive, and accepting the commodification of the individual.

If Kim represents the fate that Han must run from and reject, then is George's philosophy of life the better of the two? Whereas Han depicts George humorously, showing that he does not really take George seriously, Han shows Kim to be elitist and rejects his stubborn refusal to accept the need to live within the constraints the United States imposes. And in this way, Han admits that he has often felt more solidarity with George than with Kim: "Like George Jum I really like to walk the earth with people. I got on well with them. I did not become suffering and ironic like Kim before tastes, interests, attitudes that were not mine" (282). Overall, I believe that Kang attempts to carve a space for an alternative existence through the two men, Kim and George, who represent a spectrum of Korean/Asian masculinities. Even while Han leans toward George at the end and rejects Kim because of his tragic fate, we see that Han attempts to exercise an alternative integration of his own, learned from his experiences with these two men.

Han momentarily believes that his integration and eventual settlement in the United States depend upon his asserting a heteromasculine identity in order to survive, but in the end he imagines an alternative brought about through writing. Han attempts to turn away from the kind of masculinity that Kim represents, "ironic" and "suffering," and to turn toward George in another way, by asserting his sexuality through his love interest in the novel. Han is led to Trip through a mutual friend in Boston. He imagines Trip to be a kindred soul and an aspiring writer like himself. However, Han's desire for Trip is kept inside and not explicitly expressed to her. In Han's mind, he believes that he and Trip are embarking on a grand love affair. But in the glimpses of Trip's responses, the novel reveals that she is not interested in Han as her paramour. Moreover, when Trip does show any interest, it is in Han as an Oriental exotic. In describing to Trip his reasons for coming to the United States, Han evokes his difficult childhood, hoping to generate her interest and sympathy:

> I touched the more personal note, she looked so gentle and persuasively smiling. "When I was born, it was a famine year," I paused, dramatically. "I never had a mother. She died. And I missed her so much."
>
> However, Trip said, "*That* was probably a help. They don't seem to get on well with their mothers over here." And I was a little offended.
>
> "But my father was no help," I insisted indignantly. "He beat me for running off to attend Western schools. And he tried to make me marry, at sixteen, some girl I had never seen and did not love."
>
> Trip became interested. She marveled. She said she had known nothing about compulsory marriage for boys in the Orient at the age of fifteen and sixteen. (311)

The passage reveals Trip's racist assumptions about Orientals, particularly the stereotyped belief that Oriental mothers are not maternal. Trip sees Han as a curious Oriental friend and is interested more in his stories about Korea than in him as a potential amour. Han's eagerness to engage with Trip is, however, met mostly with silence: "She made little effort to talk. She seemed to be wondering quietly to herself, just what she was doing in here with an Oriental, Chungpa Han" (316). Trip momentarily comes alive only when she and Han are leaving a Chinatown restaurant and she is accosted by a law enforcement official who asks whether her parents know where she is. As Trip exclaims to Han: "Marvellous! detectives! danger! Just what you always expect from Chinatown, and never get. I never saw a detective before in my life. But I wish you'd taken me into that dive with you, Mr. Han. The steps you went down were pitch-black, and *very* sinister" (318). The sight of a young white woman in Chinatown at night, especially accompanied by an Asian man, incites suspicion in the detective, who, because of yellow peril stories may see Trip as a victim of white slavery. For Trip, the incident is a lurid adventure, and while Han admits that "the detective had done [him] a good turn, in making Chinatown interesting" to Trip (318–19), there is also the sense that such interest is fueled only by Oriental exoticism and adventure. There is a stark contrast, then, between Han's fantasy of Trip as a "kindred spirit" (305) and Trip's feelings for Han, which are mostly of exotic fascination. In effect, nothing really comes of this relationship. We can see this episode as Han's desperate attempt to escape Kim's fate by obtaining the white woman, Trip. As Han expresses: "I was so frantic to hear Trip's voice soon, to feel that she really existed, that I called very early. . . . But I had to be saved quickly from going quite empty like Kim. It was a real emergency" (360). Instinctively and fearfully running from Kim's fate, Han tries to exercise hope, believing that even while a more traditional romantic relationship may not develop with Trip, an alternative one must be imagined: "I would get her mind working with me. And that was a good book, she must see we had to write. . . . Oh, let me be her servant forever and put myself in paper's place!" (361). The point is not that something must happen but that some other form of relationship can be imagined out of these circumstances. Yet unlike the ways George's racial/sexual crossings destabilize racialized sexualities and power, Han's desperation for Trip is an effort to counter racialized extinction, a fear uttered by Han's Korean brethren earlier. In this way, writing, and writing with Trip in particular, holds out the promise of not "going quite empty like Kim." Han offers only an indeterminate ending, but it is one that echoes the novel's title, *The Making of an Oriental Yankee*, whereby the task of writing with Trip promises a narrative in the making.

Conclusion

In *East Goes West* we traced the difficult emergence of an Asian American male subject, as he strove to make the transition from East to West, from diasporic national subject to American. Just what the terms of integration mean became fleshed out in Han's encounters with a select group of "Americans." These encounters show Han trying to fit into America via the routes for which he believes he is best suited—intellectual, cultural ambassador, and so forth. Yet he is rebuffed in those attempts because of the overriding force of anti-Asian racism. Despite his fluency in English, his fine sense of English history and culture, his intellect, ambition, and intelligence, he is constantly displaced from the arenas he seeks entry into (employment, social spaces, and romantic relations) and forced to fall back into a community of Korean males in exile. As I showed in this chapter, this series of failed attempts to insert himself into American society point both to racist resistance to that project and to Han's lack of agency and power. The dynamic between these two forces in contradiction to each other is read here as the framework of the novel's representations of the uneven experiences of class, gender, and sexuality.

The next chapter continues the discussions of many of these issues, but on another terrain. Rather than a precise location in an eastern American urban space, against the backdrop of a lost Korea, in the film I treat in chapter 3, Frank Capra's *Lost Horizon*, we find exactly that, the loss of any real location and the receding of national identities in general. We are taken away from the migrant's transpacific voyage to a trans-Asia flight out of any space previously mapped by Western cartographers—we are taken to, and trapped in, a terra incognita. Despite this difference, we find nonetheless the persistence of key themes found in *East Goes West*. In this case, West goes East and is then lost in a land that transcends such labels in a weird amalgam of both, and we find the protagonist working out how a man should act in this situation. In a not untypical utopian narrative, the characters are meant to reflect back on their homeland and home lives from a vantage point radically different from anything they have experienced. Utopian narratives customarily are the pre-texts for critical reassessments of one's own society, and that in turn enables a realignment of one's own moral bearings. Just as in Younghill Kang's novel, where we were able to see how modern dilemmas of race, class/privilege, and masculinity were played out in the US space, in *Lost Horizon* we find issues of masculinity, aggression, and rationality, balanced by a vision of a different sort of masculinity.

My basic argument remains the same—I claim here and throughout that the particular historical crises in modern twentieth-century America, crises that raised questions about what exactly a modern American looked like, and acted like, were central questions about American national and racial identity. How did this question about what constituted an American then become doubly difficult when further logical questions were raised: how did Americans and Asians interact—commercially, spiritually, politically, sexually? In the next chapter, and the one that follows, we take these discussions into an extra-national frame. The first two chapters dealt with largely US domestic crises; these next two chapters take us onto the world stage, to dramatize the need to rethink masculinity as World War II brought Asia and America more profoundly and violently together than ever before in world history—and as a unique set of women from around the globe began to form a transpacific feminist movement.

3 / Utopias Lost and Found: *Lost Horizon* and the Revitalization of American Masculinity

In one of the most dramatic moments in Frank Capra's 1937 film *Lost Horizon*, two survivors of a plane crash, their aircraft buried in snow and their pilot dead, pore over a map, trying to situate themselves. As I point out later in my study, this moment begins the characters' vacillating assessments of the land to which they have come. They have landed presumably in an area that exists elusively in an unexplored part of Tibet or China, but where this place is actually located is unclear: is it East, West, Asia, or beyond Asia? Soon enough, the survivors are picked up by a mysterious Chinese man and taken to a hidden paradise called Shangri-La, which lies beyond the dangerous snowy Tibetan hilltops they just crash-landed on. It is precisely because of Shangri-La's liminal locale that it is recognized by its inhabitants as a utopia, filled with peace, harmony, and wonder and free of strife, illness, and discord. Presided over by a gentle former Catholic priest, the population, which includes European and American expatriates, missionaries, explorers, Chinese philosophers, and the indigenous Tibetan tribes people of the region, reinvents a community distinguished from the modern world in the aftermath of World War I, amid the sense that the rest of the world has become an aggressive and self-destructive place of warfare and greed, hallmarks of an outmoded masculinity according to Shangri-La residents. In contrast, the men of Shangri-La are pacifists, characterized by an alternative masculinity, and they create a world and even a kind of domicile defined not by territorial or cultural ties but through a communal existence based on equal distribution of resources and a philosophy of living "moderately." Yet, in the end, the film cannot seem to make that leap of faith. As I show, in tension with this desire to create new social communities and identities, the film becomes an inadvertent representative of a new kind of American empire at the outbreak of World War II, anchored, ironically, by an alternative white masculinity, one that was originally characterized by the film's protagonist, Robert Conway (Ronald Colman), but would later, and beyond the film, represent a new model of white manhood during World War II America. Indeed, it was precisely the spatial and ideological ambiguity of Shangri-La's utopia that made the film adaptable to different historical moments, first as a Depression-era narrative and then as a propaganda film for World War II.

Capra's other films, romantic comedies and dramas that typically depicted an average American man fighting a corrupt government or business, forwarded themes of basic morality on Main Street, USA. *Lost Horizon* was therefore a surprising and uncharacteristic film for Capra. It took place not only outside the United States but in an unspecified locale in Asia. It's not even a film about Americans: adapted from British author James Hilton's novella, the film is about a runaway British diplomat who discovers the hidden paradise of Shangri-La.[1] Perhaps not surprisingly, when I told people I was writing about the film *Lost Horizon*, most did not remember that Capra had made it. In fact, they generally could not remember what the film was about, except that it took place in Shangri-La, some sort of utopia somewhere in Asia. These vague reactions to *Lost Horizon* differed little from the film's critical reception in 1937. Some critics declared it too long and its subject matter too abstruse, while only a small minority praised its aesthetic qualities and its meaningful social content in the aftermath of World War I and during the Depression.[2] The negative reviews underscored the film's overall failure: *Lost Horizon* was Columbia Pictures' most extravagant and expensive film ever, costing an estimated $2 million during the height of the Depression, and neither Capra nor the studios ever made that money back.[3] Except for its brief revival during the outbreak of World War II, when Franklin Delano Roosevelt and the US War Department's interest in the film resulted in a second screening, the film was not really popular until the 1970s, when it was restored to its original pre–World War II version by the Film and Television Archive of the University of California, Los Angeles. Since then, it has become a cult film classic.[4]

Capra's *Lost Horizon* resides both on the margins of US popular culture and in its very mainstream. The immediate recognizability of Shangri-La as utopia—the pervasiveness of Shangri-La as a name for everything from streets to hotel chains, to its being synonymous, in the English language, with utopia—demonstrates how embedded Shangri-La is in our Western imaginary. Specifically, it is the placement of Capra's *Lost Horizon* both on the margins and in the mainstream of popular US imagination that has allowed the film's depiction of white masculinity and its embeddedness in American culture to be overlooked. Although most people today have, in a sense, forgotten the movie, I want to argue that the prevailing image of American masculinity in the film, that is, of pacified and nonaggressive men recoiling from the modern world outside, became the seed, ironically, of a reimagined American masculinity during World War II.

In *Lost Horizon*, the white Western man's relocation to an imaginary Eastern space allows for the critique and rejection of modern masculinity in the West, which is seen as greed-driven, warmongering, imperialistic, and dangerously nationalistic. Within the Asiatic space of Shangri-La, white men are able to articulate an alternative masculinity associated with pacifism, nonaggression, cooperation, and even, at times, nurturing. As

I argue, the film helps us reimagine not just what an ideal community could look like but, in particular, how this utopia is anchored in defining new and alternative white masculine identities. Ultimately, although the film in effect depicts a revision (and reversal) of an imperialist masculinity, this same white masculine form would later come to represent the US empire as the benevolent patriarch of democracy in the world. Whereas in the previous two chapters, I showed how the entrance and integration of Asia into the United States forced the nation to consider the integrity of its racialized gendered and sexual boundaries, in this chapter, the West (and the American) in Asia asks us to imagine letting go of the very definitions of masculinity that have thus far represented the US nation.

Lost Horizon continues the overarching theme we have traced throughout this book—how the United States, in its encounters with Asia, finds itself faced with new and radically different others. Rather than simply exclude them, as was done in the late nineteenth century, we find in the early twentieth century an attempt to integrate Asians into particular and narrow slots of American life. Yet even this cautious placement and containment was not without effect on the US social imaginary. Where expansion into and contact with Asia gave the United States the ability to imagine a much wider and broader sense of self, which was both exhilarating and anxiety provoking, *Lost Horizon* purports to offer a vision of a radical new social imaginary operating within US culture and projected into and mixed with geographic, ideological, and even spiritual notions of Asia. Similar to *East Is West*, Capra's film imagines the fusion of the two worlds; however, what emerges here is a vision of an "international" society, enabled and led by enlightened, pacified men. Crucially, in *East Is West*, Asia is perceived to penetrate into the domestic sphere of the West, whereas in *Lost Horizon* the reverse is found—the West is resituated in a mystified Asian terra incognita. The film seems to turn away from expansionist and acquisitive territorialization by modern Western nations and instead focuses inward, toward a reevaluation of the Western masculine self. In effect, "lost horizon" means the disappearance of the categories and definitions of the modern West, which are replaced by a new way of inhabiting the world, manifested in this alternative self. It is from this vantage point, having "lost" its "horizon" and unable to "orient" itself, that the West can imbibe the teachings of the still-spiritualized, out-of-time utopian society of Shangri-La.

Although Capra's film does not necessarily offer an explicit critique of imperialism, its professed antiwar and pacifist messages did run counter to and challenge the existing ideologies of US imperialism, which were premised on military occupation, territorialization, and monopolies on supposedly "open" trade relations with Asia. Such aggressive and expansionist policies did not differ from the general modality of nationalist behavior in the early twentieth century—along with the United States, key European nations, Russia, and Japan all were exercising imperialist dreams in the aftermath of the First World War. Against these ambitions was a growing sentiment, emblematized in the figure of Neville Chamberlain, of pacifism and antiaggression. Drawing from this moment in history of Chamberlain's appeasement policy, the narrative displacement of West to East allows the film's protagonists to explore notions of anti-territorialization and pacifism and thereby alternative new international masculinities unconfined by the boundaries of particular nations. These meditations, in turn, open the possibility for imagining an alternative society—a utopia. In a surprising reversal, Capra's film not only inverts US imperialism's "manifest" right and destiny but does so through a white masculine figure who recoils from its policy of aggression and territorial acquisition. The film contains at its core a reassessment of national and Western masculinity, specifically identified as aggressive and expansionist.

However, this brief moment, in which the borders of East and West, of Asia and America, are erased, will be recuperated back into an ideal of a US nation-state that is based on the very premises Capra sought to displace and erase. *Lost Horizon*'s subsequent appropriation by the US government during World War II transposed its utopian and borderless imaginary onto one bounded by first an antifascist and then a neo-imperialist agenda. In 1942 Roosevelt adopted the name of the utopian community depicted in Capra's film, Shangri-La, for his presidential retreat.[5] One can imagine that FDR envisioned himself as someone similar to the film's protagonist, Robert Conway, diplomat and war hero, who, at the film's end, returns to the sanctuary of Shangri-La to rebuild a new civilization. However, in stark contrast to *Lost Horizon*'s pacifism, FDR's version of Shangri-La was *militantly* antifascist. How, then, did history create such a trajectory, reversing the image of Shangri-La as a peaceful, antinationalistic utopia across the Pacific? The evolution of white masculinity in the modern world is here negotiated through the shifting and overlapping movement between Asia and the United States and, in this case, through the imagined fusion of the two in a utopia.

In this chapter, I begin by examining how the film's utopian aspirations depend upon its location in an Asian terra incognita. This permits the imagining of new social relations that are antithetical to the capitalist accumulation and imperialist ambitions of the world outside and specifically of the West. In the film, the characters transform and give up their former selves tied to the acquisitive world outside and adopt new selves divested of the ideologies of capitalism and accumulation. This new radical socialist imaginary within Shangri-La creates an alternative nation as individuals from different nations and cultures come together to create a new society, one that is particularly important in the imagining of an alternative masculinity as it is represented by Robert Conway, its protagonist and hero. Although we are told that elements of such beliefs in "better worlds" and gentler men were present in Conway's political writings, it is only upon his being transported to this Oriental terra incognita that his ideas can be fully realized, merged as they are with the empirical existence of Shangri-La. In the final section of this chapter, I examine how the film's masculine hero, unanchored in any real and identifiable space, contributed to a sense of the masculine hero's indeterminacy: will he stay in the West or go back to Shangri-La and give up on ever returning to Western civilization. I argue that Conway as the masculine hero was confusing to audiences, because they perhaps wanted a more predictable hero who returns to the West to save the day.

Moreover, in the end, Shangri-La's locale in an imaginary "Asia" has no physical or ideological grounding: the nowhere of utopia and Shangri-La simply cannot hold or accommodate the white male in Asia. In effect, while Shangri-La is a geographically bounded, isolated, and hidden locale, it is ideologically a place that challenges the borders of the West. The film's construction of an alternative masculinity, facilitated by the nowhere of utopia, reveals quite a lot of ambivalence about men's new role. Capra's rendition attempts to normalize the expansive characters and ideals he puts forth, creating a crisis of the masculine characters, one that, as I suggest, made the film attractive in the United States for the purpose of World War II propaganda. Reanchored in the nation-state, the film's nonaggressive masculinity comes to have a different meaning: its aims are not those of peace but of war on behalf of a neo-imperialist US nation. Thus Capra's original *Lost Horizon* was reedited and modified for the war.

Terra Incognita: The Displacement of Asia

The film begins with two images of spatial disorientation that re-place white American and European refugees out of the chaos of the modern world and into Shangri-La. In the opening scene in Baskul, China, Robert Conway (Ronald Colman), Britain's "Man of the East," desperately evacuates Euro-Americans about to be "butchered" in what appears to be a civil war. He gathers the last remaining Euro-Americans into a plane, which also contains Conway's brother, George (John Howard); a British paleontologist, Dr. Alexander P. Lovett (Edward Everett Horton); and two Americans, Gloria Stone (Isabel Jewell), a showgirl and prostitute, and Chalmers "Barnard" Bryant (Thomas Mitchell), a businessman. But the plane is hijacked by a mysterious Asian man, who dies when the plane suddenly crashes on the snowy tops of what look like the Tibetan Himalayas. Unbeknownst to these passengers, the mysterious Asian hijacker was instructed by the High Lama of Shangri-La to bring Conway there. Yet this fact is only revealed to Conway later in the movie and not to the rest of the passengers, adding to the disorientation of their arrival at Shangri-La. What ensues after the crash is the scene I described earlier, in which the survivors exit the plane and try to figure out, via a map found in the dead pilot's pocket, where exactly they have landed; however, as I show later, this location is not demarcated—they are simply off the map. Soon enough, an elderly Chinese man named Chang appears and takes the survivors to Shangri-La. Their journey through the Himalayas is treacherous and icy, but when they reach their destination, as the survivors peer into the narrow crevice between mountainous rocks, the land beneath them is lush and green, and the climate is temperate and warm. Chang leads them to a veritable paradise hidden within the Tibetan Himalayas. These two scenes of war and the plane crash and of entering Shangri-La create a stark contrast. By first showing how the outside world is a place of chaos and war, even death, the appearance of Shangri-La essentially erases the outside world.

In remapping Shangri-La as a utopia, *Lost Horizon* erases spatial and geographic markers of "civilization" and essentially declares the place a terra incognita. This is revealed in the pivotal scene in which Robert and George Conway try to determine where they have landed from the map of the dead pilot. They soon learn that they have essentially landed outside the boundaries of civilization as they know it. As Robert tries to decipher the map for George, he points to the blank "spot" on the map and describes it as "where civilization ends." Where they have apparently crashed is "thousands of miles beyond" where they were. Robert deduces that they are in "unexplored country—a country nobody ever reached." By curiously dubbing this blank space a "country," albeit one that no one has ever reached, the film displays the central contradiction of Shangri-La: it is both a known and knowable place, a "country" located nowhere. This map tells them where they are and at the same time tells them nothing.

This construction of terra incognita through the deciphering of maps is a persistent trope of empire within Hollywood cinema. Generally, the appearance and reading of maps within European and American cinema signify the West's superiority through technological knowledge, seen in the ability of the colonizer to locate, decipher, and name terra incognita. Maps "'mak[e] sense' of an obscure continent," explain Ella Shohat and Robert Stam, where terra incognita is a graphic and ideological "capitalist pretext" that simultaneously erases the presence of "savage" and "primitive" civilizations and peoples.[6] The map is a metaphor of Empire's possessions, in which the discovery of terra incognita is an invitation to the colonizer to fill in the supposedly "empty" geographic spaces with his civilizing mission.[7] *Lost Horizon*, in contrast, turns this metaphor askew by revealing that the map's "blank" spot, where Shangri-La is located, is already populated, not by primitives but by a thriving, enlightened civilization that in fact surpasses the West. Instead of "discovering" the natives, the white Westerners are themselves discovered by a group of fur-clad indigenous tribesmen of Shangri-La and led into utopia by a Chinese man.[8] This inversion of the colonial trope challenges the viewer to reconsider what makes a civilization. Shangri-La's physical removal from the West and the transposition of utopia onto an Asian/Tibetan landscape promise nothing less than a new social imaginary. However, while Shangri-La thus represents an ideal alternative to the modern nation, it is located within an unmappable and imaginary Asian space, which is fused fantastically with the best elements of Western culture: the place collects and preserves literature, art, music, and philosophy of both Asia and the West.

To open up the possibilities for this radical new social imaginary, Capra's film draws on the forms derived from both an antiquarian Orient and an enlightened and preindustrial Western civilization. Shangri-La is a society built on an idealistic precapitalist economy where people engage in unalienated forms of labor, live moderately, and exchange and barter outside of a market economy. And yet they also enjoy the aesthetic products of Western classical and Renaissance art. This abdication of materialism and capitalism sets the stage for Capra's reimagining of new social relations that exist outside the capitalist West's competitive "rat race" of acquisitive and imperialistic empire-building and yet retain an appreciation of the best of the West.

This new space of Shangri-La suggests an existence outside of national boundaries wherein residents from different parts of the world—the United States, Britain, France, Russia, China—willingly leave their own countries to live together according to new, yet shared, beliefs contrary to those in the outside world. Although Shangri-La's location in an Asian terra incognita suggests that this community exists beyond the concept of nation, in many ways Shangri-La represents the ideal modern nation in which people are brought together precisely by their shared belief in something better. As Ernest Renan's seminal essay "Qu'est-ce qu'une nation?" (1882) argues, the modern nation is based not so much on geographic boundaries, common history, or linguistic and ethnic similarities; rather, it is founded on a deeply consensual belief in its ideologies and principles.[9]

Aside from the general goodwill that its residents have for one another, what makes Shangri-La especially harmonious is the absence of want and greed. According to Chang, this is a place where needs are all met precisely because the community adheres to an economy based on a particular notion of "exchange." The difference between economies of buying and selling and the practice of exchange within Shangri-La is revealed most clearly in the following misunderstanding between Conway and Chang:

CHANG. Our valley is very rich in a metal called gold, which fortunately for us is valued highly in the outside world. So, we merely . . .

CONWAY. Buy and sell.

CHANG. Buy and sell . . . oh no, pardon me . . . exchange.

Chang explains that any desired material goods, such as literature, art, and furniture, are brought into Shangri-La by porters, who are paid with Shangri-La gold. Conway cannot help but misinterpret the gold as mere currency for goods that Shangri-La's residents desire. However, Chang explains to Conway that it is pure accident that a common mineral found within Shangri-La, "gold," is extremely valuable in the outside world. Hence gold does not circulate within Shangri-La but is exchanged only between it and the outside. Not entirely convinced, Conway continues to redefine Chang's word "exchange" to emphasize implicitly that the exchange of gold for goods is nothing more than "buying and selling" and that such exchange must surely go on inside Shangri-La.

Eventually, Chang expresses surprise that Conway, who wrote books about "better worlds," could be so amazed that a society such as Shangri-La could exist with no cash economy. According to Chang, Shangri-La's preindustrial system of barter and exchange is one of the main reasons poverty does not exist there. Chang explains to Conway not only that, in the outside world, the competition between people for material goods results from feelings of envy but also that envy comes from poverty and the unequal distribution of wealth. The inability of people to fulfill their basic needs inevitably leads to greedy competition for goods. While this reasoning may seem simplistic, Capra's film holds to such ideals to the end: Shangri-La represents an Edenic past in comparison to the contemporary world. The film underlines how "struggle" in the modern world is directly linked to the ways that capitalism fuels unnecessary and dangerous desires for accumulation—desires that lead to spiritual sickness in each of the characters.

Lost Horizon argues that a country based on communal principles will eventually heal the spiritual sickness of its new inhabitants. Chang asks Conway: "How many times have you heard of someone saying, 'Oh, he died because he worried himself to death, or he worked himself to death?'" The struggle that begets worry and excessive work is part of a larger problem in society—people's inability to obtain what they need to live a long and contented life. Shangri-La critiques the excessive desire for accumulation fueled by capitalism; in contrast, as Chang claims, "moderate expectations," which lead to being "moderately happy," are the key to the longevity of Shangri-La's residents. Unlike those in the West, who perish due to their inability to ever satisfy their immense desires, Shangri-La residents live exceptionally long lives and finally die peacefully of natural causes, because they are at one with the world, rather than alienated from it by materialism. This explains how Father Perrault (the High Lama and the original founder of Shangri-La) has lived to be 250 years old. Although Chang's explanations are at times both vague and incomprehensible, as the film progresses the new Shangri-La residents—Robert Conway, Chalmers "Barnard" Bryant, Dr. Alexander P. Lovett, and Gloria Stone—come to accept that "struggle" in modern life results from capitalist exploitation.

Although Shangri-La's terra incognita facilitates the imagining of alternative communities and economies, Capra's *Lost Horizon* also contains many of the themes and character types from his other films, reflecting a Depression-era populism that has now been displaced into Asia. To fully understand and live Shangri-La's communal existence, each of the characters must undergo a transformation, relinquishing an existence based on the marketplace and, in so doing, adopting a more fulfilling life, without the trappings of money and fame—what US populists believed contributed to the corruption of society. Even though *Lost Horizon* is purportedly not about "America," Shangri-La represents the possibilities for an ideal America in Capra's eyes. As Jeffrey Richards argues, *Lost Horizon*, despite its esoteric subject, still reflects much of Capra's populist sentiments.[10] Each character thus represents a different evil identified by the populists:

> In *Lost Horizon* the plane's passengers have been carefully chosen to illustrate different aspects of the Rat Race. Robert Conway is a soldier and a diplomat (the double-dealing world of diplomacy), Chalmers Bryant is a failed businessman (victim of Big Business), Gloria Stone is a show-girl (the empty glitter of Show Business), and Alexander P. Lovett is a paleontologist (the aridity of the Intellectual World).[11]

Chalmers Bryant struggles with the avarice that changed him from a humble plumber to a white-collar criminal. Lovett is caught up in the struggle of intellectual vanity, which is framed by his occupation as a paleontologist, an esoteric profession with no practical value for the common man. Gloria's struggles represent the world of vice and moral corruption. Characterized by Capra as a "pitiful but tough American prostitute—thrown out with the garbage from Shanghai's waterfront dives," Gloria epitomizes how money commodifies women who inevitably become damaged goods and are expendable.[12] Indeed, in Gloria, populism and progressivism come together to launch a general critique of the sexual immorality of modern US culture at the time, a critique that also reflects the concerns over white female victimization in *East Is West*. And in each of these cases, the desire to accumulate either money or fame results in a struggle with the "rat race" and its dangerous and even deadly consequences (Gloria is dying of tuberculosis). Crucially, Capra transposes Hilton's novella about post–World War I Europe and Britain to an ideologically American space, rerouting the themes of community and anti-accumulation to create a populist moral saga. In this respect, the otherworldly location of Shangri-La permits Capra to make critiques of American culture and modernity in which the terra incognita of Shangri-La represents Capra's ideal US society.

Nevertheless, while Shangri-La's location within Tibet as a terra incognita imagines new social relations through the displacement of West to East, it does not dissolve the historical colonial relations of East and West. Despite its radical socialist vision, *Lost Horizon* reveals how its enlightened community of equality, cooperation, and goodwill is, at the same time, a social order of discrete, if not overt, inequality. Shangri-La ultimately represents not a hybrid society of East and West but the almost virtual displacement of the West, albeit an ideal and miniature colonial civilization, onto an Eastern landscape. Conway queries Chang about Shangri-La's philosophy and is told that while accumulation of wealth is unknown in Shangri-La, there is the accumulation of knowledge and the preservation of great works of literature, art, philosophy, and music, all of which are shipped in from outside. Unlike the world outside, which has descended from its once enlightened heights, Shangri-La foregrounds the best of the West. Even the West's architecture and furniture can be seen in the sumptuous palaces, built in the style of Frank Lloyd Wright, that house the white residents. But more telling is that the film, like the novel, reproduces racialized colonial relations whereby the Asian/Tibetan natives serve the mostly white residents, even as the film professes an idealized democracy. The unspoken hierarchy between the leisured whites, who write, create, and rule, and the silent natives, who happily labor for them without complaint, points not only to the abiding orientalist stereotypes of early Hollywood cinema but also to the necessity of exploitation and hierarchy in maintaining the pinnacle of Western civilization. Capra's film reproduces in Shangri-La what was also in Hilton's novella, an idealized colonial empire without the problems of native rebellions or even real contact with nonwhite peoples.

While Hilton's novella can be read as a welcome fantasy of escape in the traumatic aftermath of World War I, it is also a literature of decolonization, more specifically a reaction to the decline of the British Empire.[13] After the war, the redistribution of British colonies, Irish independence, and the increasing rebellions in India and Africa all began to make a serious impact on the empire. Tomoko Masuzawa in her reading of Hilton's novella suggests that the significance of Shangri-La as an enlightened and hypercivilized nation reflects a "historical amnesia" of colonialism, its conflict and its violence:

> I suspect that the historical amnesia and the obliteration of the colonial markings happened for the usual reasons. The essentially material, political, and conflictual nature of the contact actually taking place between the West and the non-West—call it, for example, colonialist trade or imperialist possession—was displaced onto another, more spiritual, and ahistorical sphere of the East-and-West contrast. In fact, the logic of this displacement—this occlusion of conflict of representation of contrast—is conspicuously on display in the novel itself, as the protagonist repeatedly enacts it. Time and time again, he translates his compromised position (as reluctant minor representative of the British Empire stranded in an alien body politic beyond its control) into a dilemma of the one caught between two ideals, two lifestyles—that is, fiendish efficiency of the progressive West versus languid wisdom of the timeless East. In this representation of difference, the non-West is unilaterally projected outside time and history and imagined as an almost immaterial, ideal space that stands for a counterpart to the all-too-material reality of the West. In this projection, the non-West is often cast as fabulously old, pristine, prehistoric, sometimes, prehuman, whether that be a world of gods or beasts.[14]

According to Masuzawa, Shangri-La's representation of the East as a projection of that which is desired and yet missing in the West is also reflected in the character of Conway, who has recoiled from his job as a British diplomat, seeing himself as a casualty of modernity. Reenacting a common orientalist theme, the "languid" East, represented by Shangri-La, is restructured as a refuge from Western "hyperefficiency" and alienation, rather than as a place of colonial conflict or challenge to empire. Yet I also see the novella's depiction of Shangri-La as a form of colonial nostalgia and its idealization. The novella ponders the white man's future at a historical crossroads: on the eve of a declining British empire in the early twentieth century, the white man is losing his foothold in the world, through rebellions, challenges to his racial integrity, and the very fact that his own contact with others has precipitated a loss of his sense of self. In the face of this crisis, the novella depicts Conway as a man who is essentially lost in the chaos of the world as it once was, during the height of the British Empire. It is no coincidence that Conway's position is an international one: as a diplomat to Asia, he represents the British nation and helps smooth over conflict. Conway's disillusionment with his position actually makes him an alien in the modern world. Out of place, and not quite at home in this new era of decline, Conway retreats to Shangri-La, to a place that retains all that is perceived as lost in Western civilization. This move can be read as Conway's desire and need to try to hold on to that civilization, even while he is being buffeted and thrown about in the chaos of decolonization. The novella and the film title's reference to a "lost horizon" is, in this sense, a critique of its own colonial nostalgia. Horizons are optical illusions that give the observer the impression that what separates earth and sky can be measured by a pure and distinct line. The title is strange, perhaps even pointless: how can a horizon be lost when horizons are themselves illusions? The horizon is Shangri-La, a nostalgic reconstruction of an idyllic colonial world that was itself also an illusion: there were never any benevolent natives willing to give their land and resources to whites, and there were never any whites who did not fear rebellion and overthrow of their rule. That world is lost, but it was also an illusory world to begin with. Moreover, it is also this illusion that is lost. Serenity exists in Shangri-La only when racial hierarchies are maintained (and not challenged); thus Shangri-La is really a reactionary colonial and "rational" society, embalmed in imagination as the real world plunges to destruction and irrationality.

Capra's film, in its efforts to forward alternative notions of community, society, and economy, might be seen as stalled by its apparent retention of Hilton's colonial nostalgia. Like the novella, Capra's film might also be read as a white retreat from a world that was becoming increasingly heterogeneous and more difficult to navigate, particularly for white men, whose masculinity was threatened by unemployment and lower wages, and increasing competition with not only other men but also immigrants, and nonwhites, during the Depression era. However, in Capra's film, when re-placed within the context of America's social and political climate, Hilton's colonial nostalgia is transformed not into a masculine nostalgia bemoaning the way things used to be but into a critique of the way masculinity itself used to be and the imagining of a different one. As I show, Capra's film differs from Hilton's novella in the ways Conway changes from a figure who, in the novella, is more an antihero to a hero who embodies the tenets of an alternative masculinity based on anti-imperialism and pacifism. Conway comes to represent Capra's view of his film as critique of the impending world war, a social commentary and a form of art as political intervention, advancing an anti-imperialist philosophy. Yet this philosophy, mostly a simplistic interpretation of a much more complex issue, eventually paints an indeterminate portrait of masculinity. In the end, one wonders whether Conway represents this new masculinity, pacifist (and pacifying), or whether he still retains the masculinity of the outside world, the one of aggression and might. In fact, I read the film as unclear about Capra's redemption of white masculinity.

Capra's Indeterminate Man

Capra saw his adaptation of Hilton's *Lost Horizon* as a critique of the modern condition but specifically as reflecting the political climate of 1930s Europe and the world. The film's pacifist message links capitalist accumulation to aggressive masculinity and its offshoot, empire building, especially as they threatened Europe, the United States, and Asia in the late 1930s. While these concerns were far from remote for the film's European and American audiences, the critique of Western modernity and militarism through the creation of an Asian imaginary may not have been readily legible to Capra's American audiences. The rest of this chapter is devoted to understanding the reasons behind this failure. In turn, this understanding helps show how the film version was finally turned into an argument for war. First, however, the particular historical context of the film needs to be established.

At the time Capra was filming *Lost Horizon*, the war in Europe was certainly on his mind. By late 1936, the Axis powers (German, Italy, and Japan) had all signed military pacts. The invasions and territorializations of Europe, Russia, North Africa, and parts of Asia by Germany, Italy, and Japan had already precipitated an international crisis. Meanwhile, after completing the filming of *It Happened One Night* (1936), Capra suffered a nervous breakdown and was hospitalized during the film's opening night. He recounts that while in the hospital, "a little man" came to visit him and chastised him for not using his God-given talents for a divine purpose. Capra recalls that while this "little man" shamed him, "Hitler's raspy voice came shrieking out of" the radio. According to Capra, it was after that experience that he began to feel conflict over making films solely for entertainment.[15] Thus the making of *Lost Horizon* represented Capra's newfound sense of responsibility to make meaningful films in the form of social critiques, especially during those dangerous times of imminent war.

Yet Capra explained that *Lost Horizon*'s message would be more effective if it were veiled, perhaps because the American public was not quite ready for his critique: "*Lost Horizon* was essentially a morality play, a poetic saga. But poetic sagas can be dangerous. If audiences get a hint of what you are up to before they are 'conditioned'—they may resent it and shy away. That is why films about Lincoln, about saints, about Christ, are dangerous."[16] Capra's invocation of Abraham Lincoln, saints, and Christ, all martyrs for important social causes, reveals how he envisioned the Robert Conway character as a figure who represents pacifism and nonaggression during times of impending war. In making *Lost Horizon*, Capra believed that the American public was not ready to be fed antiwar messages or that Americans wanted to be involved in the political turmoil in Europe. Capra's cinematic rendition readapts Hilton's literary vision of modern angst and escapism post World War I by applying the novella's social critique of war to the situation in Europe in 1935.

In the modernist tradition, Hilton's novella expressed the alienation of war and the seduction of escapism, whereby Shangri-La is a refuge from Europe, the West generally, and its concomitant problems. Escapism becomes embodied in Hilton's protagonist, Hugh "Glory" Conway.[17] In the devastating aftermath of World War I, the fantasy of restructuring a civilization safely away from the remnants and memory of war was more attractive than engaging in the real world was. Significantly, Capra's film omits Hilton's narrator, Rutherford, who recounts the story of Hugh Conway and Shangri-La to a neurologist specializing in amnesiac patients. Hugh Conway suffers from a selective amnesia in which he can remember Shangri-La, but not his life before it. Metaphorically, Conway's amnesia is a forgetting of war, as these memories become replaced by visions of Shangri-La. The novella becomes less a political call for preventing war than an existential call for its total erasure. Capra's film retains Hilton's vision of alienation and the desire for escapism; however, unlike Hilton's novella, Capra's film reconstructs a remembering of war, particularly through Capra's revision of the Robert Conway character, who in the film more closely resembles the ethos of appeasement.[18]

While America recoiled from the brewing political conflict in Europe by taking an isolationist stance, Europe was engaged in diffusing conflict through the policy of appeasement. By 1935, Italy's occupation of Ethiopia and Germany's rearmament, in violation of the Versailles Treaty, threatened Europe with another world war. British prime minister Neville Chamberlain officially adopted a policy of "appeasement" that would last until 1938. Chamberlain rationalized that the use of peaceful negotiations, rather than military reprisal, especially in the case of

German aggression, would prevent another war. He believed that Germany had been treated unfairly under the terms of the postwar Versailles Treaty and that German national discontent resulted from a genuine inability of the nation to economically provide for its people. According to Chamberlain, political negotiation rather than war was ultimately the only humane and long-term solution.

Chamberlain's policy echoes that of Shangri-La—if nations provide for their people, greed and want will disappear; with their citizens at least moderately happy, nations will not need to wage war in order to acquire territory and resources. Within the historical context of appeasement, Capra's Robert Conway seems closely aligned with Chamberlain, whether this was Capra's intent or the interpretation of the actor, Ronald Colman, himself a British citizen. In any case, Robert Conway's character represents an entirely different masculine figure, one who sets himself apart from the kinds of aggressive policies evinced by Western nations. Capra's vision of *Lost Horizon* as a "moral" and "poetic" saga suggests that he made the film partly as a critique of the aggressive militarization of nations, but the scene I discuss below between Robert Conway and Father Perrault also suggests that Capra's original film contained a more explicit critique of nation-state territorialization.

In the film, Father Perrault, or the High Lama, envisions Conway as his future successor and leader of Shangri-La, on the basis of Conway's writings, which, the viewer is led to assume, contain Conway's beliefs calling for nonmilitaristic political negotiations between nations.[19] Since Perrault, already 250 years old, feels his death finally approaching, the fate of Shangri-La depends on Conway to continue what Perrault has built in the past two hundred years. The "better worlds" imagined in Conway's writings (previously mentioned in the film but always briefly and never elaborated upon) become a premonitory vision of Shangri-La's future.

One of the film's more liberal parts, which was severely edited down for the 1942 version, is a speech given by Father Perrault that is staunchly pacifist and can even be read as anti-imperialist.[20] Capra transcribes mostly from Hilton's novella Father Perrault's mildly spoken yet trenchant criticism of war, where Shangri-La is the alternative society derived from "a dream and a vision [for peace]"

HIGH LAMA: We have a reason. It is the entire reason and purpose of Shangri-La. It came to me in a vision, long long ago. I saw all the nations strengthening, not in wisdom, but in the vulgar passion and the will to destroy. I saw their machine power multiplying until a single weaponed man might match a whole army. I foresaw a time when man exulting in the technique of murder would rage so hotly over the world that every book, every treasure would be doomed to destruction. This vision was so vivid and so moving that I determined to gather together all the things of beauty and culture that I could and preserve them here against the doom toward which the world is rushing. Look at the world today. Is there anything more pitiful? What madness there is, what blindness, what intelligent leadership. A scurrying mass of bewildered humanity crashing headlong against each other, compelled by an orgy of greed and brutality. The time must come, my friend, when this orgy will spend itself, when brutality and the lust for power must perish by its own sword. Against that time is why I avoided death and am here, and why you were brought here. For when that day comes the world must begin to look for a new life. And it is our hope that they may find it here. For here we shall be with their books, their music, and the way of life based on one simple rule, "be kind." When that day comes it is our hope that the brotherly love of Shangri-La will spread throughout the world. Yes, my son, when the strong have devoured each other, the Christian ethic may at last be fulfilled and the meek shall inherit the earth.[21]

Perrault's effort to preserve the great works of civilization because they are in danger of perishing from man's "lust" and "brutality" refers to the accumulation of territory by nations and the inevitable destruction of culture once nations absorb other nations. Shangri-La becomes a place that deflects the destruction and brutality outside to maintain culture within; in this way, Shangri-La embodies Conway's vision of a "better world." Rerouted toward the aims of its time, Capra's vision of this world was to advocate for peace in a world threatened by fascist aggression and imperialism.

At one point, Capra's film makes an interesting connection among empire, imperialism, and masculinity. The film dislocates its critique of fascism as empire into a more generalized warning against an aggressive masculinity. As Britain's "Man of the East," soldier, diplomat, and British foreign secretary, Conway would appear to have achieved the pinnacle of Western masculine success, which is based on aggressiveness and cunning. Conway's proposal that men preserve peace by being rational can only remain a fantasy, since he is already entirely shaped by the nation-state as a man who merely takes orders and carries out its duties, whether he likes to or not. This formula, wherein masculine aggression is harnessed by the state for its purposes, effectively infantilizing the individual male before the paternalistic demands of the nation-state, becomes articulated in a key scene.

After the plane takes off from Baskul, Conway's brother, George, makes a toast to him for safely evacuating all the Europeans and Americans and also to congratulate him on his new role as Britain's foreign secretary. A bit tipsy from the alcohol, Conway interrupts George's laudatory speech and tells him of a recurring dream he has about disarmament and how it goes against the "centuries of tradition" of building a warmongering nation-state, a sentiment that will be reiterated later in the film through Conway's conversation with Father Perrault. In this fantasy, Conway concocts a familiar scenario of negotiations between antagonistic countries. But rather than approach the other country with threatening rhetoric, he would convince its diplomats through peaceful persuasion based on "common sense" and "reason."

As a result, these hypothetical enemies would come to see how reasonable he and his nation really are and then mutually disarm. Proposing to utter the unmentionable, Conway declares to George that these "centuries of tradition" of force will instead be "kicked in the back!" Conway's fantasy, fueled by his inebriated imagination, critiques the way politics are handled between nations but simplistically and naively regards diplomats and heads of states as "fellows" who can be "reasonable"; in this sense, it ultimately appeals to a belief in human beings' innate goodness. Nevertheless, this invocation of man's innate goodness makes the common man vulnerable to victimization by, as is typically understood in Capra's films, a faceless and callous nation-state. Admitting to George that he will simply not pursue any of the changes he has just confidently asserted, Conway says that he will be a "good little boy and fall right into line" because he "[hasn't] got the guts to do anything else." Thus the type of masculine virtue that Robert Conway proposes and aspires to live by can only be interpreted at this juncture as impotence, cowardice, and infantilization.

Conway himself remains unconvinced of his masculine valor, even as his brother, George, reminds him that he has just saved hundreds of lives in Baskul. Further, in a rather surprising response, Conway pointedly identifies Britain and the colonial state's double standards and retorts to George: "But do we tell them that we just left ten thousand natives to be annihilated down there? No . . . because they don't count." This statement confirms the film's critique of imperialism; however, it is but an oblique reference to empire and watered down by the film's understanding that it is conflicts between nations that result in war and genocide. This admission of imperialism's brutality thus ends only as a brief flash of the white man's enlightened recognition of genocide, as it is funneled through Robert Conway's sentiments of impotence and cowardice. The annihilation just witnessed in Baskul is recentered on Conway's inability to effect change rather than sustain a critique of imperialism: that is, he sees himself, like the colonial subjects of Britain, as victimized by the nation-state machinery.

Thus Capra's potential critique of empire can only be understood through the alternative construction of a nonaggressive masculinity within the film. Any potential critique of imperialism becomes sublimated or otherwise veiled through a heroic, alternative, masculinity represented by Robert Conway. In effect, though the film postulates a post-national ideal that also suggests how an alternative masculine hero can give rise to a society outside of the conflictual ideologies of nation versus nation, empire can only be cursorily read as a necessary evil and not systemic to the construction of nation. Ultimately, the film's critique of masculine aggression associated with the modern West's war machine remains a critique less of empire than of nationalism. Nationalism and patriotic fervor turn men into boys and even destroy them.

To make this point, the film positions George and Robert Conway as diametrically opposed versions of masculinity that represent the world outside and the world inside Shangri-La, respectively. Tellingly, George esteems Conway for his position as foreign secretary for Britain. As George puts it in congratulating Conway: "Why, Bob, no one is half the fighter, half the soldier, and half the diplomat as you." To George, his brother represents the pinnacle of masculine virtue. But Conway deplores his position as negotiator between nations, whose purpose is to further the acquisitive aims of the nation-state. Rather than feel heroic, Conway views his own inability to speak up and effect change for what he believes in—peace between nations—as an indication of his infantilization by his own country.

At the same time, this scene reveals that it is actually George who is impotent. George does not aspire to become as successful as his brother, because his mere association with his brother is enough to reflect on him favorably: "I can't wait to bask in the glow of Robert Conway. Everyone will say, 'Look, there's Robert Conway's brother, England's foreign secretary to the East.'" Whereas Conway reads his position for the state as emasculation—the "little boy who will fall in line"—George views his connection to Conway (and thereby his connection to England and nation) as virility by association. It is George who is the most disappointed by Conway's admission that he's been infantilized by the state; this failure illustrates his projections onto his brother, whom he supposes to be, in a sense, the man he can never be. The crisis of George's masculinity results from the discrepancy between what he wants to be and what he probably cannot be. George thus finds outlet and resolution in his brother, his masculine ideal. But the ideal is ultimately impossible to sustain, not only because Conway refuses to play that role but also because such an ideal, as the film suggests, will eventually self-destruct or implode. It becomes apparent within the film's narrative that George's desire to cling to England and the world outside has not only contributed to his arrested development but will also bring about his eventual self-destruction. Unlike George, Conway has an intuitive faith in the validity of utopia. Shangri-La is a realization of Conway's literary "better worlds," which reimagines a masculine virtue that is not based on military or imperialist aggression. Clearly, George cannot comprehend this precisely because of the nationalist fervor that blinds him to the true value of humanity. The film intimates that the outside world is anchored to a destructive patriotism that contributes to antagonistic relations between nations.

Capra envisioned George Conway as a jingoistic character and described him as a "there'll always be an England" type.[22] The director seemed to express through this character the fear that such nationalistic sentiments could mean another war on the horizon. George has the utmost faith in the British government and its imperial domination, as well as its choice of Robert Conway in upholding its ideologies. As a consequence of this faith, George is unable to see, as Conway and the others do, that Shangri-La is, by comparison, an enlightened civilization. Prone to frequent bouts of hysteria and uncontrollable anger, George is the living embodiment of precisely the aggressive masculinity that is associated with the modern nation-state's warfare and its imperialist adventures.

Thus if George comes to represent the values of aggressive masculinity and desire for recognition and fame in the outside world, then in Shangri-La, where such attributes have no meaning, this type of masculinity becomes panic and hysteria. Throughout the film, George's behavior in Shangri-La can be aptly described as unhinged. He is the only abductee who continues to doubt the Edenic existence of Shangri-La. While the other abductees begin to feel at home in Shangri-La, George acts like a caged animal that cannot escape a place that is "too good to be true." It is George who eventually convinces Conway that Shangri-La is the delusional fantasy of two old, insane men, Chang and Father Perrault. Another unbeliever in Shangri-La, a Russian woman named Maria (Margo), tells George that Shangri-La is a fable and that she has been trying to escape since she herself was abducted to Shangri-La several years ago. She begs George to take her out of Shangri-La when the next shipment of goods from the outside world comes in. The porters who bring the goods will escort them out, through the treacherous mountain terrain until they reach "civilization."

By this time, Conway and the others are fairly certain they want to remain in Shangri-La, but George tells Conway that Maria has been desperate to escape for years and is proof of Shangri-La's illusory and even destructive nature. In a conversation with Chang about leaving Shangri-La, Conway mentions that they would like to take Maria with them. Chang becomes disturbed and tells them that if Maria were to leave Shangri-La, she would immediately revert to her real age in the outside world—although she looks no older than twenty, Maria is really over ninety years old. Unconvinced, George only scoffs at Conway's warning and becomes panic-stricken and emotionally out of control. At one point, George takes a gun and intimates to Conway that he will kill someone in Shangri-La. The constant state of anxiety that George experiences in Shangri-La is another indication of his fears over giving up that part of himself associated with the outside world. George's lack of faith in the existence of Shangri-La, even while in the midst of utopia, indicates his unswerving belief in the world outside, the very world that creates "struggle," war, and decimation.

George implodes with masculine aggressiveness near the end of the film. After traveling for weeks in snowy terrain, Conway, George, and Maria are eventually left by the porters, who have resorted to shooting at them rather than helping them. An exhausted Maria finally lies down and dies in a cave, but when Conway and George go back to fetch her, they find instead an old woman. Conway is struck by the truth of Shangri-La's existence and its philosophies of community and moderate living, while George, as if enacting Father Perrault's vision of the modern world's inevitable self-destruction, plunges to his own death by jumping off a cliff when he realizes that Shangri-La is no illusion.

By contrast, the film's articulation of the alternative masculinity that Conway expresses and embodies flourishes in Shangri-La. Although Conway comes to understand this while in Shangri-La—that his version of masculinity, when seen through the standards of modern Western masculinity, is infantilized and castrated—nevertheless, in Shangri-La, Conway's "better worlds" and his essentially better man can be materialized in a masculinity based on cooperation, anti-acquisitiveness, and even nurturing. The film presents a white masculinity that during the interwar years and the Depression era was perhaps more welcome than the aggressive and imperialist manliness that Conway recoils from. During the Depression, unemployment and lower wages were accompanied by a decline in marriages and birthrates, especially among the middle classes.[23] In addition, women's autonomy as New Women and the desires of many not to marry or have families challenged patriarchal male authority.[24] The effects of economic decline and increased immigration and competition all conspired, as it seemed to both white male workers and the middle classes, to work against their power and authority. Sociologist Mirra Komorovsky's interviews with men during the Depression era paints a picture of how the effects of unemployment and lower wages compromised their traditional roles as workers, breadwinners, and heads of households. As one interviewee explained, "Before the Depression . . . I wore the pants in this family and rightly so. During the Depression I lost something. Maybe you call it self-respect, but in losing it I also lost the respect of my children, and I am afraid I am losing my wife."[25] The kind of masculinity associated with aggression and muscle simply was not viable anymore. In this respect, "Asia" resignified as terra incognita and Shangri-La allows for a remapping of masculinity, even a disavowal and erasure of older forms of white masculinity as they were replaced by newer ones, which Conway comes to represent. The film, through Conway as new masculine model, reconfigures the loss of manhood as a gain or at least a positive evolution. In this respect, the film thus reassures American men in bad times by giving them a sense of agency: like Conway they can choose to leave the old masculinity behind. This is only made possible in this orientalized space where there are possibilities for imagining less bounded conceptions of gender and sexuality.

Lost Horizon's articulation of an alternative masculinity opens up the possibility for a testing of gendered and even sexual boundaries, yet the film registers an anxiety over this possibility. There are few women in Shangri-La (really only two), and the men there display either a complete absence of amorous desire or a desire that is strongly reined in. Chang explains that there simply is no romantic rivalry in Shangri-La, as the philosophy of moderation includes a moderation of one's own sexual desires. For example, if two men vie for the same woman, then one merely politely abdicates his desire for her, understanding that the other man probably wants her more. With this discussion, however, the film also begins to bring up alternative desires that challenge normative gendered and sexual roles: what does it ultimately mean to paint such an alternative masculinity, especially in Shangri-La, where most of the male characters are either asexual or nonreproductive? Chang, for instance, is depicted as a type of Chinese mandarin, who is at times aloof and unreachable: the inscrutable Asian who is yet kind and amiable. He is the stereotype of the effeminized and asexual Chinese male, looking rather androgynous in his long Chinese robes. Then there is Father Perrault, who is ancient but also an ex-Catholic priest. The other men in Shangri-La, the new residents Chalmers Bryant and Dr. Lovett, are presented as comic relief in the film. Only Conway and George register any masculine sexual appeal, which is seen in their liaisons with women. Hence the one, or two, romantic stories in the film are Conway and Sondra (Jane Wyatt) and, possibly, George and Maria. Yet George is shown to be completely uninterested in Maria, except inasmuch as she can help him escape Shangri-La. Several times, the film shows Maria looking longingly at George, who pretty much ignores her. We are led to believe that the only reason Maria wants to leave Shangri-La is because George wants to leave. Hence George emerges as a problematic male character indeed—he is both overly attached to the world of men in politics and not at all interested in women. The film not only reveals an alternative masculinity but portrays Shangri-La as a potentially nonnormative space, which must be re-normativized so that Shangri-La can profess its alternative lifestyle and philosophy while not truly challenging the boundaries of gender and sexuality.

As if to counter the possibilities of this alternative masculinity that Conway now represents and which the other men in Shangri-La also embody, the film positions George as a "real man" who is a casualty of the outside world. The world of politics and diplomacy is not just aggressive and duplicitous, but it is also exclusively a man's world, one that George is fatally attached to. George is often depicted with some homoerotic undertones, which are more apparent in Hilton's novella than in Capra's film. In the novella, George is not Conway's little brother but George Mallinson, whom Conway expresses some fondness for, even though everyone else in Shangri-La despises him for his hysteria, tantrums, and insistence that Shangri-La is a hoax. In Hilton's novella, Mallinson and Conway are also romantic rivals for a Manchu woman, Lo-Tsen. However, Conway's interest in Lo-Tsen and his rivalry with Mallinson do not diminish his affection for Mallinson. The novella thus underscores a homoerotic tension between the two men, buffered by Lo-Tsen, displaying what Eve Kosofsky Sedgwick describes as the homoerotic triangle, where men display their desire for each other through women.[26] Yet the change of Mallinson to Conway's brother, George, in the film normalizes what is otherwise interpreted as a more ambiguous sexuality in the novella. In quite the reverse of the novella, in the film, it is George who cannot stand to be away from Conway and whose affections for his brother are cloying and suffocating. Not only is George unnaturally attached to the world of manly men outside of Shangri-La, but his projection of his own desires and failings onto his brother, Conway, results in an equally unnatural brotherly love. George is seen throughout the film as clinging to Conway's every word. In one scene in which Conway is talking to Chang, George walks in, and the camera cuts to his gaze at Chang and then at Conway and finally back to George's expression, which now appears surprised and betrayed. If there is a rivalry going on, it seems to be among George, Conway, and Chang. Yet the film eventually shows that it is George's jealousy, his unnatural love for his brother, and his attachment to the world of men outside that lead to his demise. It is the world of male exclusivity that kills him, an event that appears to offset a similar homosocial, possibly homoerotic, and nonnormative sexual and gendered world in Shangri-La.

Moreover, the film's changes to the female characters represent an attempt to reinstate a normative heterosexual boundary as further reassurance that these alternative men are still men. In typical Hollywood fashion, the addition of a romantic plot to the film does not just counter the possibility of homosociality that borders on eroticism but also reassures men that they are indeed real (heterosexual) men. In the absence of the typical markers that defined white men as men in the United States during the Depression era, that is, as patriarchal household heads with higher wages and better jobs than women and nonwhite men, the anxiety over manly integrity may be about not muscle and might but heterosexual potency. Whereas in Hilton's novella, the figure of Lo-Tsen as the love interest of both Conway and Mallinson actually adheres to a common orientalist male fantasy during the early twentieth century, popularized by the story *Madame Butterfly*, Capra's film does not take this route. The racialized female Other is replaced by the appearance of two women, Maria and Sondra, the latter of whom becomes Conway's love interest. Maria more closely resembles the character Lo-Tsen, since in the novella, it is Lo-Tsen who, like Maria in the film, wants to leave Shangri-La and then reverts to her true old age upon her death. Furthermore, Maria is played by the Mexican American actress Margo; though she is described as Russian in the film, her casting resembles that of Mexican American actress Lupe Vélez in *East Is West*, reflecting a common Hollywood practice of using Latinas to signify ambiguous whiteness: they are not quite white but not nonwhite either. Maria's more racialized status imbues her with an irrationality that distinguishes her markedly from Sondra, who not only appears rational in contrast but is also less passionate and more emotionally controlled. It is Maria, in what appears to be her uncontrollable desire for George, who convinces herself and George that Shangri-La is a hoax, ruled by two senile old men, Chang and Perrault, who have convinced everyone that Shangri-La offers eternal life. Maria conveniently forgets that she herself has lived in Shangri-La for more than sixty years, even though she still appears twenty. Sondra, by contrast, is portrayed as slightly aloof in the beginning. When Conway first sees Sondra, he attempts to get her attention, but each time, she evades him. Eventually, she succumbs, but not without telling Conway that she already knew who he was and that it was in fact her idea, not Chang's or Perrault's, to bring him to Shangri-La to be its next heir. Sondra explains to the surprised Conway that she has read his books about "better worlds." Sondra is thus partially the reason Conway must return to Shangri-La after he mistakenly leaves with George and Maria. In this way, the displacement of homoerotic tension through George and the insertion of heterosexual love interests represent the film's attempt to maintain some sexual and gendered boundaries as it presents alternative masculinities. However, at the end of the film, Conway's masculinity suddenly transforms into one that is antithetical to that presented in Shangri-La. Outside in the world, it is as if Conway has no choice but to revert back to the masculinity that he despises. Ultimately, the film produces paradoxical notions of masculinity, rendering the integrity of its alternative masculinity somewhat indeterminate.

The ending is ironic, given the film's efforts to present a masculine hero who is both infantilized by the state and, simultaneously, a different kind of heroic man precisely because he does not believe in the need for aggression. After George's death, Conway miraculously survives through sheer willpower and perseverance until he is found by British authorities at a Tibetan mission. Lord Gainsford (the man responsible for Conway's mission to Baskul) returns Conway to England, but Conway escapes from him. He is no longer just a missing foreign secretary, but with the British authorities hot on his trail, Conway becomes an outlaw in England. As such, Conway discovers that he must apply force and violence, the same aggressiveness that he once found deplorable, in order to return to utopia. More incredible than Conway's reappearance is his superhuman strength and perseverance, which Gainsford describes at the end; even the Asian natives, Gainsford says, described him as a "man that was not quite human" and called him the "blue-eyed devil." Although Gainsford has lost his man, he cannot help but admire Conway's persistence, courage, and even hypermasculinity in attempting to reach his destination beyond civilization's reaches in a "no-man's-land."

In Lord Gainsford's description, Conway becomes the very image of the masculine aggression that he once felt trapped in. And yet the sequence also reveals the necessity for Conway to employ the very same aggression of which he had been both a victim and, in his career as imperial functionary, a perpetrator. Even while Lord Gainsford makes a toast to the hope that "everyone" finds his Shangri-La, we are made more cognizant of how far the modern world is from this utopian possibility. At that very moment, the film immediately cuts to a distant shot of Conway, a silent figure on a snowy horizon, who eventually reaches the high mountain pass that leads to the portal of Shangri-La. If Father Perrault's predictions are true and Shangri-La emerges after the modern world self-destructs, then Conway's return is a hopeful ending signaling his future as successor and new leader of Shangri-La. But the film also gives the sense of retreat and indeterminacy.

Capra's depiction of an alternative masculinity is thus ambivalent, representing different sides of masculine identity: on the one hand, there is the depiction of masculinity based on hypermasculinity of might and aggression; on the other hand, there is the masculinity based on retreat. It is unclear, after Conway's herculean efforts to return to Shangri-La, whether he will retreat and live the rest of his life like the High Lama, governing the insular community of Shangri-La, or whether he intends to live out the High Lama's biblical prophecy that when the rest of the world has destroyed itself, the residents of Shangri-La, the "meek who will inherit the earth," will emerge in the outside world to build a new civilization. This ambivalence in many ways typified America's uncertainty regarding entering World War II. While Neville Chamberlain's policy of appeasement was initially seen as possibly preventing another world war, it was also interpreted as a retreat. At the height of Chamberlain's popularity there was widespread hope that appeasement would prevent war, but historians and politicians today read the appeasement policy as a failure.[27] During and after the war, Chamberlain was criticized for exactly his policy of appeasement, which many believed did not allay the onset of the world war but actually accelerated it. Questions arose: Would a swift barrage of military force and power have stopped Germany? Would the war have ended earlier if appeasement had ended earlier? Conway's masculinity represents this dual trajectory. The film's depiction of an alternative masculinity resulting in indeterminate outcomes made the film easily appropriable for the aims of war. The part reluctant hero, part hypermasculine Conway became a symbol of an American masculinity that resignified the US home and nation as benevolent and democratic, yet moral and strong in the face of global destruction.

From Nowhere to Somewhere in America

Eventually the alternative masculinity that Conway aspires to, inspired by his sojourn in Shangri-La, cannot be fully imagined as anchoring a new global world. This version of masculinity, which offered the possibility of an expansive pacifistic notion of nation and community, was limited by the film's own weak narrative closure and later constrained absolutely by historical events that made such a position impossible to maintain: the fascist war machine prompted a thorough revision of *Lost Horizon*'s message. But one should note especially that such revision was made possible by the latent contradictions in the film itself and the several ways its message actually was ambivalent; I return to address those issues at the end of this chapter. Suffice it to say that at this point it is the *adaptability* of even a "pacifist" male to the cause of war, and the dizzying fall from the heights of post-national utopianism to intensely nationalist conflict, that makes this film a perfect vehicle for reimaging America on the world stage in this transitional historical period. It is as if the Americans' time in Shangri-La gives them (and the Brit) the highest, most intense "dose" of the East possible: there they are residents of a terra incognita, clearly cut off from the "civilized world," free to indulge their wildest fantasies, prompted by the wise abbots.

Capra's "veiled" moral saga as a commentary on the war in Europe did not come across to many of its American viewers. Given how much money Columbia Pictures spent to produce *Lost Horizon*, expectations were especially high for the film's success at the box office. It was not until 1942 that Capra rereleased the film and found more success, especially after editing out certain "pacifist" material. While many of the film's reviewers agreed that Capra's extravagant big-budget production was aesthetically satisfying, some felt there was something terribly missing in the picture; in particular, the film's absence of social conflict, it would seem, detracted from the viewer's identification with a typical Hollywood masculine figure. The masculine hero in *Lost Horizon* is an antithesis not just of masculinity in the West but also of Hollywood conventions of masculinity. Conway's character is not the hero who tackles the problem but rather one who retreats from problems, to the refuge of Shangri-La. As a result, according to critics, there was simply nothing in *Lost Horizon* for a viewer to hold on to. As Charles J. Maland notes, "Though absence of conflict may create a wonderful society, it's no way to construct a film. Capra's best films are characterized by a problem confronting a hero who struggles to solve it. *Lost Horizon*, as a friend once told me, is all solution and no problem."[28] According to this critic, the lack of narrative conflict results from the absence of the hero's conflict and resolution, an absence that I argue produced a sense of indeterminacy. But for others, this indeterminacy produced a sense of defeatism. Eileen Creelman, a contemporary critic of Capra's confessed that though she enjoyed the film, "the picture's viewpoint has an almost defeatist quality."[29] Conway's return to Shangri-La is a pacifist stance, demonstrated by his turning away from the outside world and turning inward to remake himself within a new society. The residents of Shangri-La will continue living peacefully with their own ethics, completely uninvolved in the outside world's destruction. When the world is finally destroyed, it is predicted, those within Shangri-La will emerge as the ones to "inherit the earth." Yet inevitably, returning to this refuge can be interpreted as a retreat. Thus the themes of Capra's *Lost Horizon* were not palatable to American audiences until its World War II reinvention, as America prepared to enter the war. In Conway's ultimate retreat from the "real" world and back to Shangri-La are the seeds for a re-entrenched nationalism that was then readily mobilized for the new war effort.

The United States' entry into World War II brought about strategic changes to the film that would divert its original pacifist impulses, allowing it to become a symbol for the Roosevelt administration and its narratives and myths, which would define a new "America" during global war. Only upon being reinvented and relocated into the concrete geopolitical spaces of China and America during World War II did the film become comprehensible to American moviegoers, but by giving them a very different message. Capra was originally faithful to Hilton's novella by depicting the film's civil war opening in Baskul, India. However, in the 1942 version this location was modified to "Baskul, China." Additionally, the header describing and introducing viewers to the film's initial setting in which Conway evacuates "ninety white people" from being "butchered in a civil war" in Baskul was changed to their being "butchered by "Japanese hordes." These changes to the film were clearly made to capture American sympathy for China, which was a US ally, and also to incite sentiments of fear and hate for America's new common enemy, Japan. Further, the 1942 version deleted sections of Conway's and Father Perrault's speeches; for example, Conway's drunken speech to George about his reluctant role as politician and negotiator for Britain was taken out.[30] In addition, the US War Department made a concerted effort to tone down the film's pacifist messages. Indeed, history transformed Shangri-La from a place somewhere in an Asian terra incognita to an emphatically American location: Roosevelt renamed a military training camp "Shangri-La" and turned it into his retreat, a safe haven from which he and his advisors planned their military strategies. Roosevelt famously said that the B-52 surprise bombers that flew over Japan in 1944 "came from Shangri-La."[31] The elements of pacifism and anticapitalism and even the belief in a nonconflictual society, all of which registered very little with the average American viewer during the film's first release, became redefined as American democracy's war against fascism. Whereas the original *Lost Horizon*'s utopian vision of an anti-imperialist and anticapitalist existence supported Capra's pacifist vision, the reedited film suddenly became re-placed within an ideology of preserving American democracy. The changes, though seemingly minor, would shift the entire film onto a concrete location and ideology and resolve the issues I have elucidated above about geography, space, and the identification of the hero.

Indeed, the indeterminacy of the film's ending, especially as it is coupled with the evolution of Conway's masculinity—from a nonaggressive and at times passive man of the state machine, to a pacifist sage in Shangri-La, and finally to a hypermasculine "blue-eyed devil" at the end—left open another avenue of appropriation. In the film, Conway sees himself as a reluctant participant in advancing the nation's missions, even as his brother celebrates his role as "fighter, solider, and diplomat" for Britain. In the end, Conway's aggressive masculinity and his outlaw status reveal that he is a reluctant hero: although he does not want to be that aggressive man he was expected to be his entire life, in order to return to the sanctuary of Shangri-La he must employ the very aggressive tactics he deplores. In this way, the masculine figure that emerges at the end of the film became a kind of symbol of a new American masculinity during the war. Conway was identifiable by the young men who were themselves reluctant to go to war and yet enlisted, because they felt compelled to fight for a higher ideal, against fascism and for democracy and world peace. The 1942 version of *Lost Horizon* was shown to American soldiers before they were shipped off to the Pacific and Europe.[32] Later, it was no coincidence that it was Frank Capra whom the secretary of defense asked to make the first US propaganda films promoting the war (*Why We Fight*).[33]

The alternative masculinity that the film portrays became appropriately situated in an FDR-type masculinity that differed from an earlier and more aggressive version as defined by Theodore Roosevelt. Just as FDR reclaimed Shangri-La for war purposes, the film's representation of a new kind of manhood, a gentler, nonaggressive man who, when he needs to, can also go to battle, reflects the ways FDR projected his own brand of masculinity to the public. In ways not unlike Father Perrault, whose handicapped leg did not prevent him from presiding as Shangri-La's most effective and powerful ruler and patriarch, FDR embodied the contradiction of intellectual strength and emotional fortitude in a physically weak body. His famous fireside chats projected an image of a father figure as the head of the nation-state and created a wholeness to his polio-afflicted body. The image of FDR as a paternal and yet approachable president endeared him to citizens during the Depression. As Robert S. McElvaine argues, although the New Deal was not a very liberal policy, not benefitting the working man significantly while benefitting corporations considerably, people still saw FDR as an empathetic president who understood their plight. Americans continued to write to him about their problems, appealing to what they believed was his deep sympathy for them, even while his policies did little to alleviate their suffering.[34] The kind of masculinity that Roosevelt represented during the Depression era also demonstrated a new kind of masculinity for new times, in an America no longer defined by manifest destiny, the open frontier, and unlimited economic possibilities. Roosevelt had summed this up right before his election to the presidency in 1932:

> A glance at the situation today only too clearly indicates that equality of opportunity as we have known it no longer exists. Our industrial plant is built; the problem just now is whether under existing conditions it is not overbuilt. Our last frontier has long since been reached, and there is practically no more free land. More than half of our people do not live on the farms or on lands and cannot derive a living by cultivating their own property. There is no safety valve in the form of a Western prairie to which those thrown out of work by the Eastern economic machines can go for a new start. We are not able to invite the immigration from Europe to share our endless plenty. We are now providing a drab living for our own people.[35]

Roosevelt's call for retrenchment, through closing the United States' borders to immigrants and being realistic about the limited resources now available to generate money and support American dreams, describes a new America of the Depression era: one that changed not only the way men saw themselves in general but how they saw themselves in contrast to an earlier manhood that was typified by Theodore Roosevelt. According to Gail Bederman, US masculinity encountered a shift in its representations at the turn of the twentieth century. Fresh off the colonization of the Philippines and at the end of the Indian wars, Theodore Roosevelt self-fashioned a virile and aggressive manliness that was invested in promoting the twin goals of US Empire and white racial superiority. His masculinity was defined by the ability to conquer the frontier and decimate the "savage" Indians and other nonwhite populations of the world.[36] His persona as an avid hunter and frontiersman reflected a brand of aggressive, if not violent, masculinity that was, at the end of the frontier, no longer relevant. No longer was the muscle-rippling, animal-hunting, Indian-killing imperialist of the frontier era the ideal: the post-frontier ideal was a paternal, empathetic man, the reluctant hero.

It was not only the conception of masculinity that shifted between the two iterations of *Lost Horizon* in 1937 and 1942. Over that time, we can also gauge the shifting figurations of the East as demanded by two historically specific ideological formations: that of prewar utopianism and social critique and that of wartime national defense and propaganda. In the first instance, the unboundedness that the East represents becomes an unreadable signifier where East and West, Asia and America, ambiguously collide and interact. In the second instance, in contrast, the remapping of Shangri-La in China creates intersections with US imperialist ideologies. Certainly, the aims of US Empire were not visible in Capra's initial film because his film was about peace and anti-imperialism. The war forced an identification of Shangri-La with the specific nation of China, and in one stroke this broke the spell of utopia. Thus FDR's suggested changes to

Capra's film relocates Shangri-La as both China *and* America brought together, in a new way, redefining the two nations' relationship. Conway is positioned as both diplomat and common man and remade from confusing hero into reluctant hero for the average male citizen, a new kind of masculinity that presented a model for future soldiers of America, who also do not want to go to war but nevertheless must to save the "free" world. Ironically, the film also became appropriable for the war effort by positing a new form of imperialism through economic monopoly and military occupation. The United States' entrance into World War II, armed with reasons based on the reinterpreted themes of *Lost Horizon*, rationalized away the inconsistencies this posed for the United States as a racist nation-state. The United States' explicit and implicit anti-Semitic policies allowed it to ignore the Jewish genocide for an unconscionable length of time. And within the United States, we find the continuation of Jim Crow laws and the discriminatory treatment of blacks and other ethnic minorities, including the United States' long-standing anti-Asian policies—notably the massive constitutional violation in the incarceration of 110,000 Japanese Americans in 1942, the very year that *Lost Horizon* was rereleased.

Conclusion

Lost Horizon reveals how "Asia" is a catalyst for a radically different white male identity, one that discarded a destructive and aggressive Western masculinity for one that is pacifist and rational. At the same time, this new masculinity cannot be fully executed and only materializes when narrativized through, paradoxically, war. The white male protagonist Conway (and Capra himself) looks toward the East as a way to find new meanings for his existence. And in this way, the East and Asia represent a place in which white masculinity can reimagine itself, challenging the norms of gendered identity and even sexuality. However, we can see that, despite Capra's vision, this masculinity needs to be regrounded within a real space, "America," in order for it to be viable. Here, Asia's potentially transformative effects cannot be brought back home as is, but only have meaning when reappropriated back into the West.

In my next chapter, I again turn to issues of gendered identity, but this time to femininities and feminism, once again split between Asia and America, as found in the exchange of texts between American and Japanese feminists, again in the mid-twentieth century. I show how these feminists on both sides of the Pacific envisioned a brand of feminism across Japan and the United States, but that this imagining of common struggle broke down unevenly as "tradition" and the "modern" were distributed differently to women in Japan and in the United States. The emergence of "the modern woman" thus partook of both a transcendent gendered identity and a residual orientalist parceling out of "progress" in differential fashion. Thus, like *Lost Horizon*, the imagining of different and new forms of gendered identities and ideologies is made possible through East and West contact and specifically collaboration between the United States and Japan. However, such a vision, especially held by US feminists, cannot make that transpacific leap, instead resituating feminism and radical female identity within the confines of the US nation-state and America's orientalist fantasies.

4 / Envisioning Feminism across the Pacific: Japanese and American Feminism and the Limits of Race in *Facing Two Ways*

Transpacific co-encounters between Japanese and US feminists, specifically through the collaboration and alliance between two birth control activists, Baroness Shidzué Ishimoto and Margaret Sanger, are examined in this chapter. As I suggested in the introduction and in chapter 1, there are relatively few works that discuss the real and imagined relationships between Asian and white women during this period, and even fewer looking at comparative feminisms at this time. While I do not propose that the example of Ishimoto and Sanger constitutes "the" model of comparative feminisms during this period or that it predicts future models, this early transpacific feminist collaboration provided specific benefits to each woman that placed their feminisms within a more global and international frame. For Sanger, her friendship and collaboration with Ishimoto gave her the opportunity to expand her work in Japan, while for Ishimoto, Sanger's specific form of birth control activism, which focused on good mothering and the well-being of women, inspired Ishimoto to develop a similar activist agenda in Japan.

Similar to the ways notions of gender and sexuality were changing in the United States during the 1910s, 1920s, and1930s,

Japan's Taishô era exhibited shifts in notions of gender and sexuality within a liberalizing political and social climate. The popular cultural representations of the modern boy, the *mobo*, and the modern girl, the *moga*, in Japan corresponded respectively to the new man and the new woman of Europe and the United States. These conditions became a unique platform for Sanger and Ishimoto's feminist collaborations, and yet they differentiate the two women's views on race, class, women, culture, and nation. The influence of US feminisms broadened Ishimoto's feminist ideologies, which were more critical of nationalism and imperialism and even included a cognizance of the racial and cultural oppressions of both the United States and Japan. In contrast, Sanger's feminism belies racialized perspectives about race, nation, and culture.

Japanese feminist and birth control activist Baroness Ishimoto Shidzué's collaborations with American feminists, and her exposure to European and US socialist and feminist thought, motivated her to cultivate a feminist identity and philosophy that encouraged the potential for imagining a feminism between the United States and Japan, supported by an expansive vision of feminism and humanism across national, cultural, and racial boundaries. Ishimoto's only English-language autobiography, *Facing Two Ways: The Story of My Life* (1935), was written primarily for an American audience and was about her life growing up during Japan's nascent modernization. Her autobiography is of interest not only because of its depiction of a life few Americans knew about but also because of its vision of a more capacious feminist imaginary. Ishimoto's work is evidence that the influence of the West, and the United States in particular, resulted in not necessarily a Japanese feminism created in the image of white Western feminism but rather a vision that was less bounded by nation or culture in any absolute fashion. How the West became imagined, understood, and integrated into Japanese socialist and feminist thought, as evidenced in Ishimoto's writings, demonstrated a feminism that transcended national, cultural, and racial boundaries.

As an alternative Japanese female literary text, Ishimoto's autobiography appealed to female readers in the United States who themselves were trying to envision the New American Woman. However, despite the possibilities offered by Ishimoto's autobiography, especially in terms of new female identities, US readers seemed unable to look beyond their own Western orientalist gaze, often focusing their attention on the differences between East and West, Japan and the United States, and even Asians and whites. By the time Ishimoto published *Facing Two Ways*, there was already in the United States a fairly well-established tradition of reading about Japan: readers were thus familiar with certain representations of the Japanese woman, some of which were set within stock orientalist discourse. Interestingly, the rise and popularity of "Japanese" literary heroines such as Madame Chrysanthemum and Madame Butterfly occurred alongside the birth of the New American Woman. Thus images of these Japanese heroines worked in complex ways for American women. The latter could imagine the struggles shared by women on both sides of the Pacific Ocean. Reading about Japanese women's struggles to find selfhood against Japanese tradition and patriarchy assured white female readers of their own superiority as independent "American" and "Western" women. Such views of Ishimoto's autobiography reveal how readers orientalized her, continuing to see the Japanese woman as more oppressed than the American woman, even though Ishimoto's story actually challenges Western stereotypes and engages in radical discussions about Japanese feminism. The persistence of reading Asia and the United States in opposition to each other, reinscribing the divide between the "traditional East" and the "modern West," therefore is found even in the works of "progressive" feminists. While collaboration between Western (European and American) and Japanese feminists showed the possibilities for imagining a transpacific and even global and cosmopolitan feminism, Margaret Sanger, as I show from her writings, ultimately becomes an example of this limited vision of white American feminism.

For the most part, Ishimoto and Sanger remained lifelong friends. Their collaborations, which began in the 1920s and continued even after World War II, opened up new worlds to both women. Sanger's worldview, especially of the United States and Asia, revealed some early issues in the international collaboration of feminists and how racial and cultural domination works in subtle ways that define hierarchy between feminists and women across culture and nation. Accordingly, Sanger's writings often reveal an underlying ambivalence about Japanese women's potential as feminists, sometimes reiterating stock orientalist views of Japanese women as passive aesthetic objects of beauty, thereby undermining their ability to be feminists able to change Japanese society.

In contrast to Sanger, Ishimoto shows how feminism, when broadly envisioned, can challenge the myths and ideologies of nations and their segregation from a global world community. As in the previous chapter, in which I described how an alternative vision of gender can challenge nationalisms and even imperialisms as in the case of *Lost Horizon*, Ishimoto observes ways that alternative visions of women's roles and identities within the nation can challenge tradition and expand an understanding of the Japanese nation in the world. She uses the autobiographical form to narrate her process of self-realization and her transformation from a mostly passive and obedient girl raised in the Japanese tradition to a liberated woman of the world, thus serving as a counterexample to the Western stereotype of a Japanese female locked into blind adherence to "tradition" and locked out of the progressive temporal flow of modernity. But even more important than this developmental narrative is the fact that Ishimoto argues that gender inequities must be seen within a global phenomenon of the exploitation of women, men, the working class, and children. Concluding this chapter with a sustained reading of Ishimoto's text, I show how Ishimoto's ideas about feminism are set within a global perspective that decenters the nation-state as the determining site of feminist political and social action.

Facing Two Ways

Baroness Shidzué Ishimoto, who is more commonly known in Japan as Kato Shidzué, was a former member of the Japanese Diet and a leading figure in both the birth control and feminist movements in Japan. Although Ishimoto never settled in the United States, her alliances with American feminists before World War II made her fairly well known to American intellectuals and writers interested in Japan and Asia. After World War II, Ishimoto worked with the Allied occupation in Japan and as one of only a few Japanese citizens involved in the occupation was recruited by the US government to play an important role in the future democratization of her country. The US Office of Strategic Services listed Ishimoto and her future husband, Kato Kanju, under the file titled "Friendly Persons." Intelligence reports collected on Ishimoto from American missionaries who knew her before the war described her as "anti-militaristic, and pro-America."[1] Ruth Benedict's influential 1946 book about Japanese culture, *The Chrysanthemum and the Sword*, drew from parts of Ishimoto's autobiography. After the war, Ishimoto worked to forge stronger relations between Japan and its former colonies (especially Korea) and became the first Japanese woman to run for the House of Representatives.

Ishimoto wrote her autobiography in English for Americans at the urging of her friend and mentor, Mary Beard, who believed that Ishimoto's life would be of great interest to the American public. *Facing Two Ways: The Story of My Life* introduced Americans to a Japanese woman who was radically different from the literary and theatrical constructions of Japanese femininity popularized in the West at that time. Where popular orientalist representations of Japanese women in the West depicted Japanese femininity as passive and subordinate, especially to men, these representations also supported a Western aestheticization and depoliticization of Japanese women, who were seen as merely orientalist exotica for Western pleasure. In contrast, Ishimoto's autobiography would seem to refuse a reading of the exotic and aestheticized Japanese woman, given the highly politicized nature of Ishimoto's discussions, which cover the effects of capitalist and industrial exploitation, class and racial inequities, and even the dangers of Japanese militarism and imperialism. Situating her life in the midst of the momentous social and political changes in Japan resulting from its rapid industrialization and transformation into a world power, Ishimoto's autobiography shows how she herself underwent a social and personal awakening, making the transformation from traditional Japanese woman, raised to be an obedient wife and mother, to a socialist, feminist, and activist.

The autobiography is divided into three major sections. The first part describes Ishimoto's youth and adolescence, and the second, her marriage to Baron Keikichi Ishimoto, who first introduced her to socialist thought. As Ishimoto describes it, she married because she was raised as a traditional Japanese girl, but the baron's unconventional beliefs, and his interests in socialism, Marxism, and Christian humanism, gave Ishimoto the opportunity to transform herself from mother and wife to a labor activist, an advocate for women's rights, and a leader in the birth control movement in Japan. The third part of the autobiography is a series of essays outlining Ishimoto's views on a variety of subjects including marriage, the geisha problem, religion, socialism, and feminism.

The most compelling part of the autobiography is the second part, in which the baroness describes her growing awareness of the cost of Japan's industrialization. This understanding occurred when, shortly after marrying, she and the baron moved to the mining town of Miike, where the Mitsui Mining Corporation employed the baron as an engineer. Here she witnessed, for the first time in her life, the exploitation of laborers, particularly of female coal mine workers. Around the time of World War I, the Japanese coal mining industry was at its peak, considered the "golden age" of coal mining. The employment of women coal miners increased faster than that of male coal miners partly because coal mining companies could pay women (and their children) at a far cheaper wage than they paid men.[2] Thus it was in Miike that Ishimoto came to understand the plight of the female worker, who was exploited both by industrialists and by domesticity. Ishimoto saw women with practically no resources bearing the burden of child rearing in the most squalid and exploitative conditions, having more children than they could care for. Ishimoto did not know that birth control could alleviate these women's problems until she went to the United States and met Margaret Sanger. The baroness's experience in Miike created a humanitarian consciousness that she would be unable to fully articulate until she came to the United States for the first time and met Sanger and other feminists, writer and activist Agnes Smedley and feminist historian Mary Beard. Upon her return to Japan, Ishimoto opened a birth control clinic and traveled to various parts of Japan to speak to laborers about birth control and social reform, until the Japanese government confiscated and shut down her clinic and, in 1932, put her under house arrest. By this time, Baron Ishimoto had begun to turn away from both his radical politics and his wife and family, and he became increasingly supportive of Japanese imperialism and militarization. Eventually, he abandoned Ishimoto completely, leaving her to support their two sons on her own. Nevertheless, his wife did not give up the cause of progressivism; on the contrary, particularly inspired by the feminist cause, she retained and championed a vision that went against nationalism and chauvinism.

As Barbara Molony points out in her introduction to Ishimoto's book, Ishimoto originally intended for the autobiography to be a socialist and feminist manifesto in which she used "her life as a metaphor" to show how Japan changed "from feudalism to industrialism."[3] However, Ishimoto decided to change the title from *From Feudalism to Industrialization* to *Facing Two Ways: The Story of My Life*, which was less politicized and more marketable. More interesting and human than the original, the new title reflects a more personal story of Ishimoto's life in this period of transition. Indeed, for Ishimoto, "facing two ways" was about being trapped by both Japanese feudal traditions and Japan's growing industrialization. Thus in her view, facing backward and forward was not laden with the familiar message that the values of the East were archaic and the values of the West modern and progressive. In fact, her autobiography shows that for Japanese women, facing modernity was equally as exploitative as facing Japanese feudalism. In using her life "as a metaphor" for the changes from feudalism to modernity, Ishimoto depicts how her feminist work and activism in birth control conflicted with her responsibility to her family. Inspired by the Japanese women's movement, which gave women a forum to discuss what it meant to be a "good wife and wise mother" in the modern world, Ishimoto expressed her own personal dilemmas as wife and mother in a changing Japan and globalizing world.[4] In writing her autobiography, Ishimoto extended this conversation to the West and not only referenced the ways Japanese and American feminisms compared to each other but also provided poignant details about her maternal devotion to her sons and her despair over her failing marriage, as her husband, who helped her become a feminist, turned from a radical political activist into a Japanese militarist and imperialist.

The phrase "facing two ways" captures the dilemma of liberal Japanese women at the time: trying to fulfill traditional duties to children, husband, and family and yet also realizing that those vey fulfillments demanded that they abdicate public life and remain cloistered within the privacy of the domestic sphere. In this way Ishimoto's autobiography reflects white European and American women's desires and subsequent struggles to be the New Woman who sought to differentiate herself from the Victorian angel of the house and her responsibilities not toward the development of her own identity but to the service of her husband and children. Yet although some American readers found Ishimoto's personal and political transformation interesting, many were fascinated more by the duality of Ishimoto's life, existing between East and West, Japan and the United States. Instead of seeing Ishimoto's feminist transformation as occurring within the shift from feudalism to capitalism, American readers tended to depoliticize Ishimoto's writing, reading her as an aestheticized Japanese woman not so different from Madame Butterfly.

Reading Western Female Modernity through Japanese Femininity

Studies of women's middlebrow reading culture in the early twentieth century reveal how the mass production of literature made reading an important part of the formation of American female identity. According to Barbara Sicherman, reading could change the way women thought of themselves:

> A study of women's intense engagement with books suggests that many found in reading a way of apprehending the world that enabled them to overcome some of the confines of gender and class. Reading provided space—physical, temporary, and psychological—that permitted women to exempt themselves from traditional gender expectations, whether imposed by formal society or by family obligation. The freedom of imagination women found in books encouraged new self-definitions and, ultimately, the innovative behavior associated with the Progressive generation.[5]

As Sicherman explains, at the turn of the twentieth century and into the 1930s many American women saw themselves between two cultures, the Victorian and the post-Victorian, the latter viewed as modern. By giving them a glimpse of lives other than their own, the act of reading had potentially radical effects in the Progressive Era for women, who, though raised with Victorian mores, could now imagine female lives that did not adhere to Victorian standards of femininity, potentially leading these women to rethink their culture's gender and class roles. In addition, the empathy these readers developed for the literary characters, despite their own life experiences or goals for reading, allowed them to define themselves either in sympathy with or against the characters and, in this way, imagine new female identities.

An important new female identity that actually began as a literary figure was the New Woman. Penned by British and American women writers, the composite picture popularized a woman who bucked social conventions of Victorian domesticity, chose not to marry, and believed that the development of her individual self was more important than taking care of a husband and children. In contrast to the working-class "woman adrift," as described in chapter 1, the New Woman was a decidedly middle-class creation that came to prominence through a reading culture. New Woman authors such as Sarah Grand, Olive Schreiner, and even Charlotte Perkins Gilman, to name a few, eloquently expressed their discontent with society's traditional views of women, openly declared their right to free love and social and sexual freedom, and criticized the West's male-dominated culture, which treated women as men's subordinates.[6]

Although racially and culturally alien, the Japanese woman's experience was seen to hold some parallels to the middle-class American woman's life. Primarily, the modern Japanese woman represented to the West an antiquated female role, not unlike the Victorian woman of a generation before, bound by tradition to be obedient to her husband and family. Tied to this traditional role by feudalism and patriarchy, the Japanese woman, unlike the modern American woman, was unable to liberate herself. Reading about the continued oppression of Japanese women thus allowed American white women to better imagine themselves as liberated and modern.[7] Significantly, the belief that Japanese women would only be able to liberate themselves through imbibing Western influence reflected a white female racial and cultural sense of superiority and a belief that Western (and American) women were more progressive than Japanese women.

Before World War II, the images of Japanese femininity that circulated in American popular literature and theater were of exotic and sensuous, yet docile and submissive, characters.

Pierre Loti's *Madame Chrysanthemum* (1887) and John Luther Long's short story turned play and opera, *Madame Butterfly* (1903), introduced the Western world to the image of the Japanese geisha, whose role was to fulfill the Western white man's desire for racialized sexual adventure. This Japanese woman not only submitted readily to white male lust but was also willing to sacrifice herself for the love of a white man. *Madame Butterfly* was an international sensation in which white American and British actresses became famous for their portrayals of Japanese femininity.[8] The aestheticization of submissive and sacrificial Japanese femininity influenced other theatrical and literary productions that fed the American fascination for Japanese women.

Several Asian American women writers not only supported the perception of the Japanese woman made popular by *Madame Butterfly*; they also capitalized on its popularity. Chinese British author Winnifred Eaton, whose pen name was the Japanese-sounding "Onoto Watanna," featured Japanese female heroines in her novels and some of her short stories. *Miss Numè of Japan* (1899), for instance, is a Japanese American romance featuring an interracial relationship like that in *Madame Butterfly*. Eaton's other short stories such as "The Love of Sakura Jiro and the Three Headed Maid," "Kirishima-san," and "Miss Lily and Miss Chrysanthemum: The Love Story of Two Japanese Girls in Chicago" clearly draw from the popularity of Japonisme and especially of European and American orientalist portrayals of Japanese women.[9] By comparison, Yoné Noguchi's *American Diary of a Japanese Girl* (1902) plays with the stereotypes that Eaton's work underscored. The work purports to be an authentic diary written by a young Japanese woman traveling in the United States. Noguchi, posing as the diary's eighteen-year-old owner, Miss Morning Glory, plays on the American audience's fascination with exotic Japanese femininity and on American misperceptions of Japanese women. Although Noguchi was partially inspired to write *American Diary* after the success of John Luther Long's *Madame Butterfly*, the diary purposefully satirizes Western fascination with Japan and Japanese women. At one point, Miss Morning Glory makes fun of the white women who play Japanese women in stage productions such as David Belasco and Giacomo Puccini's *Madame Butterfly*, Gilbert and Sullivan's *The Mikado*, and Sidney Jones and Owen Hall's *The Geisha: A Story of a Tea House*. Miss Morning Glory's landlady, Miss Ada, spies her kimono and wants to try it on. As she does, she pretends to be a Japanese geisha, and Glory exclaims: "How ridiculously she stepped! It was the way Miss What's-her-name acted in 'The Geisha.'"[10] Noguchi is not only making fun of this racial masquerade but also foregrounding the pervasive white female imitation of an imitation itself—the Western orientalist stereotype of the Japanese woman. Noguchi thus highlights the artificiality of white female performers' and audiences' identification with orientalist melodramas and their heroines.

These submissive stereotypes of the Japanese woman presented a contrast to the assertive new American woman and thus were popular at a time when images of the latter were also increasing in literary and cultural production. This New Woman was defined against the woman of the late Victorian era, who was praised for her virtues as a gentle, obedient, loving, and submissive wife and mother, willing to sacrifice herself for the good of her husband and family. In this way, Victorian femininity was not unlike the popular Western representation of Japanese women: in *Madame Butterfly*, Cho-Cho San gives up her life so that her Eurasian child can live and be adopted by Lieutenant B. F. Pinkerton and his wife. This Japanese version of the angel of the house presented a contrast to the vocal and independent American New Woman. Yet, because of her racial difference, the Japanese heroine in Western literature and culture also made the new American woman feel, in contrast, more modern.

The popularity of orientalist melodramas such as *Madame Butterfly* gave white female audiences and performers the ability to contemplate modern female identities by simultaneously identifying and disidentifying with the Asiatic heroine.[11] In *Madame Butterfly*, a complicated relationship between a white female spectatorship and the Japanese heroine is produced, one that identifies with her in her female victimization and yet disidentifies with her racially. The Japanese heroine's racial difference gratifies white female audiences in ways that simultaneously challenge and yet reinscribe racialized gendered relations of power between East and West, Japanese and white. According to Mari Yoshihara, white actresses who played the Japanese heroine Cho-Cho San in the theatrical and operatic versions of *Madame Butterfly* during the early twentieth century exhibited a cross-racial performance that served to distance white modern femininity from Asiatic femininity. By donning and performing racially alterior roles, white Europe and American women reconfigured and created new roles for themselves: "The performance of Asian femininity thus provided an effective tool for white women's empowerment and pleasure as New Women. . . . Acting on stage and performing identities that were distinct from their own marked them as women of a new generation."[12] Actresses who performed *Madame Butterfly* emblematize a distinctive "New Woman" who challenged Victorian female roles and the domestic life that socially constrained women. And yet, critically, their adoption of the Butterfly role was actually a pretext for the ascension of white femininity over Asian. As Yoshihara argues: "Because ideal models of womanhood were intricately connected to the racialized notions of civilization, the insistence on [the actress's] difference from her Japanese role was important to upholding not only [the actress's] American womanhood but also American civilization itself. The lack of authenticity thus served to confirm [her] belief in American superiority to the Japanese."[13] Yet according to Traise Yamamoto, these representations of Japanese women as more passive and less liberated than American women also comes from the representation of the oppression of Japanese women as "both cause and consequence of its [Japan's] archaic backwardness," and this perception supports "the Japanese woman's ideological alignment with the West in contrast to and often against the negative aspects of Japanese culture and the threat of the Japanese nation-state."[14] In this popular Western and US logic, Japanese women, associated with a less developed Japanese culture, were thus behind US women, if not representing more traditional and outdated femininities.

Reviews of Ishimoto's book evidence such thinking, constructing her as an orientalized Japanese woman who was only masquerading as a feminist. In some ways, the reading of Ishimoto's autobiography in the United States, rather than elicit cross-cultural affiliations between Japanese and white women, worked in difference: interpreting Japanese women in literature as less liberated and more passive served to empower white women in the West as New Women. Literary reviews of Ishimoto's autobiography reveal the desire to see Ishimoto as a Japanese female stereotype despite her autobiography's details of her transformation into a feminist and even a New Woman of Japan. Images of orientalized Japanese femininity proved hard to replace, and US literary reviews demonstrated doubts about the authenticity of Ishimoto as a "New" Japanese woman, often reverting to seeing the Japanese woman as an aestheticized Oriental woman in her kimono or, like the fictional Japanese female characters in the West, as demure and soft-spoken, as opposed to the outspoken feminist activist she was.

The reviews of Ishimoto's autobiography reveal the strong desire to view the West as the only place where Japanese women can find liberation. Instead of seeing the significant changes in these women's lives as part of a more global phenomenon that was also linked to social reform, decolonization, and industrial exploitation, American readers chose instead to see a narrative of Eastern and Western difference as a reassurance that the West would indeed continue to save yellow women from yellow men well into modernity. Amy Loveman's review is exemplary in this sense: "Indeed, [Ishimoto's] volume makes excellent reading throughout, presenting as it does the picture of a society 'facing two ways,' reaching back to the feudalism of old Japan and forward to the Western civilization of the present."[15] The modern is always associated with the West, a place that Japan reaches for while looking back at its past. Other reviewers were confounded by the contradiction of Ishimoto's looking like a traditional Japanese woman but speaking like a radical Western feminist. For example, Rose C. Feld, writing for the *New York Times Book Review*, focused on the autobiography's idyllic descriptions of Japanese life and exotica rather than on its progressive political message:

> Labor reform, feminism, birth control—these are strange subjects to come from the pen of one who looks like a lovely print by an old Japanese master of the brush. And though Shidzué Ishimoto may not like it, for she is an ardent advocate of the way of the twentieth century against that of the fifteenth, it is the pages that deal with her childhood and youth that will bring the greatest delight to her American readers. It is not that she fails to depict the problems of present-day Japan, but that people grown weary of a machine age with its implications of human strife and discouragement will welcome a narrative that holds the magic charm of an exotic land of moonlight and lotus blossoms.[16]

Feld not only seems unable to accept the fact that a young woman looking like Madame Butterfly can write a text of political and cultural importance, but she also divulges a discomforting commonality between the political ideas raised by Ishimoto about Japan and the alienation of modern American life. Preferring to see Japan and the Japanese as a Western fantasy, the reviewer must justify this desire in spite of what Ishimoto's text actually invokes, which is the need for a global movement of class and gender consciousness.

Even the choices made by publishers in the production of the first edition of the autobiography attempted to highlight the differences between a past Japan, aesthetically exotic but by no means modern, and a progressive West. For example, the cover photograph of Ishimoto, smiling at the reader, runs contrary to the book's more complex contents. Although the title of the book is *Facing Two Ways*, Ishimoto is posed to directly face the

Western reader. Opposite the title page is another picture of Ishimoto dressed in a kimono and standing in front of a large circular rice-paper window. She is turned away from the viewer, her gaze averted. I find this juxtaposition between the book's cover and frontispiece interesting because of the ways Ishimoto's experience is framed, literally, as facing both East and West. Nevertheless, Farrar and Rinehart selectively chose to highlight Ishimoto's *Japaneseness.*

Almost all the pictures of Ishimoto in the autobiography show her wearing kimonos and the rest of her family wearing traditional Japanese clothing, even though Ishimoto describes her father as a Westernized man, frequently looking more like an English gentleman than a samurai. In addition, during Ishimoto's lifetime, many upper- and middle-class Japanese women wore Western clothing, saving their kimonos for special occasions. Ishimoto herself mentions that she felt uncomfortable when she wore a kimono, and she wore them only at the prodding of her American friends and hosts when she visited the United States. According to Ishimoto, this self-exoticization was necessary because Americans were more likely to trust her authenticity when she was wrapped in a kimono, but for her it was a disquieting act: "Always for public lectures and for formal dinners I wore my native costume. It seemed to create the best atmosphere for friendship. Since I wore Western costume at other times I often felt as exotic in my native dress as I doubtless looked to others" (*Facing Two Ways*, 371–72).

With the initial success of the first edition of Ishimoto's autobiography, which did very well in the United States (and in Sweden, interestingly), even making the *New York Times* best-seller list in 1935, the publishers made a shorter, cheaper version directed at older girls. This slimmer version, named *East Way, West Way: The Story of a Modern Japanese Girlhood*, contained only chapters 1 and 2, which describe the author's girlhood and adolescence in post-feudal Japan. Farrar and Rinehart understood that the larger reading public was captivated more by the first part of the novel because it focused not only on the dualities of East versus West and modernity versus tradition but on a girl rather than a woman. The change of title, from *Facing Two Ways*, which contains far more nuanced possibilities, to *East Way, West Way*, once again emphasizes the polarity of Orient versus Occident. The change in title also indicates a marketing of Ishimoto as a modern Japanese girl who must negotiate the pull of Eastern familial and societal expectations and Western modernity. Reviews from this shorter version of the autobiography also orientalize Ishimoto, even while they express cognizance of her importance in Japan as a leading feminist. One reviewer, exhibiting the belief that women's accomplishments must always be tempered by more feminine attributes, wrote that "little Shidzué, who was to become one of Japan's foremost leaders of feminism, was taught to grow in beauty."[17] In short, what we see in these reviews is that although Ishimoto demonstrated a real contrast to the other Japanese heroines popularized in American and Western literature, American orientalization of Ishimoto pointed to a specific desire to see the Japanese woman, on the one hand, as a subject of Western tutelage and rescue and, on the other, as a complex point of identification and disidentification by white women to define their own new womanhood.

Thus the New American Woman could be defined in relation to both similarities to and differences from Japanese women: the American New Woman reader is at once attracted to their shared causes in living under patriarchy and, at the same time, sees herself in difference to the more submissive docility of Japanese femininity. In other words, reading about Japanese women provided an opportunity for American women to imagine and understand Japanese and Asian women outside of their cultural and national contexts, but such an understanding was more frequently filtered through racialized images of Japanese femininity that fulfilled a specific purpose: to define white female autonomy and liberation in difference to Japanese submission and oppression.

We now see how redefinitions of white women's gender roles and sexualities in modernity are defined through real and imagined depictions and understandings of Asian women. That Japanese and white American women are defined through each other here marks a difference from the relation between Chinese and American women seen in chapter 1 of this study. They are obverse sides of the same coin: while the New American Woman was defined as liberated and more independent vis-à-vis her Japanese counterpart, she was also seen as threatening—her sexual autonomy made apparent by the focused surveillance on Chinese women that inevitably transferred to white women as well. These two different and seemingly opposing narratives, however, point to a continuing set of issues that consistently relegates Asian women to a means of making legible and articulating the desires and fears of white female autonomy.

Even progressive American feminists were susceptible to making the kinds of orientalist interpretations of Japan and Japanese women as American readers in general made. In the next section I examine Margaret Sanger's writings about Asia and Japan and her friendship and collaboration with Ishimoto. While Japanese femininity defined American womanhood as liberated and unfettered, Sanger's writings implicitly defined an American feminism in difference to Japanese women and feminists.

The Limits of White Feminisms

Although Margaret Sanger would have preferred to see herself as Ishimoto's mentor and the Japanese feminist as her protégé, an Asian version of herself, in reality their relationship was more equal and more reciprocal. In her biography of Ishimoto, Helen Hopper writes that Sanger took a keen interest in Ishimoto because she saw many of her own theories reflected in Ishimoto's ideas.[18] As I mentioned above, Ishimoto, in turn, became interested in Sanger's work with birth control after her experiences in the Miike mines. In her autobiography, Ishimoto identifies her first glimmerings of activism as occurring when, while living in the Miike mines, she realized that the greatest tragedy of industrial exploitation was women giving birth to children they could not feed. She began to see birth control, after meeting Sanger, as the remedy to the harshness of working-class women's lives and desired to make birth control a legal and available choice for Japanese women. Although this ambition was partially the result of Ishimoto's friendship with Sanger and of Sanger's mentoring, Ishimoto did not see herself as created in the image of Sanger. In fact, Ishimoto was instrumental in advancing Sanger's career on the international stage. Nonetheless, the American press often referred to Ishimoto as "the Margaret Sanger of Japan," while the Japanese press referred to her as "Madame Control."[19]

When Sanger arrived in Japan in 1922, she was immensely controversial, having been criminalized and barred from speaking or writing about birth control in the United States. Between 1914 and 1915, following the launch of her monthly publication *The Woman Rebel*, Sanger went into exile in Europe. The periodical's support of contraception and abortion violated the Comstock Act of 1873, which made the distribution of contraceptives against the law.[20] When she returned to the United States in 1916, Sanger finally underwent a public trial for *The Woman Rebel*. Baron and Baroness Ishimoto's friendship with Sanger and the Ishimotos' influence in liberal circles in Japan helped spark interest in Sanger's work there. Sanger was invited to Japan by the progressive magazine *Kaizo* (Reconstruction), which had published four of Sanger's essays.[21] However, when Sanger arrived in Japan, her ship was not allowed to dock. According to Ishimoto, the Japanese government feared that Sanger would introduce "dangerous thoughts" to Japan (*Facing Two Ways*, 226). Eventually, the Japanese government allowed Sanger to speak, but only if she agreed not to talk explicitly about birth control.

Ishimoto and Sanger's relationship showed that feminist collaboration across the Pacific was not only possible but also advantageous to both. Ishimoto writes that Sanger's birth control advocacy motivated her to spread information about birth control in Japan in order to better women's and their children's lives. At the time, the birth control movement in Japan was associated with either socialists or proponents of population control, and Ishimoto found Sanger's focus on women's well-being and ability to be good mothers more attractive. As a result, Ishimoto's birth control activism came to concentrate on motherhood and the health of children and families.

For both women, their friendship and collaboration gave them more exposure, or exposure of a different but equally valuable kind. Because Sanger was already fairly well known among Japanese intellectuals and activists, particularly those focusing on birth control, Ishimoto's relationship with Sanger gave her own birth control activism more exposure. On the other end, Sanger's friendship with Ishimoto helped give her an alternative forum for her activism during a time when she was immensely unpopular in the United States and Europe. Previously, Sanger's activism was based in radicalism; she tried to forward her cause by inciting public outrage and provoking authorities. As Sanger expanded her activism into Asia she began to change her methods; specifically, she felt the need to distance herself from other radical American activists and feminists.[22] Thus Sanger's visit to Asia brought her legitimacy with a global audience, while Ishimoto's relationship with Sanger raised her profile as a feminist activist both within and especially outside of Japan and in the United States. Even as the idea of a universal feminism was not defined at this time, these women's collaborations, particularly in the ways their ideologies formed across the Pacific and in relation to each other's work, influenced their views on birth control activism, nationalism, domesticity, sexuality, and gender. Yet Sanger's writings about Japan and Asia reveal a tension between the desire to forge a transcultural vision of feminism and an underlying national and deeply rooted racialized thinking that compromises such a vision.

Sanger's views about Japanese feminists display some ambivalence about their ability to become *leading* feminists. On the one hand, Sanger draws parallels between Japanese and white

Western women's experiences and celebrates Japanese feminists' different approach to the cause. But on the other hand, Sanger reveals a failure truly to educate herself about Japan and Japanese feminists. Like the American reviewers of Ishimoto's autobiography, Sanger saw Japanese women through the gaze of orientalism and at times did not seem to take Ishimoto very seriously. According to Helen Hopper, Sanger's relationship with Japan and the Japanese was "affectionate, if sometimes condescending," even though the Japanese "accorded her [Sanger] more adoration and respect than she ever received at home."[23]

In Sanger's memoir about her visit to Japan and Asia, "The East Is Blossoming," she reinforces many of the US literary critics' orientalist assumptions about Japanese women, detailed above. In speaking about Japanese feminists during her Japan tour, Sanger claims that the Japanese woman "did not possess in her typical psychology any strong leanings towards rebellion." Sanger attributes the failure of the women's movement in Japan not to a repressive government that was imprisoning women and men for "dangerous thoughts" but to Japanese women's inherent lack of rebelliousness. Conversely, Sanger attributes any assertiveness shown by Japanese women to the influence of the West through Christianity: "Only those who had turned Christian showed any signs of thinking independently. To be a Christian seemed to imply being a rebel or radical of some kind. They told me it with great secret pride."[24] However, this belief is contradicted by the fact that although her friend Baroness Ishimoto was not a Christian, she had been imprisoned for radical activities in 1937, the year before Sanger published her autobiography. While being a Christian during the Meiji era was considered radical, by the Taishô era Christianity was one among many other liberal movements in Japan, although it was often associated more with the West because of Europe and US missionary history.[25]

Sanger's opinions about the failures of Japanese feminism also show her ignorance not only of Ishimoto's work but of current Japanese political issues and events. In the decade leading up to the Manchurian Incident, the success of Japan's imperialism and militarism depended on the repression of any dissent.[26] By 1938, many of the leading feminists and labor activists were dead, exiled, imprisoned, or forced into silence. After being released, Ishimoto herself was still under house arrest for the following year, and for the duration of World War II she was under government surveillance. Finally, as Hopper notes, a few years after her visit to Japan, Sanger wrote in the *Birth Control Review* that Japanese men were responsible for the creation of the Birth Control League of Japan, even though Ishimoto was one of the most important contributors to its formation.[27] Why this blindness to the positive and pathbreaking work of Japanese women?

I attribute it both to Sanger's racial misconceptions about the Japanese and "Orientals" in general and to her ignorance of actual Japanese politics and history. In her memoir, Sanger's observations about Japan as a culture repeated the familiar Western misconception that "Orientals" valued human life less than whites did. Speaking about the horrors of child labor, Sanger says that "Japanese industrialism had been able to take advantage of an ancient Oriental habit of thought which placed slight value on the . . . child."[28] Sanger seems to believe that the exploitation of children is the result not of capitalism but of a racial and cultural flaw unique to the Japanese and other "Orientals." Sanger ignores the fact that prior to the passing of child labor laws, the United States had a similar "Oriental" habit of exploiting children, as well as women, immigrants, and nonwhite people.

Thus we can see in Sanger's writings an ambivalence about Asia and Japanese women, and while such sentiments may have been commonplace at that time, Sanger's writings reveal some ethnocentric limitations in her feminist visions: at times she shows ignorance of Japan's cultural histories and contemporary movements, and at others, ignorance of her own entrenched orientalist beliefs about Asia and Asians.

In contrast to Sanger, who was probably more of a product of Western Eurocentrism, Ishimoto's worldviews, her critical insights about Japan's imperialism and racism toward Koreans and Chinese and her comparative thoughts on women in Japan, the United States, Europe, and Korea, reveal her ability to imagine feminism and social and political alliances beyond nation, culture, and race. Ishimoto in her autobiography recounts her turn toward feminism and birth control and self-fashions a Japanese modern woman and feminist who is transcultural and international. Even while American readers tended to read her life's story through an orientalist gaze, one needs to keep in mind that Ishimoto also wrote the autobiography primarily for an English-speaking and American audience. In this respect, she partially gave American audiences what they wanted to read about Japanese women. Indeed, her writing reveals how acutely aware she is of her audience. She is less critical of Americans and laudatory of American culture, especially American women: "American women hold the most enviable position of all women" (*Facing Two Ways*, 268). Ishimoto credits Sanger (and other inspiring American feminists such as Agnes Smedley and Mary Beard) with her spiritual and intellectual awakening in becoming a feminist and a socially conscious individual.[29] Yet Ishimoto does not make such statements to emphasize American women's superiority. This admission and critique should be read as indicating the ways Ishimoto became broader in her thinking, having seen the differences of movements in Europe, the United States, and Japan. Her international understanding of feminisms across cultures certainly gave her the ability to see modernity, feminism, and humanism across racial and cultural boundaries.

Literature and the World in Japan

As mentioned previously, in her autobiography Ishimoto also credits her husband with her turn toward progressive politics and her future identity as a feminist. This turn was not entirely surprising, given the growth of liberal movements in Japan during the 1910s and 1920s. These movements in the Taishô period

(1912–26) also encouraged the growth of Japanese female activists, intellectuals, artists, and writers who were not only interested in new formations of gender and sexuality, particularly in the liberation of women in Japan, but also curious about how the women's movement in Europe and the United States compared and applied to their own lives in Japan. For this reason too, Baron Keikichi Ishimoto was not unusual in his early radicalism. And like many of the Japanese elite, having been influenced by the West's social movements through literature, he in turn influenced his wife, Shidzué Ishimoto, to become an independent woman.[30]

Literature about the social movements in other parts of the world, especially the experiences of people in Europe and the United States, had a progressive effect on Japanese intellectuals. As Ishimoto explains in *Facing Two Ways*, while there was a large interest in books about "nationalistic or war topics" (167), many educated Japanese also read widely about Western history, literature, and culture. Literacy was high in Japan; thus books "fed the great appetite for knowledge" as modern Japanese men and women became "earnest seekers after new knowledge" (167). Japanese publishers met much of this demand; according to Ishimoto, Japan published more books in 1925 than any other country except Germany (167). In particular, some of these interests included Marxian literature about the 1917 Bolshevik Revolution and novels by Russian authors such as Leo Tolstoy, Fyodor Dostoyevsky, Ivan Turgenev, and Maxim Gorky. The relatively liberal climate in Japan after the Sino-Russian War (1904–5) made it possible for the Taishô elite, the Japanese of the upper and middle classes, to engage in left-leaning pursuits and political activism. Moreover, Japanese industrialism's exploitation of workers, the increasing division between the haves and the have-nots, appealed to the Japanese intellectuals who identified with Russian novels' "gloomy stories of peasant life and of struggles under the despotic rule of the Czar" (168). Ishimoto describes the Japanese desire for literature about Russia, particularly after the Bolshevik Revolution, as a "fever" (168). Hence the literature of Europe and the United States, while by no means the sole influence on Japanese liberalism at this time, did inspire the Japanese, particularly the Taishô intellectual class, to form movements and ideas that were similar to other progressive movements in the rest of the world, especially in the West.

Ishimoto recalls being introduced very early in her childhood to American and Western ideas through books. In almost an inversion of the ways reading about Japanese women constructed a liberalized female identity in the United States, Ishimoto recounts how her "mental awakening" opened her up to the world outside of Japan and to ideas of emancipation. In the chapter titled "Mental Awakening," Ishimoto credits her Uncle Yusuke, her mother's younger brother, who was educated in Western schools and was a self-identified Christian humanist, with introducing her to American democracy through literature. These books fueled her girlish imaginings of the West as an exotic place very different from Japan, probably in much the same way American girls and women imagined Japan after reading Ishimoto's autobiography. For Ishimoto, the stories about emancipatory figures from European and American history, such as Joan of Arc, Abraham Lincoln, and Harriet Beecher Stowe, were especially interesting and moving:

> I also loved the story of Abraham Lincoln. His life from log cabin to White House! His act of emancipating slaves in the face of opposing guns and swords! Uncle Yusuke told us about a great book written by a Western woman which helped to promote emancipation, so *Uncle Tom's Cabin* became very dear to me and I felt that "little Eva" was my personal friend. (91)

These heroic tales of the emancipation of black slaves emerge as an example of US democracy, underscoring Ishimoto's appeal to her American audiences. In many ways, this chapter compliments Americans by revealing how these stories greatly influenced Ishimoto during her youth. She also illustrates in this chapter how she gravitated toward these American stories while her brother preferred heroic Japanese historical stories. Although Ishimoto spends a good portion of the chapter describing the American and European stories she liked, she cuts short stories of Japanese history: "But I shall not repeat it here, for tales of war occupy too much of the thoughts of the Japanese both with respect to their own history and to that of our neighbor country" (93). Thus Ishimoto both appeals to her American audiences and differentiates herself from her brother's more typical Japanese masculinity through their different desires for American and Japanese stories. Although she is not overtly critical of her brother's desire here, her husband's break from radicalism and embrace of Japanese militarism and imperialism, in her eyes, brought about his "thorough orientalization" (305). In this way, we begin to discern the outlines of her critique of a Japanese masculinity that is specifically associated with war and militarism, against which she constructs her more international vision of feminism.

Becoming a New Woman: American Self-Fashioning and Gender

"America" and its influences served to negotiate Ishimoto's transition from a traditional Japanese woman into a new kind of Japanese woman and a feminist. We can see some play with traditional gendered roles in Ishimoto's autobiography, where as a young girl, she describes herself as more like a boy, with boyish desires. Although her autobiography is staunchly antimilitaristic, often associating traditional Japanese masculinity with militarism, she unmoors masculinity here from militarism and appropriates it for herself as a way to describe her lack of passivity, associated with the Japanese feminine. Because as a child she associated freedom with masculinity, and oppression with femininity, when she later met Sanger, she was able to reconcile these gendered dichotomies and fashion the idea of a new woman and feminist by bridging femininity and masculinity.

Early in her autobiography, she associates her nascent feminist transformation with a hidden masculinity or boyish qualities.

This description of her young self as more boy-like than girl-like presents an unseen and inner nature that was already in rebellion against gender codes. That is, Ishimoto crafts herself as a girl who understood that she needed to behave in traditional feminine ways, concealing the knowledge that, inside, she was different. In this manner, she sets up an equation of freedom with boys and men and oppression with girls and women. As she describes, "I used to have more boys than girls for companions, as I liked to be out-of-doors, playing baseball and tennis, or climbing trees" (29). However, she is highly discouraged from this kind of play by her mother, who tells her, "You can't be married if you behave like a boy that way" (29). While being free and unfettered is associated with being outdoors and being physical (playing sports), being indoors and playing house is seen not only as bondage but also as something some girls prefer, though she does not. If Ishimoto describes her natural disposition as more boy-like, then, in contrast, her younger twin sisters, Kiyo and Kayo, were more authentically girls who could "be good brides" in her place because "[they] preferred to stay indoors, playing with dolls, and cooking the New Year's feast for them" (29). Moreover, it was not only Ishimoto's inherent disposition to like boyish activities: even physically, she appeared different from the other girls. In her mother's efforts to educate her to become a woman, which includes teaching her various tasks that would make her more marketable to a good family (speaking English, playing the piano, and creating flower arrangements), she finds that even her own hands cannot carry out these tasks. Her mother's warning is oppressive to her because she is expected to give up the pleasures of outdoor play so that she will become an acceptable bride one day. In her lament over her horrible flower arrangements, she says that her "awkward hands, fitted rather for a tennis racket than flower scissors" created an arrangement "with no taste or grace" and even looked like "untrained boys at school" (81–82). The flowers themselves thus begin to reflect the way she feels inside, less feminine and more masculine, even unruly. Her "awkward hands" were not the only potential obstacle to her marriageability. One uncle exclaimed, "What a tall girl you are! Poor girl, you are growing only in your height like a fire alarm thief!" (83).[31] The American equivalent would be to say that she was "growing like Jack's beanstalk" and that to steal the fire alarm bell, she could reach the top of the ladder from the ground. As Ishimoto explains further: "In those days tall girls did not fit the Japanese standard of beauty. So mother and uncle agreed that I needed some special accomplishments to offset my height" (83–84). Ishimoto crafts a young self that does not fit into the standard model of Japanese femininity. However, in the absence of models of alternative gendered identities, Ishimoto inevitably describes herself within the given model's gendered dichotomies so that she is less feminine and more masculine. These gendered notions of masculinity and femininity would later be challenged and changed when she met Margaret Sanger.

During Ishimoto's first trip to the United States, her narrative leads readers to believe, she came to reconcile the gender dichotomies she experienced as a girl, seeing that in fact another alternative was possible: to be a feminist such as Sanger but still a woman. Before she meets Sanger, Ishimoto imagines a mannish-looking woman, a picture that would seem consistent, in Ishimoto's mind, with being a radical activist and vocal feminist. However, what she does see is quite the opposite: "Her work, her fascinating career in fighting for her cause, had made me picture her in my mind as a big woman of manly proportions. Quite the contrary to my imagination, when she received me at the door of her studio, I saw a delicate little figure with charm of a thoroughly feminine type" (183). This perception returns readers to her chapter "Mental Awakening," to recall Uncle Yusuke's influential words to the young Ishimoto: "'Be ambitious, grow to be an important woman of Japan!' . . . Yet he never forgot to add, 'But always with sweet womanliness'" (94). We can see in Ishimoto's narrative how, rather than consciously play with gendered inversions and misconceptions, she tests out what it means to be a woman, especially one who refuses the role of the traditional Japanese wife and mother. What other roles and positions were there? To answer this question, Ishimoto, like other feminists in the United States and Japan, began reworking older notions of gender and placing them into new notions that incorporated the idea of women's liberation.

Ishimoto tests out these new notions of feminism and gendered identity while on her first trip to the United States and Europe. Shortly after meeting Sanger, the baron and baroness traveled to Europe, where Ishimoto noticed that while the men in post–World War I England were devastated, exhibiting injuries and handicaps that corresponded to their mental trauma, "the women of England seemed less tragic . . . even well off. Now they could vote." As she expresses it, "As a traveler from a country whose women were so behind in their social position owing to their persistent feudal background, my surprise and admiration were boundless" (196). Moreover, she compares the women in the West to women in Japan and comes to the conclusion that it is necessary to build up one's bodily strength as an indication of inner intellectual strength: "In all the Western countries where I observed these feminist activities, I associated them with strong physiques and came to conclusions concerning the need of physical development among the women of Japan—from the delicate gracefulness to healthy and strong constitutions—if they were to hope for true elevation in their intellectual and social status" (196). In this observation, she allows herself to reconcile her youthful inner feelings of boyishness, which were not always reflected in her outer appearance of being a girl. She gives herself permission to cultivate and exhibit an outer strength that would display and be consistent with her inner intellectual developments. At the end of her visit to Germany, she decides to test the ways her inner transformation could be embodied through physical strength: "I had been educated in America to be independent and energetic, [and] I decided to climb the Jungfrau with my husband. I was warned again and again that it was too much strain for a woman who had never climbed high mountains, but I did not listen" (199).

Thus Ishimoto's text attempts to understand Japanese female oppression in relation to other women in the world, especially American women, and consequently does so through a reworking of traditional gendered formations.

Ishimoto's experiences during this first visit to the West eventually became the basis of a more global notion of feminism: "I saw how others lived and operated. I compared other peoples, other conditions of life and labor, and other ideals and programs with the Japanese people, their social setting and their intelligence and I reached a firmer ground for my personal determinations" (268). Ishimoto gained this perspective through careful observation when she traveled the world with her husband, who had desired to spend a few years abroad learning about capitalist exploitation in the world and how other countries compared to Japan.

Much of Ishimoto's autobiography is devoted to explaining to the Western reader the position of Japanese women in Japanese society within a broader global economic frame. Throughout the autobiography she explicitly argues that Japanese women's position as a subordinate class within Japanese culture is an issue of human rights. Like feminists in the West, Ishimoto traces the material and legal ramifications of female exploitation and oppression. It is Ishimoto's contention that while male laborers are recognized as human beings, women are still considered inferior by men of all classes of Japanese society. Also like many feminists in the West, Ishimoto identifies the practice of marriage as a cultural, legal, and economic way to enforce the inferiority of Japanese women despite the abolition of Japanese feudal laws: "Today Japanese law solemnly declares that man and woman, high and low, rich and poor, are equal in its eyes. Human life and rights are strictly protected by its authority since the great Mikado of the Meiji era inaugurated a new culture. But when we come to the matter of customs rather than statutes, woman is still kept in an inferior position." Ishimoto goes on to draw parallels between oppression and marriage, where the Japanese woman "marries to lose her privileges as a person" (102). Ishimoto names the contradiction of Japan's modernization during the Meiji era. Even though the Meiji government ended feudalism and began modernizing the country, at the same time it disenfranchised Japanese women in the Meiji Constitution of 1889 and the Civil Code of 1898, which respectively denied women's suffrage and gave men absolute authority over their family.[32]

To illustrate women's loss of privilege as subjects, Ishimoto provides an exhaustive account of her marriage trousseau. Her list spans eleven pages in her autobiography and meticulously details her clothing, bedding, jewelry, hair ornaments, furniture, and other miscellaneous items. She prefaces this list by explaining that the trousseau was a gesture that meant "these objects were not the bride's personal possessions but were to become the property of the groom's family, like the bride herself" (116). These items and the bride are all objects of exchange, transferred from the bride's family to the husband's family, much like a dowry or a financial contract.

Ishimoto's relatively privileged life as a member of the Japanese aristocracy did not make her immune to exploitation, as her experience in marriage shows; however, it is her tales of working-class women and women in other countries (especially in Japan's colonies) that point most clearly to her desire to forge connections between feminism and humanism. She explains her feminist stance as "less feministic in a bourgeois way and more humane in [her] thinking" (351) and in one of her autobiography's last chapters, "My Relation to Feminism," describes a feminism that is neither bourgeois nor proletariat. Indeed, though Ishimoto's activist roots were founded in the proletariat movement, as she progressed in her birth control activism, she was criticized by proletariat feminists for seeming to direct her efforts mostly at educating upper- and middle-class Japanese women. As Elsie K. Tipton explains, Ishimoto wrote for the more mainstream bourgeois magazines *Shufu No Tomo* (The Housewife's Friend) and *Fujin Saron* (Women's Salon) and stayed away from writing in the more radical proletariat birth control magazines.[33] She did not agree with the bourgeois feminists' support of the capitalist class structure, but she also did not take the position of the proletariat feminists, who actually showed, in her words, "wider objectives than the bourgeois women's group" (351–52). Ishimoto may have felt the need to explain, if not defend, herself against her critics, particularly those of the Far Left who believed she was compromising her ideals by appealing to upper-class women, and she stated that her need to forge an individual path of feminism was based on "certain domestic reasons" (353). She explains that the discord between the proletariat and bourgeois feminists made her look at feminism with a more "humanistic" view. Ishimoto may also have had political reasons for staying away from affixing one label to herself, given the conflicts among various feminist, humanist, and socialist groups in Japan. Hopper notes that after the war and throughout the rest of her life, Ishimoto stayed away from calling herself a "feminist."[34] She may have done so not because she did not believe in feminism but because, even in Japan, she saw limits to calling herself a feminist. In any case, I believe we can see in her autobiography the ways her interpretation of humanism in the context of feminism not only led her on an independent path from both Japanese and Western feminisms but also allowed her to execute a broader vision of feminism in Japan and in the world.

Women and Class

As I noted above, Ishimoto's observations of the Miike mines radically shifted her thinking and broadened her understanding of feminism's relationships with humanism. It is to this transformative experience in Ishimoto's life that I now turn. Shortly after she married the baron, they moved to the mining town of Miike, where Baroness Ishimoto witnessed an outcome of industrialization she had never seen before: the exploitation of laborers. Ishimoto was disturbed by the horrible living conditions of the miners and their families, by the high fatalities not only from the work of mining but also from the deplorable living conditions. Men, women, and, most poignantly, children routinely died of disease, unsanitary living conditions, and malnutrition:

> Nothing could be compared to the sight of these crowded nests of ignorance, poverty and misery. It is the very picture of Hades! Children were born without love and reared without proper care, receiving even little affection from their parents. Westerners often say that Japan is a paradise for children. I wish this were true, but my impression of the children in the mining camps is so vivid that I can never forget the horror of the dirty little creatures who haunted the garbage box at my door. My heart ached when I saw babies coughing badly and left without medical attention till they died. (163)

Her account is shocking and revelatory, emphasizing the transformative effect it had on her: "As I watched the lives of these laborers and their women and children, these questions rose in my mind but I myself did not realize then that they were the seeds that were to grow and revolutionize my own life" (164). This is one of the real turning points of the autobiography.

In Miike, Ishimoto began to see the gendered division of labor in both work and home. By employing women and children as cheap labor in the mines, corporations could drive down wages so that men competed with their own wives and children. In addition, as previously noted, women bore the burden of motherhood, continually giving birth to children that the family could not care for. Women as workers and mothers thus served a dual purpose in capitalism—continually exploited as cheap labor, they also continued to produce children to add more workers to the system. In the two chapters about the Miike mines, "Life on $25 a Month" and "Are Miners Human Beings?," Ishimoto asks why women must both work and mother, a dual responsibility that greatly compromises women's and their children's health and well-being. Her feminist politics defines good mothering not as a given or a privilege but as a right for both women and children. In allowing women to bear only as many children as they can raise and treat humanely, birth control enables women to become better mothers. Moreover, Ishimoto's critique goes much further in showing the ways that capitalist exploitation dehumanizes women.

One of the more vivid ways she emphasizes the inhumanity of the conditions in the mines is by showing how women are defeminized, equating the stripping of their femininity with that of their humanity. She describes how men and women typically walked around with barely any clothes on because of the heat in the mines. Ishimoto's seeing women working side by side with men in these conditions leads her to conclude that "it was ridiculous to expect morality in such circumstances" (161). Indeed, these women "spoke and acted shamelessly, the last sign of feminine dignity sloughing off" (161). This lack of "feminine dignity" is further associated with dehumanization. The work in the mines physically changes these women's bodies to resemble those of insects or animals. "Women who worked in the darkness had a pale complexion like the skin of a silkworm," and even when pregnant, many women were forced to give birth "to children in the dark pit" of the mines. She concludes, "It would be hard to tell the difference between the life of pigs and the life of these miners" (161). Ishimoto's disturbing picture of these women, especially how labor defeminizes them, is fairly consistent with the ways that the Japanese proletariat movement at the time highlighted the contradictions of being both a mother and a worker. The two roles were seen as incompatible because of the ways labor exploits women's bodies for industrialization, taking away not only their ability to mother effectively but, according to Ishimoto, even their womanliness. Vera Mackie explains how pictures of women workers depicted this contradiction and were a source of anxiety: "Commentators of all political persuasions lamented the toll which factory work took on women's bodies, and struggled to come to terms with the reality of such work which made it difficult for women to bear and look after healthy children."[35] Thus Japanese proletariat propaganda posters often depicted women as "Madonna figures, suckling their children against the backdrop of factory chimneys."[36] In some ways, these images of women as mothers exploited by industry constitute a not entirely progressive gendered politics, for they still privilege women as mothers. Ishimoto's own impressions of the woman worker's defeminization also reveal her own ambivalence about eradicating traditional gendered identities, because, in this context, she privileges female chastity as one component of femininity that women workers are unable to maintain.

Thus some of Ishimoto's observations of the Miike women and her descriptions of them as defeminized and dehumanized may be problematic, especially given her aristocratic identity. She approaches the horror of labor exploitation with an inevitable distancing, looking at these women from the perspective of one who had the privilege to be feminine and who even chose, as I earlier explained, to test out gender roles as a way to transform herself into a liberated woman. Despite Ishimoto's genuine desire to cross class boundaries in her feminist and humanist activism, she cannot fully shed her position as a bourgeois woman and activist. For a woman from an aristocratic background, the opportunity to witness the conditions of laborers and their exploitation was still relatively rare. Her horror in describing these conditions is, in some ways, the result of a total lack of knowledge, not just about capitalist exploitation of workers but of a different side of life from which she was previously sheltered. As Mackie also explains, the proletariat women's movement in Japan during this time was mostly dominated by the intellectual elite; many of them had a "theoretical understanding of the mechanisms of exploitation to the situation of women workers, but few of them had shared the experience of manual labour, and their writings often dramatised the distance between themselves and the women of the working class."[37] We can see this distance between Ishimoto and the women of the mines as she describes them, and it is important to be mindful about the position she speaks from as a feminist from the elite class.

Japanese Imperialism and Race

To her understanding of the issues of class and nation, Ishimoto later added a more global view of the exploitation and oppression of women that included race and the effects of colonialism and imperialism; eventually, she would even become a vocal critic of Japanese military and territorial policies. Ishimoto thus differs importantly from American feminists such as Sanger, who avoided addressing how US imperialism and colonialism created power differences between nations, races, and cultures. Notably, although Sanger had been silent about the United States' imperialist endeavors, during her visit to Japan in 1922 she was quick to point out Japan's growing problem in the context of birth control: "The Japanese militarists hoped to increase the Japanese population to one hundred million, which doubles the population density from today. In that case it would be inevitable for the Japanese to expand overseas. Asian problems are now the prime issue and birth control is the only way to solve the problem."[38] In contrast, Ishimoto focused on birth control as a means to better individuals' lives, especially women's and children's, and, ultimately, lead to a healthier and happier nation. Ishimoto was, like Sanger, originally drawn to neo-Malthusian theory, which encouraged nation-states to adopt eugenic measures (both positive and negative) to curb population growth. However, as she states at the end of her autobiography, she now saw that theory as limiting because it "ignored the creative power of science and the cultural growth of mankind" (351).[39] She does not explain what she means here, but in examining her earlier observations about the Japanese colonization of Korea in the autobiography, we can see her gravitating toward a more anti-imperialist and antimilitarist stance as opposed to supporting the idea of population control.

For her part, Ishimoto could not abide her own country's rhetoric of racial superiority and its policies against the Koreans and Chinese. In the chapter "Trip to Korea, Manchuria, and China," which comprises excerpts from her 1921 diary, Ishimoto gives a fuller picture of Japanese racism and colonialism. During her trip to Korea, she observes the predicament of its citizens with shock and sadness and questions how Japan has benefited from exploiting these people. Although her observations about the Korean people may at times seem unfavorable, she is not necessarily condemning them but instead revealing the damage caused by colonialism: "The upper and lower Korean families alike seemed to me to exhibit a lazy attitude toward life. Everywhere in Korea I was impressed by the lack of vitality. I saw how actively the Japanese directed this annexed people. More than ever before I realized what the words 'conqueror' and 'conquered' meant as I traveled in Korea" (214). Similarly, she connects the exploitation of the colonized Korean people to that of the Chinese coolies. Reflecting the title of one of her chapters on the Miike mines, "Are Miners Human Beings?," she asks, "Coolies, are they not human beings?" She describes the Chinese coolies, like the Japanese miners, as existing only to offer their muscles or even their lives to be exploited by foreign capital, which is often their master under the beautiful name of "helping China, and developing Chinese natural resources." Without the coolies, there would be no interest luring foreign capital to this backward land. Will they ever learn to resist human exploitation? Or will they forever merely exist and breed slaves for the satisfaction of others? The pathetic picture of colonial labor saddened me. (216)

Ishimoto thus equates the exploitation of non-Japanese within colonialism to the exploitation of workers in the mines. In this way, she sees both class and race as indexes of oppression and hierarchy.

In addition, the lives of Korean women provide Ishimoto with another vantage point from which to examine her own life as a woman in Japan: "As an Oriental woman, I had been thinking a great deal of the social barrier I had known in our unreasonable conventions, but here I was driven into deeper dismay by the Korean ladies who were put under more fetters and lived a more depressing life of wasteful patience!" (214). As

I have stated, Ishimoto understands that the perception of "laziness" or other unfavorable traits in Koreans and the Chinese is the result of colonial oppression and capitalist exploitation. And it was Ishimoto's 1921 observations about racial injustice that led to her role in fostering relations between Japan and its colonies after World War II. In 1955, as part of an overall effort by the Japanese government to improve relations between Japan and its colonies, Ishimoto and her second husband, Kato Kanju, wrote a letter of apology to the government of South Korea for Japan's colonization and oppression of the Korean nation and peoples.[40]

Ishimoto employs a critical vision of the Japanese nation-state as a destructive imitation of the West:

> Again and again, I ask myself: "Where have we Japanese learned such a thing as fighting with foreign nations? Are we born fighters? Do we never appreciate a civilization of high order?" My knowledge of Japanese history forbade such a conclusion. I knew enough to answer myself: "We were once a peaceful nation. We developed a high civilization of our own, distinguished for its artistic qualities. Our fighting is only a part of our imitation of what the West has done in the past and is still doing." And I longed to have my people pass through this period of imitation and realize their own creative power for the sake of human progress! (217)

While she sees Japanese aggression and imperialism as Western derived, she also possesses a more utopian vision for Japan's future given its supposedly nobler past. Like many Japanese after the Meiji Restoration, Ishimoto idealized a preindustrial Japan. There was nostalgia for the loss of Japanese traditions after contact with the West; many of the older generation of Japanese saw the culture and life of preindustrial Japan as pure and the new modern era as tainted by materialism and individuality, attributes valued in the West but seen as negative in the East. Ishimoto clearly blames feudal tradition for its continued oppression of women and workers, and yet she imagines that precontact and preindustrial Japan organized gender, work, and class in ways that were less exploitative and aggressive. Unlike Americans and Westerners who simultaneously romanticize Japanese tradition and demonize it as inhibiting progress, Ishimoto's view is that tradition and modernity both conspire, in different ways, to exploit and oppress. In this way, Ishimoto reveals a more critical gaze not just at Japan but at Japan's relationship with the West and hence the ideals coming out of Western modernity.

Ishimoto's autobiography is unique in the ways it balances tracts on feminism, humanism, and even Japanese imperialism with more personal accounts of how cultural, economic, and social events affected her life at home and her relationship with her husband and her children. Although her autobiography was written in English and more likely for Americans, her writing shows influences from both Japan and the United States, not just in content but also in literary form.

"Good Wife and Wise Mother"

Ishimoto's autobiography incorporates many different female literary forms, both high literary and popular, that were known and consumed in Japan during her day. During the 1910s and 1920s, the rise of literacy among women in Japan was in many ways similar to the rise of literacy among women in the United States. In 1875, only 18 percent of girls in Japan were given a four-year primary education, but by 1910 that figure had risen to 97 percent.[41] As a result, there was a huge market for women readers, and the development of women's literature was especially important in the shaping of Japanese as "New Women." As Joan E. Ericson explains, at this time there were two types of popular magazines specifically for women. While one type focused on questions of being a "good wife and wise mother," the other discussed social and political issues. In these magazines Japanese women discussed aesthetics (particularly of women's creations), political issues, and personal accounts of what it meant to be a good wife and wise mother. Some of these magazines such as the famous *Seitō* (Bluestockings) defined and popularized the New Japanese Woman who was critical of Japanese traditions and, like her counterpart in the United States, was a proponent of free love and sexual liberation.[42] Largely as a result of these magazines, there was a more liberal and open atmosphere at this time for women to talk about their views and to discuss their personal issues. In addition, as Ericson explains, there were several literary forms that featured women's confessions. One was the "I-novel" or "I-fiction" (*watakushi-shōsetsu*), which featured women's depictions of their interior selves, and another was women's autobiographical fiction, *jiden shōsetsu*.[43] While the confessional character of Ishimoto's *Facing Two Ways* may fall under autobiographical fiction, her particular literary form is really not tied to any single form in Japan or in the United States. Nevertheless, we see the influences of these Japanese literary forms in her openness to discussing personal and private matters, most apparently in her chapter "A Japanese Husband." At the same time, she often consciously distances herself from these confessional forms by using herself as a mere example of other women who were experiencing similar oppressions at home. In this way she both personalizes her issues and depersonalizes her narrative, just as the more politicized parts of her autobiography demonstrate. That is, like the confessions of Japanese women in the women's literary forums, Ishimoto discusses what at that time would have been considered private issues, of her marriage, the discord between her and the baron, and her painful recognition that the marriage was disintegrating. At the same time, she often plays this personal tragedy down and depersonalizes it by referring to the similar plight of other women, as if to show that the personal is always political.

In the autobiography, Ishimoto's increasingly pacifist stance arises not only from her distrust of the government's use of ideas of family and motherhood to forward its imperialist aims but also from her own personal struggles in her marriage. In her chapter "A Japanese Husband," she compares the baron's abandonment of her and her sons to the ways Japanese nationalist propaganda supports the husband's neglect of his wife and family for the nation's cause. During the early 1920s, when Japanese labor revolts were being violently quelled by the Japanese government, Ishimoto's husband became increasingly disillusioned with liberalism and began to turn toward the idea of imperialism. By the late 1920s and into the early 1930s, Japan grew increasingly reactionary. The 1931 invasion of Manchuria in particular was an indication of the trajectory of Japan's militaristic and imperialistic future. As her husband's views changed and he pursued risky business ventures abroad in Korea and China, Ishimoto was left alone for long periods of time to take care of herself and her sons financially. Around this time, Ishimoto had also opened her first birth control clinic, and, as she remembers it, she suddenly became deeply torn between her activism and her obligations as a wife and mother. With little to no money coming from her husband, she continued to work in the yarn shop that she owned to make ends meet. The writing of the autobiography, preceding and following two lecture tours in the United States, was one way for her to make money to support herself and her sons. Ironically, her husband would send extravagant gifts from abroad, including a Korean bear and a Chinese deer, which only added to her burden. Although Ishimoto writes about these incidents with humor, the reader sees a woman growing increasingly anxious that her husband is drawing further and further away from both his former ideals and from her. The baron reverted from wanting a wife who was strong, thoughtful, and independent to insisting that his wife obey her husband with honor and duty. Ishimoto comments: "So after all I had a regular feudal lord at home. The only thing that was absent from the picture was the perfect feudal wife" (303). However, the feudal wife was serving the modern nation's cause. Often Ishimoto would write to her husband abroad and, in response, would receive either scant information about his activities or impersonal letters filled with "classical Chinese expressions." In one letter, he thanked her on behalf of the Japanese nation for fulfilling her role as a good mother and wife:

"The Japanese nation will be grateful to you, as I consider you meritorious in managing the difficult family affairs, as a good wife should do to help her husband who is fighting in the front line in behalf of a national policy" (305). Shocked that her husband is thanking her on behalf of the Japanese government, Ishimoto explains that she shares this experience not merely to divulge her personal problems to the reader but to demonstrate how pervasive the veneration of the "good wife and wise mother" really is:

> If the ensuing domestic problem and struggle had been but an isolated private affair, my melancholy plight would have been of little moment as a story. But my story is a common one among the present-day Japanese women who are trying to emerge from the condition of nonresistance to events however meaningful and take their place in the shaping of events in their own interests, in the interests of the race and of the nation. So in talking about myself, I am really talking about countless members of my sex in Japan. (301)

Thus in the excerpts from this chapter, we have seen Ishimoto negotiating the need to tell her story in these personal and painful ways and desiring to offer her life as an example of Japanese women's lives in general and of the oppression of patriarchy.

The confessional parts of her autobiography constitute a forceful critique of a masculinity forged out of imperialism and militarism. Ishimoto subtly reveals how her husband's political and even business failures eventually led him to turn toward militarism and nationalism in order to remasculinize himself, a move that turned him into a neo-feudal lord. We can see the baron start to change, particularly when Ishimoto comes back from her first visit to the United States and Europe and opens her yarn shop in Tokyo. At this time, her husband had finally decided it was not in his best interest to stay with the Miike mining company as an engineer, given his radical politics, and he opened a foreign books shop in Tokyo. Ishimoto's business became very successful, giving her the opportunity to travel and talk to women not just about knitting but about birth control. The baron's business, however, did not do well. Ishimoto attempted to reinvigorate her husband's fading ideals and divert him from his new "injurious friends" who were leading him to "shadowy corners" (303). She suggested that he run for a seat in the House of Peers, but the baron's former radical political activities made him suspect in a changing Japanese political climate, and he was denied a seat. This, as Ishimoto describes it, proved the final disappointment for the baron. It is interesting that Ishimoto describes the baron as a victim whom she can still see as a "very honest man": "He has been unable to doubt other people, whom he always takes to be just as honest as himself. This good nature of his is found in many men who have been brought up in the wealthy or well-to-do families of Japan. And this simplicity led Baron Ishimoto more and more into the entanglements of a dishonest and complex society" (303).

Yet it was not just "injurious friends" that led him to "shadowy corners" but also the geishas in teahouses, which Ishimoto sees as "fortresses for these men in this gloomy battle—fortresses which a wife could not assault" (303). In a previous chapter, "Domestic Women and Geisha Problems," Ishimoto argues that these teahouses where high-ranking men meet are not just places of pleasure but places where the most important political decisions are made. She explains that the geishas, who are trained specifically to flatter men, are highly influential in their powers of persuasion and thus are part of this decision-making process: "Their power over the prominent gentlemen of Japan is gained not by challenging in the open but by artfully and tactfully whispering" (288). Thus Ishimoto suggests that influences of flattering women, in addition to the baron's simplicity of mind and heart, boosted his failing masculine confidence. These events eventually changed the baron, who started to adopt a more masculinized identity that included being less domestic. Finding new interest and vigor in Japan's imperialist policies, he not only spent his time away from his family (as he was in

Manchuria and Korea) but also became an avid hunter (which is where the Korean bear came from). His lack of concern for her and his family really contradicts the Japanese government's celebration of the family as a symbol of national beauty and unity.

Ishimoto, in contrast, decenters the idea that the family is representative of the nation, particularly the ways women are used as symbols of family unity to justify repressive and oppressive policies in the name of preserving the health of the nation. We can see some similarities across the Pacific, in the US narratives of family protection as equated with the protection of the nation. Ishimoto's husband's renewed feudal attitude in the wake of Japan's imperialist project weds modernity again to the subordination of women as the traditional support of the family as "nation." There are similarities between how Ishimoto experienced her life with her increasingly imperialist husband and her witnessing of the exploitation in the Miike mines: Ishimoto describes how Japanese capitalist propaganda sells the idea that the Japanese are all one large family in order to ensure that workers are obedient and continue to work hard without complaint. Unlike other industries in Japan at that time (e.g., the textile industry), the coal mining industry had a history of recruiting families, but it also preferred them, employing as many (if not more) women as men and also the children. Moreover, coal mining differed from other industries because coal miners and their families were recruited by subcontractors, *nayagashiro*, who provided lodging and food, supervised their work, and gave them their wages. This system, while highly exploitative, was mystified through the sense that the *nayagashiro* were paternal and family oriented, when, indeed, it created a hierarchy between worker and employer (subcontractor) that was naturalized through the belief in the sanctity of family and obedience.[44] This idea is held together only by the exploitation of women of all classes, as Ishimoto explains in *Facing Two Ways*: "I often wondered whether the Japanese capitalists were true to their consciences in saying that the beautiful family system in Japan made men, women and children work harmoniously and pleasantly at their tasks, when they claimed Japanese exemption for women, on such grounds, in the international labor regulations drawn up at the Labor Conference in Geneva" (163). Ishimoto's text thus embodies the title of her book, as in this case that tradition and modernity work together to exploit Japanese women. This argument runs contrary to the West's view that Japanese feudal tradition alone oppresses women and that modernity offers emancipation.

Conclusion

Ishimoto's autobiography and her life's work represent a gaze back at Americans, challenging their narrow and orientalist perceptions of Japanese women and, more importantly, their feminist ideologies. Of course, the very fact that American feminists had even started to pay attention to Asia is significant; however, Ishimoto's text provides a critical engagement that reveals how even within progressive texts, abiding assumptions about the essential difference of the East can be found. Moreover, in so doing, her book provides an understanding of why and how Western feminists would make such assumptions—the East provided a convenient "empirical" example of still extant misogyny and sexism, in inflated form. The argument seemed to be that if America was to succeed in being the guiding light and political hegemon of the new modern age, it had to take the negative example of the East to see just how retrograde a country would remain if it continued to allow women to be so subjugated. And even if Japan had the excuse that centuries of entrenched "tradition" made it impossible to transition smoothly into the modern, the United States had no such alibi. While Ishimoto does not exactly repudiate this general argument, her critique of it centers on both its lack of understanding of the precise historical conditions that produced inequality and the fact that in many regards this inequality did not exist in the ways perceived of in the West—in other arenas of life, women in Japan in fact held more power and authority than their male counterparts, and than women in the West. Yet the subtlety of her writing was lost, erased, by the marketing strategies that delivered the book to a Western audience. The publisher too, of course, had its motivations. Finally, besides the influence of the framing devices of Western feminists and publishers, there were the academic disciplinary structures and conventions that deeply influenced the way the book was read in the West.

Ishimoto's work in the United States has been examined mostly within area studies, although more recently she is footnoted throughout Japanese American works about the prewar period. While the inclusion of Ishimoto within Asian American works serves the positive purpose of diluting to some degree the mystifications of popular orientalism, it also constrains the text within the container of "area" and nation. By seeing Ishimoto narrowly as a "Japanese" feminist, we obscure the history of the potential transnational feminist ties between the United States and Japan, a history that remarkably occurred before the postwar period and a history that Ishimoto's text recognizes, builds off of, and advances. And even today, the issues concerning the challenges of forging collaborative bonds between Asian and American feminists and creating a vision of global feminism across race, culture, and nation are also reflected in the disciplinary divisions among East Asian, Asian American, and American studies. While significant strides have been made in this regard, Ishimoto's autobiography presents a historical document that at once contributes to these fields of study and, at the same time, illuminates important phenomena that exceed their boundaries. In this respect Ishimoto's text offers issues and topics that are with us powerfully today: her understandings of the early forms of American feminism helps us reconsider how the formative struggles of the past illuminate the present challenges of creating a robust transnational feminism today.

Conclusion

In this book I have reflected on the ways key issues regarding the constitution of the American social, sexual, and gendered subject in the early twentieth century were articulated by way of cultural and social discourses that presented fascinating, and often fantastic, visions of contact between Asia and America. The texts I have examined disclose both the fluidity and instability of notions of race, gender, and sexuality and also how these notions and the way they helped constitute modern American social life were directly and indirectly produced through a series of imagined moments of an Asian and American encounter both in the United States and in Asia. The process through which these representations were produced was an uneven and problematic one, as "Asia" became the proxy through which crises of American identity were negotiated. My study has tried to locate and explicate that problematic and its significance: in brief, meditations on the nature of modern sexuality and gender could not easily be claimed as one's own, given the vexed and suppressed character of these topics. Instead, these reflections were displaced onto the Other—it was their problem, and "out there." These ruminations were more easily entertained if they were, precisely, couched in often wildly fantastic worlds, such as those found in the two films I treat. But they also can be found in seemingly simple, sincere autobiographical texts and autobiographical fiction such as those by Kang and Ishimoto. But even here, too, we find that these authors' thoughts on what it meant to be a man, or a woman, were filtered through the discourses of the West. Not only do these texts give us special insight into the nature of these concepts via a cross-cultural reading, but in their texts these authors also show how any discussion of sexuality, gender, race, and nation was mediated by structural and institutional histories and apparatuses. That is to say, Kang's presentation of various masculinities and Ishimoto's attempts to see the particular nature of both Japanese femininity and modern global femininity engaged, respectively, the legal mechanisms of naturalization and the economic nature of a racially biased job market and the debates about birth control and sterilization, eugenics and reproduction. It is precisely in the fact that these institutions exist today, in both similar and different ways, that my study has shown the critical importance of resetting our critical apparatuses to a broader historical timeline. We cannot assume that the issues of modern masculinity, femininity, sexuality, race, and ethnicity only began to take "real" shape in the postwar years, nor can we relegate the study of earlier periods to quaint curiosities and coincidences. My book has argued that there is a strong and abiding lineage to be found here that shows how contemporary Asian American studies is rooted in practices and discourses of these earlier periods in critical and rich ways. Not only that, but one could even more boldly argue that many of the terminological innovations we contemporaries take credit for ("transnational," "hemispheric," "diasporic," "hybrid," etc.) have their conceptual roots in much earlier times, again, not as crude precursors but as complex formulations in their own right.

I have been interested both in the ways these texts help us understand better the social, cultural, political, and historical world of the first half of the American twentieth century and in how the questions we raise today can be placed within a broader set of historical developments. Fundamentally, even the foundational idea of "identity" can be newly understood when we break through the East/West binary in concrete, empirical ways that locate the modern origins of these concepts in both likely and unlikely places. This means treating both well-known and lesser-known texts. In both cases, as I explain in my introduction, it is necessary to use a different critical lens to perceive the imaginative blending and blurring of Asia and America as a series of attempts to explore a new world that challenged old boundaries and norms regarding sexuality, gender, race, and national and transnational identity. This different critical lens is decidedly interdisciplinary and committed to engaging these texts in the ways they present both ideas similar to the ones we work with and ideas that, in their nuances, are displacements and fabrication marked by their age and are to be read as symptoms thereof. In the early twentieth century, it is no secret that sexuality and gender were key elements—for in them were found embedded massively important implications for everything from the status of individual desire to collective health, from the constitution of the family to the genetic composition of the national body, from the modes of employment of time and energy to the possibilities of the ludic pursuit of pleasure.

Each text in this book reveals how the different imagined "Asian" and "American" encounters were in fact experiments in reimagining how sexuality, gender roles, and race and ethnicity could be perceived as shifting and transforming under the historical pressures of the 1920s, 1930s, and 1940s. Rather than consider these as general problems of modern life, it was more palatable for the West to imagine them as taking place in a series of imaginary Asian and/or American spaces, safely removed from the homeland, when in fact the very problems and difficulties of, for example, modern American womanhood were there quite clearly in and of themselves, calling for attention and debate. But the questions raised in the texts were not just "Western" problems. An added and critical task of my study has been to show how these encounters inadvertently reveal the ways that both Americans *and* Asians made sense of their own racial, gendered, national, and sexual identities through the Other. We are thus talking about a double, bi-directional gaze. Not only was the "Orient" once again the phantasmic locus wherein the West attempted to work out its anxieties and desires, but in this same period we find the East trying to see how Western modernity had provided a set of pressures on the East's own sense of what sexuality and gender were. I have thus complicated the binary of domestic and foreign that Amy Kaplan defines in *The Anarchy of Empire*, wherein she explores how US expansion and incorporation of nonwhite territories, along with immigration, seriously challenged what was considered foreign and therefore alien and what was considered domestic. Kaplan's thesis is elaborated in my study to explain how ethnic/racial national subjects test this boundary and division. In fact, my book reveals how the Asian and American "Other," produced by their opposites, continually challenged these boundaries, driven by their mutual needs and desires to understand better how history had threatened to make conventional understandings of sexuality and gender obsolete. If that were to have happened, then where were the moral, ethical, social, political, even theological guidelines for modern action and behavior?

Another aspect of this study that I want to bring forward in concluding resides in the ways each of these texts is a rediscovered text—and in this rediscovery of what has been hidden, omitted, or forgotten we have both a new set of data with which to understand the past and an indication of how many of these historical concerns remain with us today, either in very similar fashion or in ways that show the change wrought by history. The "disappearance," "loss," or modification of these texts shows the work of ideology and contradiction as well, for I am arguing that the loss or suppression of these texts (in the fuller understandings of them that I have sought to produce here) was the result of the unwillingness or inability of their creators to directly confront the problematics of sexuality and gender that were native to their own soil. Instead, they had to approach these issues in an indirect and displaced fashion. In my analysis, these erasures or losses testify to precisely the richness and the power of the imagination behind these works—even their incoherence at times speaks to the ways they grappled with the issues mentioned above. The obsession with these topics in fact works through layers of repressive structures to find expression in art. In looking at these texts within the framework provided by this study, we gain new insights into the cultural ideologies in which these texts were constructed. In each of the chapters, I read texts that had flourished at the time they were produced but lay dormant until, for some, just a decade or two ago. *East Is West*, only recently recovered, has been shown at film festivals, and according to Universal Pictures there are plans to release it through Turner Classic Movies sometime in 2013. My goal in this book has been to ensure that this "rediscovery" is informed by the full cultural, historical, and racial context in which the film was made, a context that, once again, shows the intricate interplay between East and West, their contingent yet critical merging as set forth in both the title of the film and its contorted and dizzying narrative strategies.

Whereas *East Is West* was until very recently an authentically "lost" work, Kang's *East Goes West* was reprinted in 1997 and since then has been extensively written about—it is now solidly part of the canon of Asian American literature. Critics continue to discover new aspects of this text that seem to anticipate later developments in our thinking about assimilation, immigration, and cultural capital. In this book, I have argued that Kang's novel acquires more relevance in a "postracial" era of Asian American model minorities: the larger numbers of "highly skilled" Asian immigrants since the post-1965 Immigration Reform Act resulted in the 1990s backlash against affirmative action directed at larger and larger numbers of Asian Americans, who are seen as privileged vis-à-vis other ethnic minorities and even whites. This backlash, still very much alive at the time of this writing, challenges the view that Asian Americans have become fully assimilated. Turning to the subject of my third chapter, we find that some film theorists have remarked on the demise of Capra's films after World War II; they argue that the populist themes promoted by his films, themes that defined the Depression era, did not transfer into the Cold War era. Yet both the remake of *Lost Horizon* and the recovery of Capra's original pre–World War II version of the film interestingly appeared the year after Richard Nixon's historic visit to China, the beginnings of the reopening of United States–China relations, and the shifting of the United States out of the Cold War era. And thus *Lost Horizon*, in its reemergence, gives us a fascinating picture of America's aspirations as a new world leader and a way to see the reopening of United States–China relations in a different light—how much can we see a capitalist Shangri-La around us today? Finally, Baroness Ishimoto's autobiography underwent its second printing in the United States in 1984, comprised of a new edition of the 1935 version with a foreword. While feminists of color in the United States and Third World feminists have long been questioning the racial and national hegemony of First World and white feminists, the rise of postcolonial studies and the emergence of transnational feminism as a field shed new light on Ishimoto's 1930s exploration of feminist bonds across the Pacific and between the United States and Japan. Yet I have also made the argument that the flow of influence and significance moves in both directions, for Ishimoto's writings also make clear that notions of a transnational feminism were not solely the products of late twentieth-century "women's liberation." To set the origins of this idea at that time would be to ignore the struggles of women, both in America and in Asia, during the period I have placed at the center of my study and, most important, the understanding that the very problematics of "transnational" feminism (how must the "transnational" be understood as less transnational and not as a product of liberal Western ideology, how can "transnationalism" exist only at the expense of the "national," etc.) can be seen to be part of its nature, stretching back nearly a half century before the 1970s.

And, again, how was it that the particular testing out of the local/global dyad had a distinctly Asian American facet?

What might the reappearance of these texts tell us about the desire to *now* remember them and insert them into our cultural history, and how do their various appropriations and modes of integration into academic knowledge serve as indexes to the boundaries of our intellectual formations? The book has attempted to reinsert these texts back into our cultural and national imagination, not only to foreground their continued relevance but, more important, also to reveal that our nostalgia for the past sometimes produces a reading that is ahistorical and lacking in complexity. My exploration of these texts helps us understand better how our contemporary interpretations need to further consider the ambivalent and contradictory nature of any given piece of work and the ideological frameworks that structure such contemplations at that moment in time and how they can contribute to a new way of reimagining the liaisons between Asia and America. Thus these texts not only form a picture of what "American" might mean during this specific and crucial era (and reveal the social and cultural desires and anxieties of the age) in the United States, but they also reveal how "Asia," in its various forms, contributed to the discursive and imaginary manifestations in the making of US racial and gendered identities. But as critical as it is to understand this, I have also made a point of showing how Asian authors such as Kang and Ishimoto were themselves performing similar analytical acts via their wrestling with what, exactly, modern America was and the implications of that for a world that was increasingly feeling the hegemonic power not of Europe but of the United States.

The texts and the subjects herein therefore test the limits of our present-day theoretical and disciplinary reading habits, which tend to conform to neat boundaries between national and extra-national spaces and between races and genders. Indeed, this book explains that these texts are most interesting when read as transgressing those boundaries in particularly revealing ways.

In sum, it is crucial to note that the arguments I make about Asian and American works from the interwar period do not illustrate only a historical past. It is a past that, in many critical regards, remains present to us. The relationships between Asia and America imagined nearly a hundred years ago may seem naive to citizens of the twenty-first century, an age when "globalization" and the "flatness" of the world seem givens and financial, political, cultural, technological networks seem to have fused us together seamlessly. Yet it is precisely because we can and should debate the notion that we are in a "postracial" era that I contend that these works of the early twentieth century give us a glimpse of a set of problematics that remains with us today. Are we not, like Younghill Kang, still debating whether class and gender can make race invisible? Does the merging of pathological female sexuality separate out into distinct racial categories of "Asian" women and "white" women? Or have we truly achieved a transnational feminist agenda, when the specifics of religion, race, and culture and, indeed, "civilizational thinking" seem all the more binding, after 9/11? And, precisely along these same lines, have we reached, if not "Shangri-La," then at least some semblance of a stable world order? These questions all find their avatars in these texts of the 1930s that seek their answers within a terra incognita—Asian America.

Moreover, the cultural and political issues of the 1920s and 1930s suddenly, uncannily reappear—a massive economic recession that has been continually compared to that of the Depression era, the fortification of our national borders against immigrants, and the war against women through the eradication of health and reproductive rights and freedom (in the name of protecting, ironically, women and family and domesticity). The 1930s was an era both of "progressives" (who were not so progressive) and of populism—where today a similar blend of prohibition, morality, and the protection of family and nation mix and mingle with a rising up of "people's power." We can look at contemporary historical phenomena such as the Tea Party and Occupy movements and the anti-ethnic studies laws in the state of Arizona, where much of this book was written, and see the abiding influence of the issues raised by *East Is West, East Goes West, Lost Horizon*, and *Facing Two Ways*. And yet, what I see in these texts are also moments of creating and expressing, sometimes as forms of resistance or agency and other times as simply the desire and will to imagine something else beyond what is proscribed to individuals. These desires challenge normative definitions of gender, sex, race, and class and show the immense value of close critical analysis of cultural texts rigorously analyzed within the context of their age and the period of our reading. Indeed, not unlike these authors, who each looked to the other side of the Asian and American divide, we can benefit from a temporal, historical doubleness that uses the past to teach us about the present as much as we use the critical tools that have been advanced over the years to better understand the past.

Notes

Introduction

Epigraph: *East Is West*, directed by Monta Bell, with performances by Lupe Vélez, Lew Ayres, and Edward G. Robinson (Los Angeles: Universal Pictures, 1930), DVD. The film's screenplay was adapted by Winnifred Eaton from *East Is West: A Comedy in Three Acts and a Prologue*, by Samuel Shipman and John B. Hymer (New York: Samuel French, 1924).

1. Historical and cultural works on the formation of white racial identity and superiority in the United States in the early twentieth century point to the ways new immigrants from Asia, southern Europe (Italians and Greeks), eastern Europe (Jews), and Ireland contributed to a destabilizing notion of nativist white identity. Whiteness continued to become more inclusive, mostly of Europeans (though not always, as Jews continued to be marginal white people), through socially and legally establishing nonwhiteness. US naturalization laws that allowed only white persons to become US citizens became inclusive of the Irish, Italians, and Greeks but excluded Asians as ineligible to become citizens. David Roediger, *The Wages of Whiteness: Race and the Making of the American Working Class* (New York: Verso, 2007); Noel Ignatiev, *How the Irish Became White* (New York: Routledge, 2008); Ronald Takaki, *A Different Mirror: A History of Multicultural America, rev. ed. (New York: Back Bay Books*, 2008); Tomàs Almaguer, *Racial Fault Lines: The Historical Origins of White Supremacy in California* (Berkeley: University of California Press, 1994).

2. Pervasive gendered and sexual orientalist stereotypes within US history depict Asian women as castrating dragon ladies, while Asian men are routinely consigned to characterizations of asexuality and effeminacy, on

the one hand, and of predatory deviancy, particularly toward white women, on the other. These images have become quite familiar as stock orientalist stereotypes. They point to the persistence of representing Asian men and women as sexually deviant and, in turn, normalize, within a white US racist paradigm, white male and female sexuality and gendered identities. The construction of Asian men and women as sexual deviants has been covered extensively, but probably most notably in the documentary *Slaying the Dragon*, directed by Deborah Gee (San Francisco: Asian Women United, 1988), DVD. The early twentieth century's cinematic portrayals of Asian women and men as sexual yellow peril menaces are examined in Gina Marchetti, *Romance and the "Yellow Peril": Race, Sex, and Discursive Strategies in Hollywood Fiction* (Berkeley: University of California Press, 1994); and Robert G. Lee, *Orientals: Asian Americans in Popular Culture* (Philadelphia: Temple University Press, 1999), chaps. 3 and 4 ("The Third Sex" and "Inner Dikes and Barred Zones").

3. George Anthony Peffer, *If They Don't Bring Their Women Here: Chinese Female Immigration before Exclusion* (Urbana: University of Illinois Press, 1999); Eithne Luibhéid, *Entry Denied: Controlling Sexuality at the Border* (Minneapolis: University of Minnesota Press, 2002); Nayan Shah, *Contagious Divides: Epidemics and Race in San Francisco's Chinatown* (Berkeley: University of California Press, 2001); Sucheng Chan, ed., *Entry Denied: Exclusion and the Chinese Community in America, 1882–1943* (Philadelphia: Temple University Press, 1991).

4. Shah, *Contagious Divides*, 77–104.

5. Luibhéid, *Entry Denied*, 1–54.

6. Susan Koshy explains how the antimiscegenation laws directed at Asian American men were "shaped by a need to police the sexuality of a primarily male immigrant labor force; the laws worked to impede their incorporation into America through marriage or through the creation of a subsequent generation of American-born citizens." Susan Koshy, *Sexual Naturalization: Asian Americans and Miscegenation* (Stanford, CA: Stanford University Press, 2004), 6–7. Antimiscegenation laws were also passed against Chinese on the US West Coast, but even in areas without such laws, social prohibitions were often as powerful as legal ones. The social prohibition of miscegenation in the absence of laws continued to construct deviant Asiatic male sexualities as a threat to white womanhood and the family. The difference between states that did or did not pass antimiscegenation laws against Asians had to do with the relative size of Asian immigrant populations in different areas (ibid., 7).

7. Like Filipino men, Chinese men were similarly suspect as predators of young white women, even though, for the most part, Chinese (and even Japanese) relations with white women were not nearly as rampant as many white Americans believed. Mae M. Ngai points out that Filipinos' migratory work, which required them to move repeatedly,

and their relationships with white and Mexican women combined to make them appear sexually deviant and unattached to family life, while disregarding racial boundaries. The furor over Filipino men's supposed deviancy justified the exclusion of Filipinos with the passing of the 1934 Tydings-McDuffie Act. The Tydings-McDuffie Act (or the Philippine Independence Act) was approved to provide for Philippine independence from the United States. As a result, Filipinos were reclassified from American nationals to "aliens," and thus the number of Filipinos immigrating to the United States was greatly reduced (to approximately fifty per year). Mae M. Ngai, *Impossible Subjects: Illegal Aliens and the Making of Modern America* (Princeton, NJ: Princeton University Press, 2005), 11, 121.

8. Rachel F. Moran, *Interracial Intimacy: The Regulation of Race and Romance* (Chicago: University of Chicago Press, 2001), 28–41. Moran describes how antimiscegenation laws directed at East Asian men served more to define their racial inferiority than to deter interracial relations, while for Filipinos, the laws were about the sexual threat these men posed to white womanhood. I am not sure that I agree with this division, though questioning the degree of assimilation of different Asian men in the United States at this time is important and demands more careful thought. I take this up in more detail in chapter 2 in my discussion of Korean and East Asian male sexuality. For more in-depth discussions of Filipino sexuality in the early twentieth-century United States, see Linda España-Maram, *Creating Masculinity in Los Angeles's Little Manila: Working-Class Filipinos and Popular Culture, 1920s–1950s* (New York: Columbia University Press, 2006); Antonio Tiongson, Edgardo Gutierrez, and Ricardo Gutierrez, eds., *Positively No Filipinos Allowed: Building Communities and Discourse*, annotated ed. (Philadelphia: Temple University Press, 2006); and Yen Le Espiritu, *Filipino American Lives* (Philadelphia: Temple University Press, 1995).

9. The New Woman was born around the fin de siècle as a literary creation by writers such as Sarah Grand, Olive Schreiner, and Elizabeth Robins. By the 1920s and 1930s, this New Woman figure represented mostly middle-class women who wanted to work and be treated as equals to men and chose not to marry or have families. As Wendy Kline explains:

[This] new generation of middle-class women also provoked consternation. The "new woman" challenged the existing social order by demanding "rights and privileges customarily accorded only to white middle-class men." Between 1890 and 1910, the number of women attending college tripled, and by 1920 women accounted for nearly 50 percent of the university population. Choosing college and careers over marriage and motherhood, these women violated the nineteenth-century "cult of true womanhood," which placed middle-class women in the home. As a result, they raised questions about gender and morality. (Wendy Kline, *Building a Better Race:*

Gender, Sexuality, and Eugenics from the Turn of the Century to the Baby Boom. [Berkeley: University of California Press, 2005], 10)

10. Ibid., 97.

11. For the purposes of this book, the masculinity in question in these texts refers to a hegemonic masculinity that I identify as white and middle-class American. In both chapter 2's reading of Younghill Kang's *East Goes West* and chapter 3's reading of the film *Lost Horizon*, the white and Asian men are decidedly middle class (or upper middle class).

12. According to Gail Bederman, the idea that "manliness" was in crisis only during the early twentieth century is inaccurate. She argues that masculinity—its normative and hegemonic definitions and representations, who embodies it and who does not, what a less masculine or more masculine man says about society at large at specific historical times—is essentially always in crisis, always reforming new definitions and identities. However, she does suggest that middle-class white men were preoccupied with what their masculinity actually meant, given the growth of the women's movement, the influx of immigrants (and thus the changing nature of labor and capital that resulted from the migration of blacks to the industrial centers and from immigrant laborers), and the rise of the working-class man, who was seen as a counterpoint to middle-class masculinity, which increasingly appeared weakened. Gail Bederman, *Manliness and Civilization: A Cultural History of Gender and Race in the United States, 1880–1917* (Chicago: University of Chicago Press, 1996), 11–15.

13. Here I am referring to some of the major Asian American studies books whose predominant or partial focus is the early twentieth century. These include David Palumbo-Liu, *Asian/American: Historical Crossings of a Racial Frontier* (Stanford, CA: Stanford University Press, 1999); Lee, *Orientals*; and Colleen Lye, *America's Asia: Racial Form and American Literature, 1893–1945* (Princeton, NJ: Princeton University Press, 2004).

14. For the purposes of my study, I choose not to use the term *Asian American* in describing Kang. Even though he is now considered an early Korean American writer, and he himself in his novel *East Goes West* attempts to define a culturally hybrid identity between Korea/Asia and America ("Oriental Yankee"), to describe him as Asian American during the early twentieth century warrants a lengthy discussion of what that means outside the post–civil rights, politicized, and pan-Asian designation of *Asian American*. That discussion is outside the scope of this book.

15. As Kang writes in his novel: "Kim and I came when the Village spirit was upon America. It was the time when everybody wanted the artist's and rebel's life. Marriage was a failure. Exile was the only refuge. Men and women everywhere tried free love, companionateness, everybody wished hard to live the life that did not smell of baby diapers, corned beef and cabbage." Younghill Kang, *East Goes West: The Making an Oriental Yankee* (1937; New York: Kaya Production, 1997), 366.

16. Palumbo-Liu, *Asian/American*, 20.

17. The early Japanese American author Etsu Inagaki Sugimoto, who wrote *A Daughter of the Samurai*, expressed some similar sentiments about Japan's modernization, frequently citing the adopted "American ways" that compromised Japanese traditions, even as she was quick to criticize those traditions after her transformation into a Japanese American. Etsu Inagaki Sugimoto, *A Daughter of the Samurai* (Honolulu: University Press of the Pacific, 2003).

18. Palumbo-Liu, *Asian/American*, 17.

19. Significant overseas expansion of Asia and the Pacific started with the 1854 opening of Japan by Commodore Matthew Perry and then the signing of treaties between the United States and China, significantly the 1868 Burlingame-Seward Treaty, which opened the doors to Chinese immigration. The rapid growth of the US empire was empowering and even intoxicating for many white Americans. Josephine Nock-Hee Park argues that some early twentieth-century American poets wrote "ecstatic meditations on the Asiatic," though these were not just expressions of exotica or a racial othering of Asia. Rather, these poets demonstrated that the "alliances that structure American Orientalism" were actually "fueled by the dream of commerce." Josephine Nock-Hee Park, *Apparitions of Asia: Modernist Form and Asian American Poetics* (New York: Oxford University Press, 2008), 7.

20. Kaplan loosely identifies the beginning of US imperialist policy with the colonization of the Philippines in 1898, but she also sees this moment as a continuation of national policies of internal colonization and territorialization through the Indian wars, the Mexican-American War (1846–48), and the Treaty of Guadalupe Hidalgo (1848). Amy Kaplan, *The Anarchy of Empire in the Making of U.S. Culture* (Cambridge, MA: Harvard University Press, 2005). Others such as Shelley Streeby and Susan Koshy identify the start of US imperialism with the Mexican-American War. Shelley Streeby, *American Sensations: Class, Empire, and the Production of Popular Culture* (Berkeley: University of California Press, 2002), 4–37; Koshy, *Sexual Naturalization*, 17.

21. Kaplan in *The Anarchy of Empire* (25) examines citizenship, territorialization (of Puerto Rico, the Philippines, and Hawaii), the incorporation of Indians, and the regulations over domestic and foreign commerce—all of which forced the contemplation of what it might mean to incorporate, assimilate, annex, and even to tax.

22. Many now argue that the 1875 Page Law, and not the 1882 Chinese Exclusion Act, should be seen as the first race-based exclusion law passed by the United States. See Peffer, *If They Don't Bring Their Women Here*. Moreover, the 1924 National Origins Act continued this race exclusion and greatly reduced the number of legal immigrants from Asia during the 1930s. As Ngai states in *Impossible Subjects* (3), the 1924 act was "the nation's first comprehensive restriction law. It established for the first time

numerical limits on immigration and a global racial and national hierarchy that favored some immigrants over others."

23. Nativist and anti-Asian sentiments also led to the passing of a series of exclusion acts between 1882 and 1943 (deemed by Asian American historians as the "exclusion period"). While not exhaustive, the list of national immigration exclusion laws includes the 1875 Page Law, the 1882 Chinese Exclusion Act, the 1907 Gentlemen's Agreement and the 1921 Ladies' Agreement, the 1922 Cable Act, and the 1924 Johnson-Reed Act (Immigration Act of 1924), which included the National Origins Act. In the naturalization cases of Takao Ozawa (1922) and Bhagat Singh Thind (1923), Asian immigrants were prevented at the federal level from becoming citizens. More specific state-by-state laws in the late nineteenth and early twentieth centuries focused on preventing Asian immigrants from owning land (Alien Land Laws in California, 1912–13, and in Arizona, 1915–17). See Sucheng Chan, *Asian Americans: An Interpretive History* (Boston: Twayne, 1991); Timothy P. Fong and Larry H. Shinagawa, *Asian Americans: Experiences and Perspectives* (Upper Saddle River, NJ: Prentice Hall, 2000); and Timothy P. Fong, *The Contemporary Asian American Experience: Beyond the Model Minority* (Upper Saddle River, NJ: Prentice Hall, 2008).

24. See Chan, *Asian Americans*; Erika Lee, *At America's Gates: Chinese Immigration during the Exclusion Era, 1882–1943* (Chapel Hill: University of North Carolina Press, 2003); and Ngai, *Impossible Subjects*. For more detailed accounts of antimiscegenation acts, see Susan Koshy, introduction to *Sexual Naturalization*, 1–25. Moreover, the construction of Asian Americans as foreign and alien is an ongoing phenomenon, based on a legacy of immigrant exclusion and anti-naturalization acts that legally codified Asians as "aliens ineligible to become citizens." Robert G. Lee astutely observes in *Orientals* (3) the different and historically specific ways that Asian Americans are continually seen as "pollutants" and "outsiders" from the early days of Asian immigration exclusion, through the Cold War era, and into the Reagan-Bush years.

25. Lisa Lowe, *Critical Terrains: French and British Orientalisms* (Ithaca, NY: Cornell University Press, 1994), 5. Lowe complicates Edward Said's rather totalizing interpretation of orientalism (and, to that effect, a Foucauldian interpretation of power). Instead of seeing the discourses and representations of orientalism as always powerful and oppressive, she reveals how the structures of orientalisms exhibit weaknesses, fissures, and contradictions.

Rather I argue for a conception of orientalism as heterogeneous and contradictory; to this end I observe, on the one hand, that orientalism consists of an uneven matrix of orientalist situations across different cultural and historical sites, and on the other, that each of these orientalisms is internally complex and unstable. My textual readings give particular attention to those junctures at which narratives of gendered, racial, national, and class differences complicate and interrupt the narrative of orientalism, as well as to the points at which orientalism is refunctioned and rearticulated against itself.

I suggest that the elucidation of these heterogeneous sites may prove useful, in terms of both method and political strategy, because they mark the places where orientalism is vulnerable to challenge. (Ibid.)

26. Mary E. Odem, *Delinquent Daughters: Protecting and Policing Adolescent Female Sexuality in the United States, 1885–1920* (Chapel Hill: University of North Carolina Press, 1995), 1; Joanne J. Meyerowitz, *Women Adrift: Independent Wage Earners in Chicago, 1880–1930* (Chicago: University of Chicago Press, 1988), xvii; Ruth Rosen, *The Lost Sisterhood: Prostitution in America, 1900–1918* (Baltimore: Johns Hopkins University Press, 1983).

27. Koshy argues in *Sexual Naturalization* that romantic and sexual relationships between Asian women and white men thrived in Asia. These relationships were seen as exotic and often tolerated because they existed outside of the United States. Yet interracial relationships between Asian men and white women, because they existed primarily within the US nation, were less tolerated and thereby greatly prohibited.

1 / How Yellow and White Women Are Sold

Epigraphs: "*East Is West*: Songs and Dialogue," script, 1930, New York State Archives, Albany.

1. Sing-song girl is a Western term used to refer to a Chinese courtesan.

2. In the Universal Pictures film, the emphasis is that Ming Toy's "white looking" features fetch a higher price, though this does not appear in the final film version.

3. The Hays Commission (or Hays Office) I refer to is the Production Code Administration created under the leadership of William Hays, the first president of the Motion Picture Producers and Distributors of America, or MPPDA. The Production Code was created in 1930 to limit what was perceived at that time to be explicit or offending material that dealt with sex and social, cultural, and political issues. See Richard Maltby and Ian Craven, *Hollywood Cinema* (Oxford: Blackwell, 1995), 364–69.

4. Many films required a code certificate for specific regions, cities, and countries to ensure that content relating to sexuality, profanity, anti-Christianity, and even race and culture would be edited out according to the regulations of specific areas. There was disapproval from China, for which the film's depiction of Chinese prostitution reflected badly on Chinese nationalism globally. Criticism from the Hays Commission's foreign division explained that the Chinese government protested that the film was an affront to its nation, especially after the 1911 nationalist revolution, when China declared itself a fully modern nation—in part by eradicating female foot-binding—and declared men and women equal in the new Chinese republic. China was thus particularly incensed by the film's depiction of the "selling of Chinese girls," which the government flatly denied had ever occurred in Chinese history. In 1935 Universal Pictures made the final

attempt to obtain the "code certification" for *East Is West* but was again rejected. Universal Pictures, memorandum to Colonel Jason S. Joy, January 15, 1931, Margaret Herrick Library, Academy of Motion Picture Arts and Sciences, Beverly Hills, CA.

5. Page Law, US Code, sec. 141, 18 Stat. 477 (1875). Between 1875 and 1882, the number of Chinese and other Asian women immigrating to the United States drastically declined.

6. Henry Yu notes that there was as much interest in scholarly studies as there was in dime-store novels and serials regarding the subject of interracial relationships between Asians and whites. Henry Yu, *Thinking Orientals: Migration, Contact, and Exoticism in Modern America* (New York: Oxford University Press, 2001), 56–59. Similarly, Koshy argues in *Sexual Naturalization* (1–20) that despite the small numbers of interracial relationships between Asians and whites during the early twentieth century, this pairing was a pervasive literary image in US popular culture.

7. Margit Stange, *Personal Property: Wives, White Slaves, and the Market in Women* (Baltimore: Johns Hopkins University Press, 1998), 77. Although Progressives were known for their crusades against vice and crime in the cities, including Prohibition, they focused not on prostitution in general but on white slavery.

8. "Progressive Era reformers, unlike their Victorian counterparts, no longer saw these girls as the victims of unscrupulous male seducers. Instead, they acknowledged female sexuality and worked to contain and control its expressiveness in adolescent girls." Mary Ting Yi Lui, *The Chinatown Trunk Mystery: Murder, Miscegenation, and Other Dangerous Encounters in Turn-of-the-Century New York City* (Princeton, NJ: Princeton University Press, 2005), 92.

9. Peffer, *If They Don't Bring Their Women Here*, 36.

10. While the Page Law's purpose was to stop the immigration of Chinese prostitutes, it successfully limited the immigration of Chinese and other Asian women in general. In the absence of any evidence supporting the prostitute theory, it is clear that empirical evidence was trumped by evidence fabricated from dubious sources and put forward to play to public fears. See ibid., 1–11, 57–86.

11. Lucie Cheng, "Free, Indentured, Enslaved: Chinese Prostitutes in Nineteenth-Century America," in *Labor Immigration under Capitalism: Asian Workers in the United States before World War II*, ed. Lucie Cheng and Edna Bonacich (Berkeley: University of California Press, 1984), 421. Ironically, the passing of the Page Law also resulted partially from the sensational accounts of Christian missionary women's rescues of Chinese prostitutes. Donaldina Cameron was an especially notable figure in these rescues, publicizing the exploits of Chinese women and the need to "save" them from unscrupulous and abusive Chinese men. These high-profile rescues led by Cameron and other missionary women contributed to the public perception

that there were more Chinese prostitutes in the city than was actually the case. See Peggy Pascoe, *Relations of Rescue: The Search for Female Moral Authority in the American West, 1874–1939* (New York: Oxford University Press, 1990), 78.

12. Ronald Takaki, *Strangers from a Different Shore: A History of Asian Americans*, updated and rev. ed. (New York: Back Bay Books, 1998), 41.

13. Almaguer, *Racial Fault Lines*, 160–62. Part of the anti-Chinese sentiment over the influx of Chinese immigrants—the opposition was mostly about Chinese workers as strikebreakers and the perception by white workers that the Chinese were depressing the white working man's wage in California—also targeted Chinese women, who were seen as unclean and diseased and a menace to white families because they were supposedly coming into the United States solely for prostitution.

14. Asian Americans were early targets of the nation's fears over the social ills of urbanization and also served as specimens of germ theory and the study of infection. As early as the mid-nineteenth century, Chinese were viewed as carriers of certain germs to which, it was widely believed, they but not Anglo-Americans were immune. The exclusion of Asian women was based, in part, on how new theories and research on viruses and diseases intersected with eugenics and social Darwinism to explain the inherent differences between whites and Asians. See Shah, *Contagious Divides*, 77–104.

15. Ibid., 79–81.

16. Ibid., 81–86.

17. Ibid., 86.

18. According to Luibhéid:

That photography enabled new forms of subjection through the body is hardly surprising. As Alan Sekula describes, many official uses of photography developed from and further extended a philosophical paradigm that held that "the surface of the body, and especially the face and head, bore the outward signs of inner character." This paradigm found expression in the various strands of "scientific" studies of "race," as well as in sexology and criminology, in which bodies were photographed, divided into zones, and classified into taxonomic schemes. Thus, the photograph also served as an index of other processes that shaped Chinese women's immigration possibilities. (Luibhéid, *Entry Denied*, 47)

19. Ibid., 45.

20. Ibid., 44. See also Sucheng Chan, "The Exclusion of Chinese Women," in Chan, *Entry Denied*, 100.

21. As Shah describes:

The urgency in targeting Chinese prostitutes, however, unleashed confusion in identifying the signs of prostitution and distinguishing a professional prostitute from other women. The motives, location, and conduct of Chinese women had to be deciphered and classified. In the 1850s and 1860s, police singled out women who were observed peering out their windows or standing outside a door or who worked in small, first-floor rooms. Police presumed that in these rooms women allowed the frequent arrival and departure of seemingly anonymous men. These women were interpreted to be crib prostitutes. However, there were also women who lived in more secluded, upper-story apartments who lavishly entertained regular clients, primarily Chinese merchants. These women were identified as courtesans who charged premium prices for the entertainment and companionship they provided. (Shah, *Contagious Divides*, 82)

22. The 1882 Chinese Exclusion Act is typically referenced and cited as the first racially based exclusion law. However, this overlooks the earlier Page Law, as George Anthony Peffer argues. In Asian American studies the omission of a critique of racialized gendered identities within a cultural and historical critique of nation can be partially attributable to the privileging of the 1882 Chinese Exclusion Act as the first race-based immigrant exclusion law over the Page Law. Peffer, *If They Don't Bring Their Women Here*, 10.

23. Chan, "The Exclusion of Chinese Women," 100.

24. Erika Lee in *At America's Gates* (94) also discusses the ways in which Chinese and Asian immigrant women were often considered prostitutes to be proven innocent. The detailed questions, the need for copious biographical material from these women, and visual scrutiny (looking at their ways of dressing and their bodies: did they exhibit class privilege, did they wear finer clothing, and were their feet bound, as would befit a merchant's wife?) often made it impossible for supposedly legitimate and "exempt" Chinese and Asian immigrant women to pass (ibid., 92–99).

25. For sensational accounts of Chinese men as predators of white women in newspapers, serials, plays, and short fiction, see Lee, *Orientals*, 72–89; Philip P. Choy, Lorraine Dong, and Marlon K. Hom, eds., *The Coming Man: Nineteenth-Century American Perceptions of the Chinese* (Seattle: University of Washington Press, 1995), 107; and Lui, *Chinatown Trunk Mystery*, 81–110. Probably the most popular narrative about evil Asiatic men comes from the Sax Rohmer tales about Chinatown and Fu Manchu. For other accounts of interracial marriage between Asian men and white women, see John Kuo Wei Tchen, *New York before Chinatown: Orientalism and the Shaping of American Culture, 1776–1882* (Baltimore: Johns Hopkins University Press, 1999), 75–86, 159–63. See also the sociological study of Chinese immigrant men in Paul C. P. Siu, *The Chinese Laundryman: A Study of Social Isolation*, ed. John Kuo Wei Tchen (New York: New York University Press, 1987), 272–93.

26. *Broken Blossoms*, directed by D. W. Griffith (Los Angeles: United Artists, 1919), DVD.

27. Lui, *Chinatown Trunk Mystery*, 86. See also K. Scott Wong, "'An Eagle Seeks a Helpless Quarry': Chinatown, the Police, and the Press; The 1930 Boston Chinatown Raid Revisited," *Amerasia Journal*, 22, no. 3 (1996): 89. Wong discusses some similar liaisons between white and Chinese men in Boston's Chinatown.

28. Victor Jew, "'Chinese Demons': The Violent Articulation of Chinese Otherness and Interracial Sexuality in the U.S. Midwest, 1885–1889," *Journal of Social History* 37, no. 2 (2003): 401.

29. Lui, *Chinatown Trunk Mystery*, 92–93. See also Ruth M. Alexander, *"The Girl Problem": Female Sexual Delinquency in New York, 1900–1930* (Ithaca, NY: Cornell University Press, 1993), 3, 52–53.

30. Meyerowitz, *Women Adrift*, xvii.

31. For a history of prostitution in America, see John D'Emilio and Estelle B. Freedman, *Intimate Matters: A History of Sexuality in America* (Chicago: University of Chicago Press, 1997).

32. Rosen, *Lost Sisterhood*, xiii.

33. The ongoing fears and discussions over controlling white women's sexuality and behavior in metropolitan and industrial centers of the United States resulted in the social surveillance of white women. More disturbing to the public was the possibility that these white women were not necessarily lured or did not choose to escape from the life of prostitution or the abodes of nonwhite men. In these narratives, white women's sexuality also became part of this unholy alliance with immigrant and racialized Others. See Lui, *Chinatown Trunk Mystery*, 82–110; Moran, *Interracial Intimacy*, 17–75; and Stange, *Personal Property*, 75–103.

34. Stange, *Personal Property*, 1–3.

35. Stange argues in *Personal Property* (76–84) that the fears over white slavery began in Europe and Latin America as early as the mid-nineteenth century. She suggests that the white slavery panic did not exclusively target nonwhite immigrant men as predators and exploiters, but forged a more general warning about the commodification of (white) women. Many believed that the commercialization of white slavery in the United States was more destructive to the nation than nonwhite immigrant men were. The belief that white slavery was an organized, commercializing business corresponded to progressivist fears over trusts and corporate monopolies. Viewed as "commodity" in a growing commercialized vice industry, the white woman, as the "white slave," became the poster child for progressivist social reform.

36. Luibhéid, *Entry Denied*, 14–15.

37. *East Is West* script, 4.

38. Arthur Fitz-Richard, script synopsis of *East Is West*, August 28, 1935, 1, Margaret Herrick Library, Academy of Motion Picture Arts and Sciences, Beverly Hills, CA.

39. This refusal to evolve into modernity points to what Ali Behdad describes as an orientalist trope of civilizational difference that undermines Asia as coeval with the United States and Europe. The historical inaccuracies reflect US and European perceptions of the East as a place that will always be mired in an archaic and preindustrial past. In many of the exotic dramas of Hollywood, Asia remains unchanging, geographically

and culturally distinct from the Occident. These films are interested more in giving viewers a temporary experience of voyeuristic tourism through the cultural and racial Other, only to return them safely home to the West—where east and west will never really meet. Ali Behdad, *Belated Travelers: Orientalism in the Age of Colonial Dissolution* (Durham, NC: Duke University Press, 1994), 12.

40. *East Is West* script, 5.

41. Ibid.

42. In the 1915 silent version of *Madame Butterfly*, directed by Sidney Olcott, the title role was played by Mary Pickford; in the 1932 version, directed by Marion Gering, it was played by Sylvia Sidney.

43. As the proprietor in the play version says of Ming Toy: "She very near like white woman. Chinese always pay high price for girl what look like white woman. Chinese like you—he like variety." Shipman and Hymer, *East Is West*, 12. The script synopsis draws from the play but changes "whiteness" to a "pronounced European cast." Fitz-Richard, script synopsis of *East Is West*, 1–2.

44. Before the incorporation of the Southwest into the United States, Mexican and Anglo marriages were considered acceptable and even favorable because of land rights afforded to the white settlers from these marriages. After the incorporation, there was no economic or political need for these mixed marriages. Moran, *Interracial Intimacy*, 50–53. While antimiscegenation laws did not specifically forbid Mexicans from marrying whites, cultural practices and social disapproval highly discouraged it. Mexicans were viewed by Anglo-whites as culturally nonwhite, and Mexican women, in particular, formerly seen as desirable, after incorporation were viewed as sexually promiscuous and racially inferior. Koshy, *Sexual Naturalization*, 6.

45. *East Is West* script, 4.

46. Ibid., 7.

47. Ibid., 8.

48. Ibid., 21.

49. One issue that emerges from this easy shift from Chinese to white racial identity, beyond the simple explanation that it resolves the story's obstacle of miscegenation, is the larger one of racial fluidity and the racial/social/political formations of Asian and white identity during the early twentieth century.

50. *East Is West* script, 27.

51. Ibid., 5.

52. Shipman and Hymer, *East Is West*, 20.

53. Ibid., 48–49.

54. Ibid., 40–41.

55. *East Is West* script, 8. Winnifred Eaton adapted the play to the film, and thus her inserted dialogue here points to her ability to make fun of Americans' ignorance of the Chinese.

56. In the script synopsis, the writers describe how Benson's father was the US ambassador to China. This detail is not clear at all in the film. Fitz-Richard, script synopsis of *East Is West.*

2 / Masculine Racial Formations in Younghill Kang's *East Goes West*

1. Katherine Woods, "The Making of an Oriental Yankee," *New York Times Book Review,* October 17, 1937, quoted in Sunyoung Lee, "The Unmaking of an Oriental Yankee," afterword to Kang, *East Goes West,* 378. All page references to Kang's novel are cited in the main text.

2. "Life in America Viewed by Korean," review of *East Goes West: The Making of an Oriental Yankee,* by Younghill Kang, *Springfield Sunday Union and Republican,* September 26, 1937, quoted in Lee, "The Unmaking of an Oriental Yankee," 378.

3. In real life Kang was married to Frances Keely, a Wellesley graduate and a poet. Sunyoung Lee, "Chronology: The Life and Work of Younghill Kang," in Kang, *East Goes West,* 404.

4. Lee, "The Unmaking of an Oriental Yankee," 376. Kang was the first Asia to receive a Guggenheim.

5. Lee, "Chronology," 407.

6. Ibid.

7. Lee, "The Unmaking of an Oriental Yankee," 375.

8. Both of the literary critics I mentioned at the chapter's outset conflate the novel's narrator with Kang, seeing the work as autobiographical even though Kang envisioned *East Goes West* as a fictional piece. The reduction of Kang's work of fiction to an autobiographical portrait contributes to the continual marginalization of women and writers of color. Within this logic of white and Western cultural superiority, where great works of fiction were an indication of an author's talent and ability to objectively critique his or her contemporary culture, literary works by writers of color did not have such epic aspirations or effects. They were personal accounts, almost always autobiographical and nonfiction, lesser literary achievements.

9. On how the March First movement actually brought Korea onto the world stage, making visible Korean protest against Japanese imperialism and colonization, see Michael Edson Robinson, *Korea's Twentieth-Century Odyssey* (Honolulu: University of Hawaii Press, 2007), 47. Some of the more notable Korean nationalists resided in the United States and sustained the Korean American community's ethnic and nationalist solidarity. Chan, *Asian Americans,* 98–99.

10. Lee, "Chronology," 403.

11. Takaki, *Strangers from a Different Shore,* 284–85.

12. See Harold Isaac, *Scratches on Our Minds: American Images of China and India* (New York: John Day, 1958), 11–35; and in *Orientations: Mapping Studies in the Asian Diaspora,* ed. Kandice Chuh and Karen Shimakawa (Durham, NC: Duke University Press, 2001), see Kandice Chuh and Karen

Shimakawa, "Introduction: *Mapping Studies in the Asian Diaspora*," 6–11; Dipesh Chakrabarty, "Notes toward a Conversation between Area Studies and Diasporic Studies," 108–9; and Rey Chow, "Leading Questions," 189–212.

13. Dale Carnegie, *How to Win Friends and Influence People* (New York: Pocket Books, 1990), 53.

14. Lawrence Levine, *The Unpredictable Past: Explorations in American Cultural History* (New York: Oxford University Press, 1993), 224.

15. Koshy, *Sexual Naturalization*, 4. Although antimiscegenation laws prohibiting marriage and sexual relations between Asians and whites did not exist in eastern US states such as New York, Massachusetts, and Washington, DC (where most of the novel takes place), there was clear and virulent social disapproval of these partnerships in the United States. In an examination of Asian-white interracial relationships during this period, Koshy explains how antimiscegenation laws and the exclusion of Asian immigrant women in the United States "curtailed but did not end interracial relationships between whites and Asians" and that couples found ways to circumvent the laws (ibid., 3).

16. In this episode, Han is actually defending George to his employer, Lively, whose wife spied George and his white girlfriend, June, kissing outside their house during a visit with Han. In some ways, Han's explanation to Lively attempts to redraw racial and cultural boundaries of decorum, where George is to some extent exempt because of his Americanization.

17. Melinda de Jesús, "Reclaiming Queerness in Carlos Bulosan's *America Is in the Heart* and Bienvenido Santos' *Scent of Apples*," *Journal of Asian American Studies* 5, no. 2 (2002): 95.

18. Ibid. De Jesús quotes from David Eng, "In the Shadows of a Diva: Committing Homosexuality in David Henry Hwang's M. Butterfly," in Asian American Sexualities: Dimensions of the Gay and Lesbian Experience, ed. Russell Leong (New York: Routledge, 1996), 132.

19. David Palumbo-Liu's reading of *East Goes West* interprets Kim as "Han's projection of an ego ideal—a figure that represents precisely that subjectivity that resolves the contradictions he senses in himself and also those between his temporal frame of reference and his spatial location." Palumbo-Liu, *Asian/American*, 119.

3 / Utopias Lost and Found

1. James Hilton, *Lost Horizon* (New York: Pocket Books, 1933).

2. Eric Smoodin found that in addition to being a box-office disappointment, *Lost Horizon* ran less successfully at smaller theaters outside major US cities, where some patrons considered the film to be "a little above their heads." Eric Smoodin, *Regarding Frank Capra: Audience, Celebrity, and American Film Studies, 1930–1960* (Durham, NC: Duke University Press, 2004), 110–11n102.

3. *Lost Horizon*, directed by Frank Capra, with performances by Ronald Colman, Jane Wyatt, John Howard, and Thomas Mitchell (Culver City, CA: Columbia Pictures, 1937), DVD. In the text discussion, I quote directly from the film. *Frank Capra: The Name above the Title; An Autobiography* (New York: Macmillan, 1971), 191.

4. A few years after its initial release, *Lost Horizon* then reappeared in different forms, all during US conflicts with Asia. In 1956, three years after the Korean War, *Lost Horizon* inspired a Broadway musical called *Shangri-La*. The musical, based on Capra's *Lost Horizon*, opened at the Broadway Winter Garden Theatre in New York City on June 13, 1956. In 1960 this stage musical was adapted for an NBC television *Hallmark Hall of Fame* special.

5. FDR converted the former military training camp into a retreat and renamed it the USS Shangri-La. See The White House, "Camp David," http://www.whitehouse.gov/about/camp-david (accessed May 17, 2012).

6. Ella Shohat and Robert Stam, *Unthinking Eurocentrism: Multiculturalism and the Media* (New York: Routledge, 1994), 147.

7. The colonial/imperial trope of new lands as empty spaces absent of people and civilization is symbolically displayed in the ways Europeans drew their maps of the world. Typically, Europe is the center of civilization, while the lands in the Americas and Africa are denoted as blank and unpopulated, even dangerous, spaces. These blank spaces beckon the European traveler to make meaning out of the land by giving him the authority to inscribe landscapes, peoples, and cultures. For example, this colonial knowledge production through the map is evident in the first few pages of Joseph Conrad's novella, *Heart of Darkness*, in which Charles Marlowe's boyhood fantasy of traveling to "blank spaces" is described. Joseph Conrad, *Heart of Darkness* (1902; New York: Penguin Group, 1999), 12. Mary Louise Pratt and Anne McClintock both discuss the significance of the colonial/imperial map as knowledge production. Anne McClintock, *Imperial Leather: Race, Gender, and Sexuality in the Colonial Contest* (New York: Routledge, 1995); Mary Louise Pratt, *Imperial Eyes: Travel Writing and Transculturation* (New York: Routledge, 1992).

8. Both Hilton's and Capra's *Lost Horizon*s have inspired a number of fantastic speculations about the existence of Shangri-La, from finding plane wreckage believed to be part of the original hijacked plane to mysterious sightings of Robert Conway. A lamasery that was found in the Zhongdian County region in China, bordering Tibet, may have been Hilton's inspiration for the creation of Shangri-La. All of these sensational discoveries and sightings certainly increased the tourist value of the Zhongdian region in China. In 2001, capitalizing on the myth of Shangri-La, China allowed Zhongdian County to rename itself Shangri-La County, in order to draw even more international tourism to the already booming area. What this reveals is not only that the Asian imaginary is a figment of Western orientalism but that orientalism has become transnational. Even in China, Shangri-La is an

elusive and mystical entity and one that represents an imagining of an East and West hybridity. Ben Hillman, "Paradise under Construction: Minorities, Myths, and Modernity in Northwest Yunnan," *Asian Ethnicity* 4, no. 2 (2003): 177.

9. Ernest Renan, "What Is a Nation?," trans. Martin Thom, in *Nation and Narration*, ed. Homi K. Bhabha (New York: Routledge, 1990), 8–22.

10. Richards argues that most of Capra's films contained populist ideology, which explains why, after World War II, Capra's films were no longer popular, because populism and its beliefs were no longer relevant in a post–World War II American culture. Jeffrey Richards, "Frank Capra and the Cinema of Populism," in *Movies and Methods: An Anthology*, ed. Bill Nichols (Berkeley: University of California Press, 1976), 1:65–77.

11. Ibid., 1:75.

12. Capra, *Name above the Title*, 193.

13. Hilton's *Lost Horizon* was originally published in 1933. Although Capra's version of *Lost Horizon* differs from Hilton's novella, the important themes of communal existence, pacifism, and even escapism remain, especially as embodied in its main characters, Robert "Hugh" Conway (as he is referred to in Hilton's novella) and Father Perrault.

14. Tomoko Masuzawa, "From Empire to Utopia: The Effacement of Colonial Markings in *Lost Horizon*," *positions: east asia cultures critique* 7, no. 2 (1999): 545.

15. Capra, *Name above the Title*, 176.

16. Ibid., 196.

17. In Hilton's novella, Rutherford, an old schoolmate of Conway, provides the reader with most of the perspective on Conway. The novella's narrative is told through Rutherford, who is trying to piece together a story told by an amnesiac Conway. It is thus unclear in the novella whether Conway's stories are delusion or truth. At certain moments in the novella, Conway is viewed multiply as insane, delusional, and perhaps even a pathological liar. Masuzawa, in "From Empire to Utopia" (551), interprets the novella's Conway as "possibly an insane liar." Without the character Rutherford, the film conveys less ambivalence about the validity of Robert Conway's stories about Shangri-La.

18. I thank Gordon Chang for drawing out this connection to appeasement.

19. Conway's book about "better worlds" does not exist in Hilton's novella. Rather, in Hilton's text a book is being written by the neurologist studying amnesia (Hugh Conway is one of his subjects). I am extrapolating about what Conway's writings contain, given Robert Conway's fantasy of disarmament mentioned during a conversation with George, and on which I elaborate at greater length later in this chapter.

20. Only a small portion of Perrault's monologue remains in the 1976 restored cinematic version of *Lost Horizon*. Capra claims that two entire

reels of footage were burned after the embarrassingly unfavorable opening night in Santa Barbara; however, it is unclear what exactly was taken out, as no one can verify Capra's claim, not even Capra himself. Charles Champlain and Robert Gitt, "Restoration Commentary (1998)," from *Lost Horizon*, directed by Frank Capra *(1937; Culver City, CA:* Columbia TriStar Home Video, 1999), DVD.

21. *Lost Horizon script,* February 16, 1937, New York State Archives, Albany.

22. Capra, *Name above the Title*, 193.

23. During the Depression era a number of factors helped contribute to men's feeling a lack of virility and manhood. Marriages declined markedly in 1929, while during the 1930s the birthrate also dropped (three million fewer babies were born). White middle-class couples limited their families to two children, whereas poorer women were producing more children. Kline, *Building a Better Race*, 96–97.

24. Ibid., 10.

25. Mirra Komorovsky, *The Unemployed Man and His Family* (New York: Dryden Press, 1940), 355, 357; quoted in Michael Kimmel, *Manhood in America: A Cultural History* (New York: Free Press, 1996), 201.

26. Eve Kosofsky Sedgwick, *Between Men: English Literature and Male Homosocial Desire* (New York: Columbia University Press, 1985). Sedgwick's work argues that the forbidden desires between men in Western compulsory heterosexual culture can only be expressed through sanctioned heteronormative relations, such as between men and women.

27. One result of Chamberlain's appeasement policy was the 1938 Munich Agreement, which allowed Germany to take the Sudetenland in exchange for the promise that Germany not take any more territory. Ultimately, Chamberlain's policy was criticized as an ineffectual means of diffusing Nazi Germany's military aggression in Europe, given that Germany violated the terms of the agreement shortly after it was signed.

28. Charles J. Maland, *Frank Capra* (Boston: Twayne, 1980), 101.

29. Eileen Creelman, "The New Talkies," *New York Sun*, March 4, 1937.

30. In the 1942 re-release, titled *Lost Horizon of Shangri-La*, the lengthy drunken speech delivered by the character of Robert Conway, in which he cynically mocked war and diplomacy, was deleted because it was feared such sentiments expressed at the height of World War II would prove to be unpopular with audiences. Capra felt the film made no sense without the scene, and in later years film critic Leslie Halliwell described the missing twelve minutes as 'vital.' A ninety-two-minute version of the film was later released in 1952, with the aim "to downplay the supposedly Communist themes associated with utopia, as well as to limit the sympathy shown towards the Chinese, whose relationship with the American government grew strained in the years following World War II." *Wikipedia, s.v. "Lost Horizon (1937 Film)," http://en.wikipedia.org/wiki/Lost_Horizon_(1937_film)*

(accessed May 17, 2012). See also Leslie Halliwell, *Halliwell's Hundred: A Nostalgic Choice of Films from the Golden Age* (New York: Scribner's, 1982), 180–83.

31. The naming both of the first US air strike on Japan and of FDR's presidential retreat as "Shangri-La" is fairly common knowledge. A Google search of "FDR and Shangri-La" on May 17, 2012, yielded 127,000 sources that reference both his retreat and the air strike.

32. Interestingly, Eric Smoodin in his work on *Lost Horizon* in *Regarding Frank Capra* (170–72) reveals that after World War II, German prisoners of war were required to watch the revised *Lost Horizon* as part of their reeducation.

33. John Dower, *War without Mercy: Race and Power in the Pacific War* (New York: Pantheon, 1986), 249. See also Champlain and Gitt, "Restoration Commentary (1998)," included in the 1999 Columbia TriStar Home Video edition of *Lost Horizon*. Peter C. Rollins, "Frank Capra's *Why We Fight* Film Series and Our American Dream," *Journal of American Culture* 19, no. 4 (1996): 81–86.

34. Robert S. McElvaine, *The Great Depression: America, 1929–1941* (New York: Three Rivers Press, 1993). See also Geoffrey Perrett, *Days of Sadness, Years of Triumph: The American People, 1939–1945* (Madison: University of Wisconsin Press, 1985).

35. Franklin Delano Roosevelt's Commonwealth Club Address, delivered in San Francisco, September 23, 1932, http://www.emersonkent.com/speeches/commonwealth_club_fdr.htm.

36. Bederman, *Manliness and Civilization*, 170.

4 / Envisioning Feminism across the Pacific

1. Helen Hopper, *A New Woman of Japan: A Political Biography of Kato Shidzué* (Boulder, CO: Westview Press, 1996), 157.

2. Between 1909 and 1919, the growth of female colliers increased from thirty-eight thousand to ninety-five thousand. During this time there was a larger increase of female workers than of male workers (104 percent compared to 147 percent). Janet Hunter, *Japanese Women Working* (New York: Routledge, 1995), 105.

3. Barbara Molony, introduction to *Facing Two Ways: The Story of My Life*, by Baroness Shidzué Ishimoto (Stanford, CA: Stanford University Press, 1984), xv. Subsequent references to the autobiography are to this edition and are cited in the main text.

4. According to Laurel Rasplica Rodd, during the 1910s and 1920s, prominent Japanese feminists helped lead debates on the meaning of modern womanhood. As "new women," these feminists sought to redefine the Meiji Era's definition of women as "good wives and wise mothers." A prominent women's literary magazine *Seitō* (Bluestockings) provided a forum for literary pieces, editorials, and dialogues between women about new female

identities in Japan. Sometimes these conversations included women outside of Japan, involving groups such as the British feminist Bluestockings and authors such as Sarah Grand and Olive Schreiner. Thus Japanese feminists were not just witnessing their own progression into modern womanhood, but they were also able to compare and contrast their experience to that of other modern women in the world. Laurel Rasplica Rodd, "Yosano Akiko and the Taishô Debate over the 'New Woman,'" in *Recreating Japanese Women, 1600–1945*, ed. Gail Lee Bernstein (Berkeley: University of California Press, 1991), 175–98.

5. Barbara Sicherman, "Sense and Sensibility: A Case Study of Women's Reading in Late Victorian America," in *Reading in America: Literature and Social History*, ed. Cathy N. Davidson (Baltimore: Johns Hopkins University Press, 1989), 202.

6. Teresa Lynn Mangum, *Married, Middlebrow, and Militant: Sarah Grand and the New Woman Novel* (Ann Arbor: University of Michigan Press, 1999), 1–5.

7. Karen Kuo, "*The Shanghai Gesture*: Melodrama and Modern Women in the East/West Romance," *Quarterly Review of Film and Video* 29, no. 2 (2012): 95–113. In my essay I suggest that the Japanese Cho-Cho San in *Madame Butterfly*, read as a tragic Victorian heroine, represents an antiquated image of white women, who were now seen as contemporary and emancipated.

8. Mari Yoshihara, *Embracing the East: White Women and American Orientalism* (New York: Oxford University Press, 2003), 46–77.

9. Unlike her sister Edith Maude Eaton, who adopted a Chinese pen name, Sui Sin Far, Winnifred decided to write as a Japanese woman. Given virulent anti-Chinese sentiment in America from the turn of the century until the 1920s, her choice to masquerade as Japanese both protected her and capitalized on the cultural popularity of *Madame Butterfly* and other similar narratives. Some have argued that Winnifred's success as a writer, which was greater than that of her sister Edith, was due to her willingness to give the American public Japanese characters that conformed to the *Madame Butterfly* stereotype. See Onoto Watanna, *"A Half Caste" and Other Writings*, ed. Linda Trinh Moser and Elizabeth Rooney (Urbana: University of Illinois Press, 2003).

10. Yoné Noguchi, *The American Diary of a Japanese Girl, ed. Edward Marx and Laura E. Franey, annotated ed.* (Philadelphia: Temple University Press, 2007), 31. In a discussion of how Noguchi makes fun of Japonisme, see the introductory essay by Franey (xii).

11. In many ways, *Madame Butterfly*'s appearance a decade or so after Loti's *Madame Chrysanthemum* is effectively read as a criticism of masculinity deriving from the East/West liaison. The story of *Madame Butterfly* is thus a dramatization of a specific problem of white male colonial behavior in Asia, mainly the entitlement of white males to take native

women as temporary companions. Not only does the resulting taint of interracial sexual contact lead to domestic problems, but it also leads to a general crisis of masculinity. The play, in showing Pinkerton and his friend Sharpless as "Ugly Americans" shirking responsibility and behaving dishonestly in both their domestic and colonial affairs, expresses a sentimentalized and nostalgic desire for a lost chivalric masculinity. Despite the double standard that allows Pinkerton and Sharpless to cross racial boundaries, albeit temporarily, Cho-Cho San is the sole heroic character. Consequently, Cho-Cho San's victimization criticizes a white masculinity within a specific colonial setting of Western encroachment on the East. See Susan McClary, "Mounting Butterflies," in *A Vision of the Orient: Texts, Intertexts, and Contexts of Madame Butterfly*, ed. Jonathan Wisenthal, Sherrill Grace, Melinda Boyd, Brian McIlroy, and Vera Micznik (Toronto: University of Toronto Press, 2006), 21–35. McClary rereads the play and opera as a performance of female victimization intended to make men responsible.

12. Yoshihara, *Embracing the East*, 78.

13. Ibid., 86. Yoshihara argues in *Embracing the East* that these orientalist roles were not necessarily viewed as authentic. For example, one critic, in reviewing *Madame Butterfly* and other melodramas centered on Japan and Japanese women, derided the lofty and ostentatious translation of Japanese into English. In addition, Yoshihara argues that white actresses were fully aware of performing these Japanese female roles inauthentically to accentuate the polarity between white and Asiatic femininity.

14. Traise Yamamoto, *Masking Selves, Making Subjects: Japanese American Women, Identity, and the Body* (Berkeley: University of California Press, 1999), 24.

15. Amy Loveman, "Born to Change," review of *Facing Two Ways*, by Baroness Shidzué Ishimoto, *Saturday Review of Literature*, August 31, 1935, 13.

16. Rose C. Feld, "A Woman of Old and New Japan," *New York Times Book Review*, August 25, 1935, 5.

17. Molony, introduction to *Facing Two Ways*, xvi.

18. Hopper, *New Woman of Japan*.

19. "My activity at the front line in our birth control propaganda was a cause of alarm to the people of my own class. It was taken as a fancy of a romantic person or of one not quite sound in her head. They called me 'Madame Control' and drew caricatures of me in papers and magazines." Ishimoto, *Facing Two Ways*, 232.

20. Sanger was finally able to open a legal birth control clinic after 1923 due to a loophole in the Comstock Act that allowed a licensed medical doctor to distribute contraception.

21. Malia Sedgewick Johnson, "Margaret Sanger and the Birth Control Movement in Japan, 1921–1955" (PhD diss., University of Hawaii, 1987), 51.

See also Margaret Sanger, *My Fight for Birth Control* (New York: Farrar and Rinehart, 1931), 239.

22. Elsie K. Tipton, "Ishimoto Shidzué: The Margaret Sanger of Japan," *Women's History Review* 6, no. 3 (1997): 341–42. As Tipton notes, Sanger began distancing herself from other radical feminists such as Emma Goldman, who was deported to the Soviet Union in 1919. Sanger also focused more narrowly on the birth control movement with the aim of garnering the support of middle- and upper-middle-class women in the United States (ibid., 342–43).

23. Hopper, *New Woman of Japan*, 24.

24. Margaret Sanger, "The East Is Blossoming," in *Margaret Sanger: An Autobiography* (New York: W. W. Norton, 1938), 331.

25. While the adoption of Protestant Christianity during the Meiji era was important in the modernization of Japan and seen as a progressive influence, by the late nineteenth century Christianity had fallen out of favor with the growing anti-Western sentiments. And yet during the Meiji era many of the key intellectuals who were Christian converts became influential in the social and humanitarian progressive movements into the Taishô era. See Mioko Fujieda, "Japan's First Phase of Feminism," in *Japanese Women: New Feminist Perspectives on the Past, Present, and Future*, ed. Kumiko Fujimura-Fanselow and Atsuko Kameda (New York: Feminist Press at the City University of New York, 1995), 329. Still, for the aristocratic and later the middle class, a Christian education, particularly for girls, was common and favored. Ishimoto's mother, like many aristocratic Japanese, was educated at Canadian mission schools in Tokyo, which, as Ishimoto explains in her autobiography "was considered a progressive education for girls." But as Ishimoto also says, her mother's education in the mission schools "helped her a good deal in understanding her father as befitted the wife of a Japanese businessman" (*Facing Two Ways*, 11).

26. The Manchurian Incident was an event staged by Japan to rationalize an invasion of northern China in 1931. The Japanese military engineered the bombing of a northern Chinese railroad in order to provoke Chinese retaliation and thereby justify the ensuing invasion of Manchuria. Japan's invasion of Manchuria was denounced by the League of Nations.

27. Hopper, *New Woman of Japan*.

28. Sanger, *An Autobiography*, 330.

29. Beard was both a friend and collaborator of Ishimoto's. Ishimoto called Beard her "sensei," and Beard not only encouraged Ishimoto to publish *Facing Two Ways* for American readers, but she also edited it. In addition, Ishimoto and other Japanese feminists contributed to a multivolume work on women's history that Beard was editing with other European feminists.

30. Tipton, "Ishimoto Shidzué," 342.

31. The reference to being as tall as, or taller than, a fire alarm thief dates back to pre-high-rise modern buildings in Japan. As Ishimoto explains:

Before Japan erected skyscrapers in her modernized cities, the towns were flat, being filled with only one- or two-story houses and the tallest object in each ward in the town was a ladder with a big fire alarm bell on the top. My uncle meant to say that I was growing like "Jack and the Beanstalk" and could reach to the top of the ladder from the ground if I wanted to steal the bell. (*Facing Two Ways*, 83)

32. Fujieda, "Japan's First Phase of Feminism," 323.

33. Tipton, "Ishimoto Shidzué," 343.

34. Hopper, *New Woman of Japan*, 25.

35. Vera Mackie, *Feminism in Modern Japan: Citizenship, Embodiment, and Sexuality* (Cambridge: Cambridge University Press, 2003), 75.

36. Ibid.

37. Ibid.

38. "Mrs. Sanger Takes a Strong Attitude: Leaving for Japan without a Visa," *Rafu Shimpo*, February 19, 1922, quoted in Kyoko Kakehashi Fujisaka, "Japanese Immigrant Women in Los Angeles, 1912–1942: A Transnational Perspective" (PhD diss., University of Wisconsin–Madison, 2005), 54.

39. There are some works on Sanger that reveal her collaboration with eugenics, but in general she was not a proponent of positive eugenics, which called for selective reproduction of white Anglo-Americans. See Angela Davis, *Women, Race, and Class* (New York: Vintage Books, 1983), 213–14. Scc also Linda Gordon, *Woman's Body, Woman's Right: Birth Control in America*, rev. and updated ed. (New York: Penguin Books, 1990); Dorothy Roberts, "Margaret Sanger and the Racial Origins of the Birth Control Movement," in *Racially Writing the Republic: Racists, Race Rebels, and Transformations of American Identity*, ed. Bruce Baum and Duchess Harris (Durham, NC: Duke University Press, 2009), 197–98; and Nancy Ordover's chapter on Margaret Sanger in *American Eugenics: Race, Queer Anatomy, and the Science of Nationalism* (Minneapolis: University of Minnesota Press, 2003), 137–58.

40. Hopper, *New Woman of Japan*, 258.

41. Joan E. Ericson, "The Origins of the Concept of 'Women's Literature,'" in *The Woman's Hand: Gender and Theory in Japanese Women's Writing*, ed. Paul Schalow and Janet Walker (Stanford, CA: Stanford University Press, 1996), 82.

42. The New Woman did not usually refer to the *moga*, or the Modern Girl, who was seen more as a depoliticized creature, but one who believed in free love and social and economic independence.

43. "Women writers of the 1920's also often favored a confessional style; however, their works were generally categorized not as *watakushi-shōsetsu* [I-novel or I-fiction], but rather as *jiden shōsetsu* (autobiographical fiction)." Ericson, "The Concept of 'Women's Literature,'" 91–92.

44. The growth of the coal mining industry began as an opportunity for sideline work in the mid-nineteenth century, whereby rural farming families would take on extra work in the coal mines to make ends meet. At that time, small mines were independently owned by entrepreneurs; they were later replaced by large corporations, which found that the recruitment of families made the worker more stable and easier to control and supplied a large amount of cheap labor—women and children. Hunter, *Japanese Women Working*, 104.

Bibliography

Alexander, Ruth M. *"The Girl Problem": Female Sexual Delinquency in New York, 1900–1930*. Ithaca, NY: Cornell University Press, 1993.

Almaguer, Tomàs. *Racial Fault Lines: The Historical Origins of White Supremacy in California*. Berkeley: University of California Press, 1994.

Bederman, Gail. *Manliness and Civilization: A Cultural History of Gender and Race in the United States, 1880–1917*. Chicago: University of Chicago Press, 1996.

Behdad, Ali. *Belated Travelers: Orientalism in the Age of Colonial Dissolution*. Durham, NC: Duke University Press, 1994.

Capra, Frank. *Frank Capra: The Name above the Title; An Autobiography*. New York: Macmillan, 1971.

Carnegie, Dale. *How to Win Friends and Influence People*. New York: Pocket Books, 1990.

Chakrabarty, Dipesh. "Notes toward a Conversation between Area Studies and Diasporic Studies." In *Orientations: Mapping Studies in the Asian Diaspora*, edited by Kandice Chuh and Karen Shimakawa. Durham, NC: Duke University Press, 2001.

Chan, Sucheng. *Asian Americans: An Interpretive History*. Boston: Twayne, 1991.

———. "The Exclusion of Chinese Women." In *Entry Denied: Exclusion and the Chinese Community in America, 1882–1943*, edited by Sucheng Chan. Philadelphia: Temple University Press, 1991.

Cheng, Lucie. "Free, Indentured, Enslaved: Chinese Prostitutes in Nineteenth-Century America." In *Labor Immigration under Capitalism: Asian Workers in the United States before World War II*, edited by Lucie Cheng and Edna Bonacich. Berkeley: University of California Press, 1984.

Chow, Rey. "Leading Questions." In *Orientations: Mapping Studies in the Asian Diaspora*, edited by Kandice Chuh and Karen Shimakawa. Durham, NC: Duke University Press, 2001.

Choy, Philip P., Lorraine Dong, and Marlon K. Hom, eds. *The Coming Man: Nineteenth-Century American Perceptions of the Chinese*. Seattle: University of Washington Press, 1995.

Conrad, Joseph. *Heart of Darkness*. 1902. New York: Penguin Group, 1999.

Creelman, Eileen. "The New Talkies." *New York Sun*, March 4, 1937.

Davis, Angela. *Women, Race, and Class*. New York: Vintage Books, 1983.

de Jesús, Melinda. "Reclaiming Queerness in Carlos Bulosan's *America Is in the Heart* and Bienvenido Santos' *Scent of Apples*." *Journal of Asian American Studies* 5, no. 2 (2002): 91–111.

D'Emilio, John, and Estelle B. Freedman. *Intimate Matters: A History of Sexuality in America*. Chicago: University of Chicago Press, 1997.

Dower, John. *War without Mercy: Race and Power in the Pacific War*. New York: Pantheon, 1986.

East Is West. Directed by Monta Bell, with performances by Lupe Vélez, Lew Ayres, and Edward G. Robinson. Los Angeles: Universal Pictures, 1930. DVD.

Enloe, Cynthia. *Bananas, Beaches, and Bases: Making Feminist Sense of International Politics*. Updated ed. Berkeley: University of California Press, 2000.

Ericson, Joan E. "The Origins of the Concept of 'Women's Literature.'" In *The Woman's Hand: Gender and Theory in Japanese Women's Writing*, edited by Paul Schalow and Janet Walker. Stanford, CA: Stanford University Press, 1996.

España-Maram, Linda. *Creating Masculinity in Los Angeles's Little Manila: Working-Class Filipinos and Popular Culture, 1920s–1950s*. New York: Columbia University Press, 2006.

Espiritu, Yen Le. *Filipino American Lives*. Philadelphia: Temple University Press, 1995.

Feld, Rose C. "A Woman of Old and New Japan." *New York Times Book Review*, August 25, 1935, 5.

Fong, Timothy P. *The Contemporary Asian American Experience: Beyond the Model Minority.* Upper Saddle River, NJ: Prentice Hall, 2008.

Fujieda, Mioko. "Japan's First Phase of Feminism." In *Japanese Women: New Feminist Perspectives on the Past, Present, and Future,* edited by Kumiko Fujimura-Fanselow and Atsuko Kameda. New York: Feminist Press at the City University of New York, 1995.

Fujisaka, Kyoko Kakehashi. "Japanese Immigrant Women in Los Angeles, 1912–1942: A Transnational Perspective." PhD diss., University of Wisconsin–Madison, 2005.

Gordon, Linda. *Woman's Body, Woman's Right: Birth Control in America.* Rev. and updated ed. New York: Penguin Books, 1990.

Halliwell, Leslie. *Halliwell's Hundred: A Nostalgic Choice of Films from the Golden Age.* New York: Scribner's, 1982.

Hillman, Ben. "Paradise under Construction: Minorities, Myths, and Modernity in Northwest Yunnan." *Asian Ethnicity* 4, no. 2 (2003): 175–88.

Hilton, James. *Lost Horizon.* New York: Pocket Books, 1933.

Hopper, Helen. *A New Woman of Japan: A Political Biography of Kato Shidzué.* Boulder, CO: Westview Press, 1996.

Hunter, Janet. *Japanese Women Working.* New York: Routledge, 1995.

Isaac, Harold. *Scratches on Our Minds: American Images of China and India.* New York: John Day, 1958.

Ishimoto, Shidzué, Baroness. *Facing Two Ways: The Story of My Life.* 1935. Stanford, CA: Stanford University Press, 1984.

Jew, Victor. "'Chinese Demons': The Violent Articulation of Chinese Otherness and Interracial Sexuality in the U.S. Midwest, 1885–1889." *Journal of Social History* 37, no. 2 (2003): 389–410.

Johnson, Malia Sedgewick. "Margaret Sanger and the Birth Control Movement in Japan, 1921–1955." PhD diss., University of Hawaii, 1987.

Jusová, Iveta. *The New Woman and the Empire.* Columbus: Ohio State University Press, 2005.

Kang, Younghill. *East Goes West: The Making of an Oriental Yankee.* 1937. New York: Kaya Production, 1997.

Kaplan, Amy. *The Anarchy of Empire in the Making of U.S. Culture.* Cambridge, MA: Harvard University Press, 2005.

Kim, Daniel. *Writing Manhood in Black and Yellow: Ralph Ellison, Frank Chin, and the Literary Politics of Identity.* Stanford, CA: Stanford University Press, 2005.

Kimmel, Michael. *Manhood in America: A Cultural History*. New York: Free Press, 1996.

Kline, Wendy. *Building a Better Race: Gender, Sexuality, and Eugenics from the Turn of the Century to the Baby Boom*. Berkeley: University of California Press, 2005.

Komorovsky, Mirra. *The Unemployed Man and His Family*. New York: Dryden Press, 1940.

Koshy, Susan. *Sexual Naturalization: Asian Americans and Miscegenation*. Stanford, CA: Stanford University Press, 2004.

Kuo, Karen. "*The Shanghai Gesture*: Melodrama and Modern Women in the East/West Romance." *Quarterly Review of Film and Video* 29, no. 2 (2012): 95–113.

Lee, Erika. *At America's Gates: Chinese Immigration during the Exclusion Era, 1882–1943*. Chapel Hill: University of North Carolina Press, 2005.

Lee, Robert G. *Orientals: Asian Americans in Popular Culture*. Philadelphia: Temple University Press, 1999.

Lee, Sunyoung. "The Unmaking of an Oriental Yankee." Afterword to *East Goes West: The Making of an Oriental Yankee*, by Younghill Kang. New York: Kaya Production, 1997.

Levine, Lawrence. *The Unpredictable Past: Explorations in American Cultural History*. New York: Oxford University Press, 1993.

Lewis, Reina. *Rethinking Orientalism: Women, Travel, and the Ottoman Harem*. New Brunswick, NJ: Rutgers University Press, 2004.

Lost Horizon. Directed by Frank Capra, with performances by Ronald Colman, Jane Wyatt, John Howard, and Thomas Mitchell. Culver City, CA: Columbia Pictures, 1937. DVD.

Loveman, Amy. "Born to Change." Review of *Facing Two Ways*, by Baroness Shidzué Ishimoto. *Saturday Review of Literature*, August 31, 1935, 13.

Lowe, Lisa. *Critical Terrains: French and British Orientalisms*. Ithaca, NY: Cornell University Press, 1994.

———. *Immigrant Acts: On Asian American Cultural Politics*. Durham, NC: Duke University Press, 1996.

Lui, Mary Ting Yi. *The Chinatown Trunk Mystery: Murder, Miscegenation, and Other Dangerous Encounters in Turn-of-the-Century New York City*. Princeton, NJ: Princeton University Press, 2005.

Luibhéid, Eithne. *Entry Denied: Controlling Sexuality at the Border*. Minneapolis: University of Minnesota Press, 2002.

Lye, Colleen. *America's Asia: Racial Form and American Literature, 1893–1945*. Princeton, NJ: Princeton University Press, 2004.

Mackie, Vera. *Feminism in Modern Japan: Citizenship, Embodiment, and Sexuality*. Cambridge: Cambridge University Press, 2003.

Maland, Charles J. *Frank Capra*. Boston: Twayne, 1980.

Maltby, Richard, and Ian Craven. *Hollywood Cinema*. Oxford: Blackwell, 1995.

Mangum, Teresa Lynn. *Married, Middlebrow, and Militant: Sarah Grand and the New Woman Novel*. Ann Arbor: University of Michigan Press, 1999.

Marchetti, Gina. *Romance and the "Yellow Peril": Race, Sex, and Discursive Strategies in Hollywood Fiction*. Berkeley: University of California Press, 1994.

Masuzawa, Tomoko. "From Empire to Utopia: The Effacement of Colonial Markings in *Lost Horizon*." *positions: east asia cultures critique* 7, no. 2 (1999): 541–72.

McClary, Susan. "Mounting Butterflies." In *A Vision of the Orient: Texts, Intertexts, and Contexts of Madame Butterfly*, edited by Jonathan Wisenthal, Sherrill Grace, Melinda Boyd, Brian McIlroy, and Vera Micznik. Toronto: University of Toronto Press, 2006.

McClintock, Anne. *Imperial Leather: Race, Gender, and Sexuality in the Colonial Contest*. New York: Routledge, 1995.

McElvaine, Robert S. *The Great Depression: America, 1929–1941*. New York: Three Rivers Press, 1993.

Meyerowitz, Joanne J. *Women Adrift: Independent Wage Earners in Chicago, 1880–1930*. Chicago: University of Chicago Press, 1988.

Molony, Barbara. Introduction to *Facing Two Ways: The Story of My Life*, by Baroness Shidzué Ishimoto. Stanford, CA: Stanford University Press, 1984.

Moran, Rachel F. *Interracial Intimacy: The Regulation of Race and Romance*. Chicago: University of Chicago Press, 2001.

Ngai, Mae M. *Impossible Subjects: Illegal Aliens and the Making of Modern America*. Princeton, NJ: Princeton University Press, 2005.

Noguchi, Yoné. *The American Diary of a Japanese Girl*, edited by Edward Marx and Laura E. Franey, annotated ed. Philadelphia: Temple University Press, 2007.

Odem, Mary E. *Delinquent Daughters: Protecting and Policing Adolescent Female Sexuality in the United States, 1885–1920*. Chapel Hill: University of North Carolina Press, 1995.

Ordover, Nancy. *American Eugenics: Race, Queer Anatomy, and the Science of Nationalism*. Minneapolis: University of Minnesota Press, 2003.

Palumbo-Liu, David. *Asian/American: Historical Crossings of a Racial Frontier*. Stanford, CA: Stanford University Press, 1999.

Park, Josephine Nock-Hee. *Apparitions of Asia: Modernist Form and Asian American Poetics*. New York: Oxford University Press, 2008.

Pascoe, Peggy. *Relations of Rescue: The Search for Female Moral Authority in the American West, 1874–1939*. New York: Oxford University Press, 1990.

Peffer, George Anthony. *If They Don't Bring Their Women Here: Chinese Female Immigration before Exclusion*. Urbana: University of Illinois Press, 1999.

Perrett, Geoffrey. *Days of Sadness, Years of Triumph: The American People, 1939–1945*. Madison: University of Wisconsin Press, 1985.

Pratt, Mary Louise. *Imperial Eyes: Travel Writing and Transculturation*. New York: Routledge, 1992.

Renan, Ernest. "What Is a Nation?" Translated by Martin Thom. In *Nation and Narration*, edited by Homi K. Bhabha. New York: Routledge, 1990.

Richards, Jeffrey. "Frank Capra and the Cinema of Populism." In *Movies and Methods: An Anthology*, vol. 1, edited by Bill Nichols. Berkeley: University of California Press, 1976.

Roberts, Dorothy. "Margaret Sanger and the Racial Origins of the Birth Control Movement." In *Racially Writing the Republic: Racists, Race Rebels, and Transformations of American Identity*, edited by Bruce Baum and Duchess Harris. Durham, NC: Duke University Press, 2009.

Robinson, Michael Edson. *Korea's Twentieth-Century Odyssey*. Honolulu: University of Hawaii Press, 2007.

Rodd, Laurel Rasplica. "Yosano Akiko and the Taishô Debate over the 'New Woman.'" In *Recreating Japanese Women, 1600–1945*, edited by Gail Lee Bernstein. Berkeley: University of California Press, 1991.

Rollins, Peter C. "Frank Capra's *Why We Fight* Film Series and Our American Dream." *Journal of American Culture* 19, no. 4 (1996): 81–86.

Rosen, Ruth. *The Lost Sisterhood: Prostitution in America, 1900–1918*. Baltimore: Johns Hopkins University Press, 1983.

Sanger, Margaret. *My Fight for Birth Control.* New York: Farrar and Rinehart, 1931.

Sedgwick, Eve Kosofsky. *Between Men: English Literature and Male Homosocial Desire.* New York: Columbia University Press, 1985.

Shah, Nayan. *Contagious Divides: Epidemics and Race in San Francisco's Chinatown.* Berkeley: University of California Press, 2001.

Shipman, Samuel, and John B. Hymer. *East Is West: A Comedy in Three Acts and a Prologue.* New York: Samuel French, 1924.

Shohat, Ella, and Robert Stam. *Unthinking Eurocentrism: Multiculturalism and the Media.* New York: Routledge, 1994.

Sicherman, Barbara. "Sense and Sensibility: A Case Study of Women's Reading in Late Victorian America." In *Reading in America: Literature and Social History,* edited by Cathy N. Davidson. Baltimore: Johns Hopkins University Press, 1989.

Siu, Paul C. P. *The Chinese Laundryman: A Study of Social Isolation.* Edited by John Kuo Wei Tchen. New York: New York University Press, 1987.

Smoodin, Eric. *Regarding Frank Capra: Audience, Celebrity, and American Film Studies, 1930–1960.* Durham, NC: Duke University Press, 2004.

Stange, Margit. *Personal Property: Wives, White Slaves, and the Market in Women.* Baltimore: Johns Hopkins University Press, 1998.

Stoler, Ann Laura. *Carnal Knowledge and Imperial Power: Race and the Intimate in Colonial Rule.* 2nd ed. Berkeley: University of California Press, 2010.

———. *Race and the Education of Desire: Foucault's "History of Sexuality" and the Colonial Order of Things.* Durham, NC: Duke University Press, 1995.

Streeby, Shelley. *American Sensations: Class, Empire, and the Production of Popular Culture.* Berkeley: University of California Press, 2002.

Sugimoto, Etsu Inagaki. *A Daughter of the Samurai.* Honolulu: University Press of the Pacific, 2003.

Takaki, Ronald. *Strangers from a Different Shore: A History of Asian Americans,* updated and rev. ed. New York: Back Bay Books, 1998.

Tchen, John Kuo Wei. *New York before Chinatown: Orientalism and the Shaping of American Culture, 1776–1882.* Baltimore: Johns Hopkins University Press, 1999.

Tiongson, Antonio, Edgardo Gutierrez, and Ricardo Gutierrez, eds. *Positively No Filipinos Allowed: Building Communities and*

Discourse. Annotated ed. Philadelphia: Temple University Press, 2006.

Tipton, Elsie K. "Ishimoto Shidzué: The Margaret Sanger of Japan." *Women's History Review* 6, no. 3 (1997): 337–55.

Watanna, Onoto. *"A Half Caste" and Other Writings*. Edited by Linda Trinh Moser and Elizabeth Rooney. Urbana: University of Illinois Press, 2003.

Wong, K. Scott. "'An Eagle Seeks a Helpless Quarry': Chinatown, the Police, and the Press; The 1930 Boston Chinatown Raid Revisited." *Amerasia Journal* 22, no. 3 (1996): 81–103.

Yamamoto, Traise. *Masking Selves, Making Subjects: Japanese American Women, Identity, and the Body*. Berkeley: University of California Press, 1999.

Yoshihara, Mari. *Embracing the East: White Women and American Orientalism*. New York: Oxford University Press, 2003.

Yu, Henry. *Thinking Orientals: Migration, Contact, and Exoticism in Modern America*. New York: Oxford University Press, 2001.

Index

About the Author

Karen Kuo is an Assistant Professor of Asian Pacific American Studies in the School of Social Transformation at Arizona State University.

(Continued from the series page.)

Thomas P. Kim, *The Racial Logic of Politics: Asian Americans and Party Competition*

Sucheng Chan, ed., *The Vietnamese American 1.5 Generation: Stories of War, Revolution, Flight, and New Beginnings*

Antonio T. Tiongson Jr., Edgardo V. Gutierrez, and Ricardo V. Gutierrez, eds., *Positively No Filipinos Allowed: Building Communities and Discourse*

Sucheng Chan, ed., *Chinese American Transnationalism: The Flow of People, Resources, and Ideas between China and America during the Exclusion Era*

Rajini Srikanth, *The World Next Door: South Asian American Literature and the Idea of America*

Keith Lawrence and Floyd Cheung, eds., *Recovered Legacies: Authority and Identity in Early Asian American Literature*

Linda Trinh Võ, *Mobilizing an Asian American Community*

Franklin S. Odo, *No Sword to Bury: Japanese Americans in Hawai'i during World War II*

Josephine Lee, Imogene L. Lim, and Yuko Matsukawa, eds., *Re/collecting Early Asian America: Essays in Cultural History*

Linda Trinh Võ and Rick Bonus, eds., *Contemporary Asian American Communities: Intersections and Divergences*

Sunaina Marr Maira, *Desis in the House: Indian American Youth Culture in New York City*

Teresa Williams-León and Cynthia Nakashima, eds., *The Sum of Our Parts: Mixed-Heritage Asian Americans*

Tung Pok Chin with Winifred C. Chin, *Paper Son: One Man's Story*

Amy Ling, ed., *Yellow Light: The Flowering of Asian American Arts*

Rick Bonus, *Locating Filipino Americans: Ethnicity and the Cultural Politics of Space*

Darrell Y. Hamamoto and Sandra Liu, eds., *Countervisions: Asian American Film Criticism*

Martin F. Manalansan, IV, ed., *Cultural Compass: Ethnographic Explorations of Asian America*

Ko-lin Chin, *Smuggled Chinese: Clandestine Immigration to the United States*

Evelyn Hu-DeHart, ed., *Across the Pacific: Asian Americans and Globalization*

Soo-Young Chin, *Doing What Had to Be Done: The Life Narrative of Dora Yum Kim*

Robert G. Lee, *Orientals: Asian Americans in Popular Culture*

David L. Eng and Alice Y. Hom, eds., *Q & A: Queer in Asian America*

K. Scott Wong and Sucheng Chan, eds., *Claiming America: Constructing Chinese American Identities during the Exclusion Era*

Lavina Dhingra Shankar and Rajini Srikanth, eds., *A Part, Yet Apart: South Asians in Asian America*

Jere Takahashi, *Nisei/Sansei: Shifting Japanese American Identities and Politics*

Velina Hasu Houston, ed., *But Still, Like Air, I'll Rise: New Asian American Plays*

Josephine Lee, *Performing Asian America: Race and Ethnicity on the Contemporary Stage*

Deepika Bahri and Mary Vasudeva, eds., *Between the Lines: South Asians and Postcoloniality*

E. San Juan, Jr., *The Philippine Temptation: Dialectics of Philippines-U.S. Literary Relations*

Carlos Bulosan and E. San Juan, Jr., ed., *The Cry and the Dedication*

Carlos Bulosan and E. San Juan, Jr., ed., *On Becoming Filipino: Selected Writings of Carlos Bulosan*

Vicente L. Rafael, ed., *Discrepant Histories: Translocal Essays on Filipino Cultures*

Yen Le Espiritu, *Filipino American Lives*

Paul Ong, Edna Bonacich, and Lucie Cheng, eds., *The New Asian Immigration in Los Angeles and Global Restructuring*

Chris Friday, *Organizing Asian American Labor: The Pacific Coast Canned-Salmon Industry, 1870–1942*

Sucheng Chan, ed., *Hmong Means Free: Life in Laos and America*

Timothy P. Fong, *The First Suburban Chinatown: The Remarking of Monterey Park, California*

William Wei, *The Asian American Movement*

Yen Le Espiritu, *Asian American Panethnicity*

Velina Hasu Houston, ed., *The Politics of Life*

Renqiu Yu, *To Save China, To Save Ourselves: The Chinese Hand Laundry Alliance of New York*

Shirley Geok-lin Lim and Amy Ling, eds., *Reading the Literatures of Asian America*

Karen Isaksen Leonard, *Making Ethnic Choices: California's Punjabi Mexican Americans*

Gary Y. Okihiro, *Cane Fires: The Anti-Japanese Movement in Hawaii, 1865–1945*

Sucheng Chan, *Entry Denied: Exclusion and the Chinese Community in America, 1882–1943*